Philosophy and Finance: A Love Story

Paule Ansoleaga Abascal

Philosophy and Finance: A Love Story

Bridging Ancient Wisdom and Modern Finance in a Journey Toward Awareness, Interconnection, and Human Flourishing

palgrave
macmillan

Paule Ansoleaga Abascal
Arcano Partners
Milan, Italy

ISBN 978-3-032-22217-6 ISBN 978-3-032-22218-3 (eBook)
https://doi.org/10.1007/978-3-032-22218-3

Translation from the Italian language edition: "FILOSOFIA E FINANZA: UNA STORIA D'AMORE" by Paule Ansoleaga Abascal, © Paule Ansoleaga Abascal 2025. Published by Il Sole 24 Ore . All Rights Reserved.

Cover Image Credit: Hoika Mikhail

This Palgrave Macmillan imprint is published by the registered company Springer Nature Switzerland AG
The registered company address is: Gewerbestrasse 11, 6330 Cham, Switzerland

For my mother, Belén—the wisest and most generous soul I know.

When I was a child, I went on many outdoor school trips. I remember sitting on the grass with my friends as we unwrapped our lunches. Theirs were bocadillos de tortilla*—lovingly prepared over at least half an hour. Mine was always simpler: a two-minute* bocadillo de jamón, *or something alike.*

You were the mother of three, rising before dawn to go to work. You didn't have time for elaborate meals. But you always had time—for Love, for Wisdom, for the most astonishing and enriching conversations. For timeless insight drawn from East and West, ancient and modern. The world seemed to grow calmer the moment after you spoke.

I remember looking at my sandwich and smiling, because I knew: you gave me something far richer—life-changing advice, the kind of guidance that lasts forever.

This book, like my life, is shaped by your presence.

Foreword

There are books that inform and there are books that remind. *Philosophy and Finance: A Love Story* is very much the latter—a generous, soulful work that reminds us of something we have always known but somehow managed to forget: That how we deploy capital is an expression of who we are, and that who we are is, in no small part, a matter of deliberate reflection and cultivation.

I have spent much of my career arguing, in various registers and to various audiences, that value is not monolithic. The Blended Value framework holds, at its core, that economic, social, and environmental value are not separate things to be traded off, one against the other, but dimensions of a single, unified phenomenon.

One cannot, in the end, separate a company's financial performance from its human, social and environmental capital any more than one can separate a person's bank account from their personal understanding of the purpose of that capital. Both are braided together, as interlocking strands of DNA, whether we acknowledge it or not. The market has simply not yet built the conceptual framework much less accounting system sophisticated enough for the mainstream to see this clearly. Works such as this, help us advance in this critical direction.

What Paule Ansoleaga Abascal does in this luminous book is something complementary and, in many ways, more fundamental. She asks not merely how we should measure value, but how we should understand it—and how the ancient project of living well, which philosophy once held at its centre, might be restored to its proper place at the heart of economic and financial life.

This is a question that runs through my own work in ***The Purpose of Capital***, where I trace the deep roots of our relationship to money and wealth, to ask why we invest at all—not just how. Paule takes that inquiry yet further, returning us to the Stoics (to Epictetus and Marcus Aurelius and Seneca) to remind us the examined life and ethical economy were never supposed to be separate undertakings.

This is not an abstract concern. When finance serves only capital accumulation and concentration—when capital is organized purely around the logic of separation, as Paule so aptly frames it—it does not merely fail to generate social good. It actively concentrates power in ways that erode the conditions for democratic life and economic flourishing. The financialization of everything, untethered from moral imagination, becomes one of the structural preconditions for the world we do not wish to inherit and a future we must all now work to co-create on terms best for all and not for the few.

The solution for our global drift toward authoritarianism is not primarily a technical challenge. We do not lack for sustainability frameworks or impact measurement tools. What we lack is the practice of awakening philosophy has always offered. And that awakening comes as an outcome from our operating within a set of habits and disciplines that make us capable of seeing our choices clearly. That clarity is what helps us understand more fully the consequences of those choices even as the system around us is nudging us elsewhere.

This is precisely what this valuable volume offers. Consider the resonance of her journey through Stoic practice, via Pierre Hadot's spiritual exercises. Or her description of the stories of Epictetus and Socrates and Thales. She is equipping readers with what the ancient philosophers would have recognized as an askesis—a practice of self-formation—adapted for the people who are, right now, making decisions regarding how capital moves in the world. The inner work she describes is not separate from systemic change; it is its precondition and starting place. We cannot build an economy oriented toward flourishing if the people steering it have not done the work of asking what flourishing actually means.

I am struck by the structural elegance of this book. Paule moves us along a four-part flow—from the philosophical case for reunion and reintegration, then to the lived practice of ancient wisdom, back yet again through the moral history of finance, and then forward into a vision of what could be. This journey mirrors something important regarding how change happens in the world. Change does not begin with shifts in policy, but rather perception. Paule affirms the willingness to see what is really going on and to be honest with ourselves regarding the gap between our stated values and our operational ones.

We have the tools we need to build a different kind of economy. What we lack is the will—and that will, I now believe, is a function of character which is the province of philosophy. Paule understands this. Her book is, in the best sense, an act of education in the classical meaning of that word. She champions a leading out, an awakening and preparation for responsible citizenship in a world that desperately needs people who think and act from their deepest values.

The figure she conjures—what she calls the Financial Alma, the investor or entrepreneur who operates from wisdom, conscience, and care—is not a utopian fantasy. It is a portrait of what becomes possible when human beings take their inner lives seriously. We have seen glimpses of this figure throughout history. She is present in the financial reformers and ethical investors Paule profiles, and we see glimpses of it today in the growing movement of people who refuse to believe capital and conscience are inherently at odds.

This book will find its readers at a moment when that refusal is of critical import. In a world drifting toward the consolidation of power in ever fewer hands, the act of returning finance to its philosophical roots is itself a political act—a quiet, sustained, deeply personal act of resistance. The cultivation of wisdom and insistence on human dignity are not soft alternatives to structural change. They are its hard challenge and core. They are our foundation.

I am grateful to Paule for writing this book. I commend it to anyone who suspects the world we want cannot be built by people who have never asked themselves why they want it.

Jed Emerson
New York City

Emerson is the originator of the Blended Value framework and, among other books, author of *The Purpose of Capital: Elements of Impact, Financial Flows and Natural Being.* His ongoing writing on democracy, value, and the Antidote to Authoritarianism may be found at blendedvalue.substack.com.

Introduction to the Book

Prologue: A Canvas for Creation

"As if you could kill time without injuring eternity." –**Henry David Thoreau**, Journal, 1851.

These words have lingered in my mind for years. As if we could kill time without injuring eternity. To me, they are a gentle yet powerful reminder of life's ultimate purpose: to awaken—to live not just on the surface, but with depth, integrity, and meaning. Not merely for ourselves, but for others, for those yet unborn, for eternity.

Thoreau warns us that to "kill time" is to squander the moments that shape our existence. Every thought, every action, every investment ripples outward into infinity. Nothing is insignificant. And yet, how often do we live as though our choices do not matter? How often do we let distractions, ambitions, and fleeting concerns pull us away from the profound?

The tragedy of humanity lies in its failure to recognise its own greatness. Too often, we define ourselves by what we **do**—our jobs, achievements, possessions—while remaining blind to the immeasurable depth of who we truly **are**. We skim the surface of life, absorbed in external pursuits, forgetting to explore the inner landscape where our true potential resides. This disconnect is not only a personal loss; it is a collective one. When we fail to nurture the greatness **within**, we limit our capacity to contribute meaningfully to the world.

Thoreau's insight is a call to live with purpose. To remember that the fleeting moments of our daily lives are woven into something far greater. When we neglect our values, when we forget our responsibility to one another and to the world, we can injure eternity.

But here lies the beauty: each moment is a choice. A chance to step off the treadmill of distraction and treat time as a canvas—for creation, connection, and reverence. Each moment is an opportunity to awaken.

Thoreau's wisdom cuts to the heart of what it means to live well. It invites us to honour time, to cultivate purpose, to leave a legacy that transcends and endures. It reminds us that true wealth is not measured by what we accumulate, but by what we leave behind—the love we give, the knowledge we share, the beauty we create.

Philosophy, for me, has been this awakening. It has taught me to look beyond the immediate and to see life as a grand composition in which every choice contributes to the whole. It has revealed that wealth is not just an economic concept, but a moral one. True wealth is found not in accumulation, but in wisdom, in kindness, in the steady formation of character—in learning to live in a way that honours what came before us and safeguards what will come after.

To honour our time is to brighten eternity.

Introduction: Where the Journey Begins

We are living in an age of rupture: climate collapse, rising inequality, digital overload, eroded trust. The crises we face are urgent, complex, and deeply interwoven. But beneath them lies a quieter crisis—harder to see, easier to ignore: a moral disconnection. An ethical forgetting. An oblivion of *being*.

And yet, something ancient is stirring. A sense that the answers we seek may not be entirely new, but beautifully old. That wisdom—deep, lived, humble wisdom—might offer a light through the fog. That what we need is not only policy and progress, but presence. **Philosophy, in its truest form: philia + sophia—the love of wisdom.**

This is where our journey begins: not in the markets, but in the mirror. Before we can rebuild the world, we must remember who we are—and how we choose to live, love, lead, and learn.

We begin with time—how we spend it, how we waste it, and how, through reflection and inner work, we can learn to honour it. We explore not only the necessity of systemic change, but the foundation of that change: the *Self.* Inner work. Because a sustainable world can only be built by sustainable beings.

Yet reflection alone is not enough. Awareness must lead to alignment—between our values and our systems, our inner thoughts and our outer choices.

In our modern world, power flows through finance. Capital fuels innovation, ambition, and growth—but it can also deepen inequality, exploit nature, and accelerate harm. Finance is not neutral. It mirrors our values. So we can ask: *What are we financing? What future are we building with each investment?*

This book traces a continuum. It learns from the past—to understand how we arrived here. It listens to the present—where something promising is unfolding, where conscience and capital begin to converge in the form of *impact investing*. And it dreams forward—toward a future that could emerge if finance, entrepreneurship, and life were guided by the *Love of Wisdom*, and the *Wisdom of Love*.

It reminds us that the most powerful revolutions are not only technological or political. They are ethical. And they begin within.

This is not a book of easy answers. It is a map of questions. An invitation to reconnect: wisdom with wealth, **being** with **doing**, soul with system. Because the world we long for cannot be outsourced. It begins here. Within us.

About the Author

Life enthusiast, mother of two angels, and industrial engineer turned financier, Paule is on a journey to harness ancient philosophy to become the best version of herself.

With over 20 years of experience in Capital Markets and Asset Management, she is now Managing Director Italy at Arcano Partners. She has lived and worked in Milan, London, Paris and Madrid with firms such as Rothschild & Co and Bank of America Merrill Lynch.

She co-founded Inclusive Finance and serves on the board of Alice for Children. She holds an MBA, a Master in Sustainability, and is a certified ESG Analyst (CFA UK).

She is passionate about ancient philosophy, nature, animals, books, sport, yoga, meditation, and everything that cannot be bought or measured.

She believes that outer change begins within, and that finance—when guided by the love of wisdom—can become a powerful force for good.

Acknowledgements

Andrea Bozza: My husband, my partner. This book is also thanks to you. Thank you for making space—for holding the fort during endless weekends dedicated to writing. I know it has not always been easy, but you persisted. I could not have done this without you.

Nike and Chloe: If Daddy was the practical support, you were the emotional. You were my rocks. My heroes. My personal advisors—"Mummy, put stickers; otherwise, nobody will buy it!" I am so thankful to you both. I know Mummy spent too much time writing, and I'm sorry we missed out on so many adventures. But I hope it's worth the effort. I hope you will read this book one day (when you no longer like stickers!) and, most importantly, I hope you realize that there is far more magic in the depths than on the surface of life. And thank you for the marvellous drawing, my love, Nike. Chloe will illustrate the second one.

Karen Nahum: I have no words to thank you. This book exists because of you. Thank you for insisting, for believing I could do it—even before I did. Most people write a book and then find an editor. I had an editor before I even had a book. You read a few of my articles and immediately saw something in me. Your trust lit the first spark. I will carry that gift always. And I will be forever grateful.

Jed Emerson: Thank you for writing the preface to this book, and for inspiring me for years through your pioneering vision of impact investing and mutual impact. The Purpose of Capital holds a special place in my library and in my journey. Your work helped me see more clearly that finance, guided by wisdom and values, can become a force for human and planetary flourishing.

Antonio Lagala: Thank you for being such a kind, grounded presence. It has been a true pleasure working with you. Your calm and clarity brought peace to this process.

Ben Granger: For being the most brilliant and generous English teacher I've ever had. Your guidance helped me shape this book in a language that is not my own—but is now a part of me. Thanks to you for the most enlightening English lessons ever.

Odile Robotti: For being a friend, a coach, and a role model. Epictetus was right: we must surround ourselves with those who uplift us. That's you.

Luca Mentasti and Gianfilippo Mancini: Thank you for your thoughtful *last-minute* proofreading support. Your encouragement and timely feedback were greatly appreciated.

To my mother, Belén: To whom this book is dedicated. Thank you for a lifetime of wisdom shared with love—for the conversations, the books, and the quiet understanding. No one has lived a life so different from mine, and yet understood mine so completely. Not sure where I would have been without you.

To Daniel Lumera , Epictetus, Mario Alonso Puig, and all the remarkable authors, philosophers, and visionaries mentioned in these pages—thank you for your light. Your words have shaped the questions I've asked and the path I've chosen to walk.

Thank you to all the **Entrepreneurial Almas**, mentioned and unmentioned, and the **Financial Almas**—and to the **Almas** in general.

To all those whose names do not appear here, but whose love and presence have quietly shaped this book—thank you.

And to you, **my dear reader**—thank you for the time you've dedicated to these pages. If these pages stirred something within you, then they have fulfilled their purpose. If you feel like sharing your thoughts, reflections, or simply saying hello, I would love to hear from you: pauleansoleagaabascal@gmail.com

The Journey Ahead

Part 1

Why Philosophy and Finance, Together

This first block explains why I decided to write this book, and why I am bringing together two disciplines that seem, at first glance, worlds apart: Philosophy and finance. It is not a prescription, nor a set of answers to heal the world's problems—I would not dare. It is, rather, a personal journey. A map of questions. Questions that have followed me quietly for years: Why are we here? What do we truly value? What is the purpose of capital? And the purpose of life? How might our economic systems reflect the deeper currents of the human spirit? Why are we treating just symptoms, without addressing the root causes of our problems?

Along the way, I stumbled upon surprising bridges. Thales of Miletus, the first philosopher in Western history, was also the first known financier. The connection between philosophy and finance was there from the very beginning—though somewhere along the road, we seem to have forgotten it.

In this block, I share stories—of eagles and wolves, seekers and sages, philosophers and emperors—to make the journey not only profound, but also, and most importantly, playful. Each of these tales, in its own way, gestures toward the same truth: that it is time to reunite what we have long held apart—numbers and values, capital and wisdom, prosperity and purpose, system and soul.

1

Philosophy's Useless, Transformative Beauty

Life is a wondrous unfolding—a journey of learning, growing, and deepening our understanding of the world and ourselves. When we realise that true peace is not found in the endless pursuit of consumption and distraction, but in introspection and connection, everything changes. Suddenly, beauty reveals itself in unexpected ways.

For each of us, this realisation arrives differently. For me, it was Philosophy that unlocked the door. By sharing my humble experience, I hope to offer a window of reflection, an invitation to pause and consider a path that has profoundly transformed my own life. If it resonates with even one person, if it sparks even the smallest shift towards a more thoughtful, intentional way of living, then these pages will have been worth writing.

Yet, Philosophy's power did not reveal itself to me through mere intellectual study. Reading the Sages fed my soul with fleeting moments of wonder, but their wisdom remained abstract, easily swept away by the demands of daily life—until I began to **live** it. Philosophy became transformative only when I committed to putting it into practice, when I allowed its lessons to shape my choices, my character, my way of being in the world. This is why I fell in love with Ancient Philosophy—a tradition not confined to academic discourse, but devoted to guiding how we live.

The French philosopher Pierre Hadot captured this distinction perfectly. In his masterpiece Philosophy as a Way of Life, he reminds us that, for the ancients, Philosophy was not an abstract system but an art of living—a practice meant to transform one's way of being. Only later did philosophy retreat into technical language, increasingly confined to specialists and academic circles.

P. Ansoleaga Abascal, *Philosophy and Finance: A Love Story*,
https://doi.org/10.1007/978-3-032-22218-3_1

Philosophy was a way of being, a daily discipline of mind, heart and soul. It meant engaging in spiritual exercises, practicing virtue, progressively shaping one's character through conscious action. It was not an abstract pursuit, but a lived commitment—a path toward wisdom, self-mastery, and inner peace.

This is the Philosophy I love. The Philosophy that will inhabit these pages. Philosophy with capital P.

The very word Philosophy comes from two Greek roots: **philia** (love) and **sophia** (wisdom). To love wisdom—to seek it, to cherish it, to let it illuminate our path—is, I believe, one of the noblest pursuits.

And yet, Philosophy is often dismissed as impractical, abstract, or *useless*. A luxury reserved for those with time to spare. But is it really *useless*? I would argue quite the opposite. It is life-changing, the most *useful*—and beautiful—discipline of all.

Perhaps my disillusionment lies not with Philosophy, but with the narrow way we define *usefulness* in our modern world. From childhood, we are taught to pursue only what is productive—what leads to measurable success. We study, exercise, eat well—not for the simple joy of learning, moving, or nourishing ourselves—but to achieve: to secure a high-paying job, to maintain a certain image, to meet external expectations. **This obsession with usefulness strips ordinary life of its magic. It blinds us to the beauty of the present moment.**

At 45, I feel I have pursued enough *useful* endeavours. Now, I am drawn to the **useless**—to standing still, to staring in awe, to savouring life as it unfolds. To expanding my sense of now. As the Welsh poet W. H. Davies so beautifully wrote:

What is this life if, full of care,
We have no time to stand and stare?

–W. H. Davies, Leisure (1911)

Philosophy invites us to do just that. To pause. To look beyond surface distractions and into the depths of what truly matters. It turns out that the most *useless* of all disciplines is also the most precious, the most transformative, the most essential.

Philia and *Sophia*, Love and Wisdom, Strength and Freedom

Love makes us strong. Love—by which I mean **Philia** (brotherly love) and **Agape** (universal, selfless love)—makes us strong. It gives us the courage to face our fears, the resilience to uphold our values, and the generosity to extend ourselves toward the well-being of others.

Wisdom makes us free. True wisdom is not just knowledge, but a deep, harmonious understanding of life—an integration of intellect, experience, and inner clarity. It is the light that guides us toward virtue, helping us live with integrity and purpose. Wisdom frees us from the need for external validation. It allows us to walk our own path, unapologetically yet compassionately, with the grace to respect and support the paths of others.

Is there anything more beautiful—more profoundly human—than possessing strength and freedom?

> *Philosophy offers us a beauty that is not fleeting, not bound to appearances. It is a beauty that radiates from within—shining through clarity of thought, the light in one's eyes, the warmth of the heart, and the quiet, boundless power to make the world better for all.*

My Father's Three-Legged Stool, and My Mother's Epictetus Book

When I was a child, my father used to say that the body, mind, and soul could be distinguished—but never separated.

"We," he used to tell me, **"are like a three-legged stool. If one leg is missing, we cannot stand steady—we wobble, or worse, we collapse."**

He often observed that in the Western world, we tend to care for the **body** and cultivate the **mind**, but the **soul**—the spiritual dimension—is too often neglected, dismissed as impractical or irrelevant. Yet without it, we remain incomplete. Something essential is missing.

Though I did not fully understand his words as a child, I felt their truth.

Years later, life led me to an engineering school, an MBA, and a career in the financial heart of London. I was apparently successful, yet I felt something was missing. I was living what Socrates called an *unexamined life*—one driven by achievement, but disconnected from my true essence. I felt like an actress playing a role that was not my own.

Then, my mother—herself a psychologist, and someone who knew me better than I knew myself—gently placed a book in my hands: **Discourses** by **Epictetus**.

Reading Epictetus, I finally understood my father's words. The wisdom of the Stoics awakened me to a deeper way of living—one in which external success pales in comparison to inner character. It was the beginning of a journey back to myself.

Through **Socrates**, I learned that Philosophy is not an academic pursuit, but a way of life. Through **Aristotle**, I discovered the *golden mean*—the delicate balance between excess and deficiency in the cultivation of virtue. **Seneca** taught me that time is our most precious resource, and that wasting it is life's greatest tragedy. My beloved **Epictetus** revealed the *dichotomy of control*—the power of focusing only on what lies within us, and letting go of all the rest. **Marcus Aurelius** showed me the strength of daily reflection. **Lao Tzu and Nietzsche** offered the wisdom of *Wu Wei* and *amor fati*—to flow with life rather than force it, to love one's fate and embrace existence as it is, not as we wish it to be. The **Buddha** helped me understand the restless nature of the mind, and the peace that emerges through stillness. And **Daniel Lumera** has illuminated my path with the power of forgiveness, the discipline of meditation, and the idea that kindness not only softens the soul—but brightens and lengthens life itself.

The list is longer than I can name—spanning centuries, cultures, and voices. Some are well known, others barely remembered. Yet all carried the same truth: the **outer** world reflects the **inner** one. Yes, **the world outside mirrors our world within.**

As **William James**, one of the founders of modern psychology and a pioneer of pragmatist philosophy, observed, one of the most profound revolutions of modern thought is the realisation that by changing our inner attitudes, we can transform the outer conditions of our lives.

I did not want to live a *limping life*. I wanted to live fully, with purpose, peace, and boundless joy. And I wanted to share that joy with others.

In a world obsessed with speed, success, and material gain, Philosophy offers an oasis of peace. It calls us to step back. To ask: *Am I living in alignment with my values? Am I seeking wisdom, or just chasing achievement?*

Philosophy offers us not just answers, but the courage to ask better questions.

This book is my way of giving back—of sharing the beauty of Philosophy, the love of wisdom, with those who seek a more meaningful way forward.

Who knows? If we infuse finance with Philosophy, numbers with ethics, and investing with integrity, perhaps the world might grow a little fairer, a little kinder, a little more alive with possibility. And that, after all, is the whole point.

2

The Eagle and the Wolf

Once upon a time, a Navajo Sage sat down with his grandson to share a lesson about life.

> "*My soul is a battlefield,*" the elder said. "*On one side, there is a majestic Eagle. She soars above the clouds, her every action guided by truth, love, peace, goodness, and beauty. Though she sometimes descends into the valleys, she always lays her eggs high in the mountains, close to the heavens.*
> *But within me also dwells a terrible Wolf. He is filled with anger, envy, greed, arrogance, and resentment. He is the embodiment of my Ego, the voice that justifies every selfish impulse. He watches my falls with satisfaction, whispering that he, too, is part of me.*"

The grandson thought for a moment before asking, "**Which one wins the battle, Grandfather?**"

The elder replied, **"The one I feed every day."**

P. Ansoleaga Abascal, *Philosophy and Finance: A Love Story*,
https://doi.org/10.1007/978-3-032-22218-3_2

Nikole Bozza Ansoleaga

I do not know whether this story truly originates from the Navajo people. Many attribute it to the Cherokees, calling it the *Two Wolves* parable instead. Whether it is *The Eagle and the Wolf* or *The Two Wolves* does not concern me much—though I confess a fondness for the Eagle, with her majestic flight and noble spirit.

What matters is the truth this story conveys. Within each of us, there is both light and shadow, virtue and vice. We are not passive recipients of our nature but active participants in shaping our character. The Eagle and the Wolf remind us that **who we become is determined by what we cultivate within.**

I love this story because it gives me a visual language for my own struggles. I can picture my Eagle and my Wolf battling for control over my thoughts, words, choices and actions. When I act with kindness, generosity, or courage, I see my Eagle in flight. When I crave external validation or succumb to resentment, I feel my Wolf stirring. In most cases, my Wolf is simply my Ego—the part of me that fears, clings, and seeks to be fed.

This story could have been written by my favourite philosopher, Epictetus. Like the elder teaching his grandson, Epictetus taught that our character is not fixed but formed through daily choices. We become what we practise, what we give our attention to.

"We become what we give our attention to." –Inspired by Epictetus, Discourses (paraphrase)

Few philosophers have influenced me as profoundly as Epictetus. Born into slavery in the first century AD, physically disabled, and later exiled from Rome, he was intimately acquainted with suffering. Yet he lived with a rare and enduring freedom—one rooted in the mind.

His teachings, recorded by his student Arrian, remain among the most powerful guides to a meaningful life. For Epictetus, happiness did not depend on circumstances, but on the cultivation of inner virtue. He invited his students to attend carefully to what lies within their control, and to release what does not—a simple insight, endlessly demanding, and quietly transformative.

Through Epictetus, I learned to nourish my Eagle consciously: to practise patience in moments of frustration, gratitude in times of difficulty, humility in the face of success. I learned that Philosophy is lived before it is understood. That wisdom, like any craft, takes shape through daily attention.

Building Character: Striving Toward *Arête*

For Epictetus, Philosophy was not about abstract theories but about shaping one's soul. To live well, he believed, one must cultivate **arête**—excellence of character—through three essential and interconnected disciplines.

The first is **physics**, or natural philosophy: understanding the nature of the cosmos and our place within it. Without this perspective, we become frustrated by life's unpredictability and resistant to what cannot be changed.

The second is **logic**: learning to think clearly, critically, and coherently. Without reason, we can fall prey to confusion or distorted judgments.

The third is **ethics**: using our understanding of nature and our capacity for reason to act justly and to contribute to the common good. Without ethics, knowledge becomes hollow and intelligence loses its moral compass.

These three pillars were deeply intertwined. To live virtuously, one had to **understand the world, think clearly, and act justly**. Without a grasp of nature's laws, we become frustrated by life's unpredictability. Without reason, we are at the mercy of impulse. Without morality, knowledge becomes an empty pursuit.

This integrated vision of wisdom is largely absent today. Science advances at extraordinary speed, while ethical reflection struggles to keep pace. We celebrate intelligence, yet overlook character. We build powerful technologies without pausing to ask whom they serve, or at what cost.

I often return to Epictetus' teaching that we become what we give our attention to. If we devoted the same care to forming character as we do to accumulating knowledge, our scientific and economic progress would be guided by a deeper sense of responsibility—and a truer concern for the common good.

An Inflection Point in Human History

We are at a turning point. We have outlined bold visions for the future—frameworks for sustainability, shared prosperity, and a more conscious form of capitalism. On paper, the solutions are there. And yet, implementation remains our Achilles' heel. We are not losing the battle of ideas, but the courage to act upon them. Too often, our Wolves still overpower our Eagles.

What prevails today is an EGO-system: a world organised around self-interest, competition, and short-term gain. It crowds out the ECO-system we urgently need—one grounded in collaboration, interdependence, sustainability, and shared prosperity. We continue to model our economies on **Homo Oeconomicus**, the isolated, rational, self-interested individual. We design education systems that reward performance over wisdom, productivity over purpose.

And so, we find ourselves in a paradox. Never before have we possessed so much knowledge, and yet so little wisdom. We are scientifically and technologically advanced, yet deeply divided, anxious, and unfulfilled. The crises we face—climate change, inequality, war—are not merely external challenges. They are symptoms of a deeper rupture: a crisis of values, a loss of meaning, an erosion of ethics, a growing disconnection from ourselves, from one another, and from nature.

And yet, I believe we can still turn the tide. The deepest and most enduring revolutions are not technological, but moral. Before we change our world, we must change our minds and hearts. As Einstein once observed, the problems we face cannot be solved with the same patterns of thinking that created them. They call for a transformation in how we see and understand the world.

We can think differently. We can act differently. Science, business, and innovation—the **head**—can be guided by wisdom, empathy, and responsibility—the **heart**. Moral Philosophy can once again inform our institutions, our economies, and our decisions. We can restore the balance between intellect and ethics, reason and compassion, progress and purpose.

Pope Francis often reminded us that economic and political objectives cannot stand on their own. Without ethical foundations, they lose their legitimacy. And ethics, in turn, requires an inner transformation—a true change of heart.

The Stoics expressed this insight in their own way: when virtue leads the way, every step becomes safe.

We can reawaken the wisdom of the past to shape the future we seek. We can embrace a new paradigm—one in which finance fuels not only growth, but wellbeing; where success is measured not by accumulation, but by contribution; where our Eagles, once again, lead the way forward.

3

The Road of Being or the Road of Having

I am convinced we can choose between two roads in life: the road of **being** or the road of **having**.

The **road of being** is the path of love, kindness, empathy, and generosity. It is the road of harmony with all beings and with nature. It is a journey of meaning, where even the smallest steps are guided by a greater vision. It is the road of creativity, of work that is not merely productive but deeply fulfilling—work that adds value, that uplifts, that contributes. It is the path of a **eudaimonic** life. On this road, we consciously choose to feed our Eagles.

The **road of having**, on the other hand, is the road of accumulation, external validation, and the endless pursuit of more. Detached from purpose, it can grow dangerous—sliding into egoism, greed, extractive labour, or ruthless competition. It can become a life shaped by outward measures, where accumulation replaces meaning, success becomes identity, and consumption replaces connection. A purely hedonistic existence—the path on which our Wolf comes to rule our life.

To me, the road of being leads to true happiness, authentic relationships, inner peace, and a life of profound fulfilment. The road of having leads to dissatisfaction, transactional relationships, and an inner void that manifests as stress, anxiety, and loneliness.

Extensive psychological and economic research shows that the more individuals prioritise money, image, and social status, the lower their overall well-being and the higher their levels of distress. Materialistic values are consistently associated with reduced life satisfaction, fewer positive emotions, and a greater prevalence of anxiety, depression, anger, and fear. They are also linked

P. Ansoleaga Abascal, *Philosophy and Finance: A Love Story*,
https://doi.org/10.1007/978-3-032-22218-3_3

to poorer physical health, higher substance use, and an increased risk of psychosomatic and cardiovascular disorders.

Economist Stefano Bartolini, in **Manifesto for Happiness**, synthesises decades of this empirical evidence to show how societies centred on consumption and status undermine both individual flourishing and collective well-being. Similar conclusions have been reached by psychologists studying materialism and well-being, including Tim Kasser and Richard Ryan.

Choosing the road of being is not easy. It requires conscious effort, resilience, and the courage to question inherited values and deeply rooted beliefs. Our societies are designed to nudge us onto the road of having—to chase external achievements, what the Stoics called *preferred indifferents*, like wealth, career success, or status. The more, the better. We are conditioned to believe that our worth is measured by accumulation—of possessions, accolades, influence. But in this restless pursuit of more, we lose sight of the richness of simply being.

This is where Philosophy becomes our refuge. Philosophy—the love of wisdom—reminds us of what truly matters. It transforms life into a journey of learning and growth, guiding us towards self-mastery and inner peace.

Patagonia, the outdoor clothing brand, offers a striking example of what happens when those at the helm of a business choose the road of being. Founded by **Yvon Chouinard**, Patagonia has always placed ethics before profit, purpose before unchecked growth. From pioneering sustainable materials to encouraging customers to buy less, Patagonia defies the mainstream corporate obsession with endless expansion. In 2022, Chouinard and his family made an extraordinary decision: they gave away Patagonia. Instead of selling the company or taking it public, they transferred ownership to a trust dedicated to environmental protection. The business still earns revenue, but that wealth is now entirely directed toward sustaining the planet. The company continues to thrive—demonstrating that rejecting the road of having does not mean rejecting success. It means redefining it.

Financial leaders can choose the road of being too. **Jacqueline Novogratz**, the founder of Acumen, is one such leader. She has redefined finance not as a tool for accumulation, but as a force for dignity and human flourishing.

Both ancient wisdom and modern science show that the *road of having* can become a labyrinth—a twisting, noisy maze that traps us in cycles of desire and dissatisfaction.

But there are threads that can guide us out.

Religion, Philosophy, Spirituality—all offer pathways back to the road of being. Each thread is different, yet all point to the same truth: fulfilment is not found in external acquisition but in inner peace, alignment, and love.

This book is about one of those threads—just one among millions—and it is called Ancient Philosophy.

Not Philosophy as a mere intellectual pursuit, but Philosophy as a way of life. The love of wisdom, as practised by the ancients. The wisdom that strengthens our Eagles, allowing them to soar above the illusions of the world, while our Wolves—our Egos—hibernate, growing quieter, weaker, until, one day, they disappear altogether.

4

The Story of Eliahu and Hakim

In an oasis hidden deep in the desert, old Eliahu knelt beside a palm grove, digging in the sand. His neighbour, Hakim, a wealthy merchant, stopped to water his camels and saw Eliahu sweating, labouring under the scorching sun.

Hakim: **"How are you, old man? Peace be with you."**
Eliahu: **"And with you,"** he replied, without stopping his work.
Hakim: **"What are you doing here, in this heat, with that shovel in your hands?"**
Eliahu: **"I am sowing."**
Hakim: **"Sowing what?"**
Eliahu: **"Dates,"** he said, gesturing toward the palms around them.
Hakim: **"Dates?"** Hakim repeated, narrowing his eyes. **"The heat must have clouded your mind, my friend. Come, leave this, and let's have a drink."**
Eliahu: **"I must finish planting first. Then, if you wish, we will drink."**
Hakim: **"But tell me, Eliahu, how old are you?"**
Eliahu: **"Sixty, seventy, eighty… I don't know. I've forgotten. But does it matter?"**
Hakim: **"Of course it matters! Date palms take more than fifty years to bear fruit. I hope you live to a hundred, but you know you will never reap what you sow today. Leave this foolishness and come with me."**
Eliahu: **"Look, Hakim, I ate the dates that someone else planted, someone who never dreamed of tasting them. I sow today so that others may eat tomorrow. Even if only in honour of that stranger, I must finish my task."**
Hakim: **"You have given me a great lesson, my friend. Let me repay you."** And with that, he placed a leather bag of coins in Eliahu's hand.

P. Ansoleaga Abascal, *Philosophy and Finance: A Love Story*,
https://doi.org/10.1007/978-3-032-22218-3_4

Eliahu: **"I appreciate your kindness, Hakim. But you see? You said I would not reap what I sowed. And yet, before I've even finished planting, I have already harvested a bag of coins—and the gratitude of a friend."**

Nikole Bozza Ansoleaga

Today, most of us think like Hakim. We measure life by immediate rewards. We ask what we can gain, rather than what we can give. We plant only when we are certain we will be the ones to harvest—ourselves, or at most our closest circle of family and friends. We see ourselves as separate from the rest of humanity, divided by borders, skin colour, generations, and ideologies. We allow differences of race, religion, gender, and politics to define us, building walls where bridges are needed.

Decades of neglecting philosophical, religious, and spiritual wisdom have left us with a hyper-rational, materialistic worldview—one that mistakes hyper-individualism for freedom. Market values—*EGO-system* values—have displaced human values—*ECO-system* values—encouraging relentless competition while quietly eroding relationships, families, and communities. The result is an existential void that material wealth cannot fill.

We chase external rewards—money, power, status—at the expense of deeper, intrinsic ones: fulfilment, connection, purpose. Companies, too, prioritise short-term profits over people and planet. This mindset lies at the root of our climate, social, and economic crises. The climate emergency, in particular, is not only an environmental issue; it is a symptom of our disconnection from the world around us, and of our false belief in separation.

We fail to act because we do not feel part of the whole. We experience these crises as distant—melting ice at the poles, consequences deferred to future generations. Even when disaster strikes closer to home—wildfires in California, floods in Valencia—our memories are short. Like Hakim, we ask: why sow seeds that will not bear fruit in our lifetime?

But Eliahu understood something profound: we are part of a greater whole, and we are happiest when we contribute to it.

I think of Eliahu every day when I cycle to work. As I pass through the Duomo of Milan, I see five centuries of collaboration: architects, sculptors, and artisans working across generations. Each contributed their talent without knowing whether they would ever see the final masterpiece.

Ancient Philosophy invites us to adopt Eliahu's perspective. It reminds us that wisdom, inner peace, and virtue are the foundations of a eudaimonic life, a life truly worth living. By looking inward, we cultivate the clarity and compassion needed to inspire change outward. Eliahu's decision to plant date palms, knowing he would never harvest their fruit, reflects long-term vision and devotion to the common good. He seemed genuinely at peace with himself and with his place in the world. His joy did not come from what he owned, but from what he gave.

Happiness is one of the greatest gifts we can offer the world. And it spreads. Research shows that fulfilment ripples through social networks: when we are at ease within ourselves, others tend to feel it too. Just as Eliahu awakened something in Hakim, inner joy can awaken those around us. Happier people build stronger communities. They look beyond consumption in search of meaning. They care more deeply for the planet. A shift toward inner fulfilment naturally gives rise to more conscious, more compassionate, and more sustainable ways of living.

Contemporary writer and spiritual teacher **Rebecca Campbell** often speaks of the quiet power of inner light. When we live in alignment with who we truly are, our presence alone begins to awaken others. One illuminated life invites another, and then another, until transformation spreads gently, almost imperceptibly, through the world.

Creating a better world requires more than balance sheets and net-zero commitments. It calls for systemic transformation: new economic thinking, sustainable policymaking, bold investment choices, and unprecedented global cooperation.

Yet all enduring change begins within. A better world cannot emerge without a shift in human consciousness, one that embraces unity, gratitude, and interdependence. A movement from me to we, from short-termism to long-term vision, from having to being, from fear to love. From Hakim to Eliahu.

When we transcend the ego and reconnect with one another and with nature, we do more than increase our own happiness. We help heal the planet. And we create a world in which our children, grandchildren, and those who come after them can enjoy the dates we plant today.

5

The Role of Inner Work in Reimagining Capitalism

The world stands at a crossroads. We are living through a convergence of crises that no longer unfold in isolation: war and climate breakdown, ecological overshoot and rising inequality, mental distress and forced migration, technological power without ethical restraint, the erosion of social bonds, the loss of shared meaning. Together, they are straining human flourishing and planetary balance.

The urgency of this moment is no longer in question. Economic shocks, ecological disruption, and persistent conflict have made one thing unmistakably clear: our current economic paradigm has failed too many. Sustainable development is no longer an aspiration or a moral add-on. It has become a condition for continuity.

Across boardrooms, financial conferences, and business schools, this awareness has been building for over a decade. Long before today's crises became impossible to ignore, voices within business and finance were already questioning a model centred exclusively on profit. And this has continued despite growing backlash and a global environment marked by conflict, insecurity, and the temptation to retreat into narrow, short-term priorities. There is now widespread recognition that capitalism must evolve—no longer oriented solely toward profit, but toward people and the planet as well. And yet, while the need for change is broadly acknowledged, the path forward is still understood in very different ways.

Some argue that reimagining capitalism begins with redesigning the **corporation**—embedding social and environmental purpose at its core. They champion the triple bottom line: People, Planet, and Profit. In this view, financial success becomes a means, not the ultimate goal. Companies,

P. Ansoleaga Abascal, *Philosophy and Finance: A Love Story*,
https://doi.org/10.1007/978-3-032-22218-3_5

they argue, should exist to create long-term value, not merely short-term gains. And they have a point: businesses are the backbone of our economies. Without responsible, visionary companies, the future we hope for cannot be built. Governments and philanthropies alone cannot shoulder this burden.

Others believe that **finance** itself must evolve—enabling and encouraging business leaders to focus on long-term value creation instead of quarterly performance. In this vision, capital allocation becomes a lever for sustainability, channelling investment into enterprises that generate positive impact, not just shareholder returns. If business is the backbone of the economy, finance is its lifeblood.

Still others advocate for bold **government** action to ensure markets serve the greater good. They call for public investment in green technologies, stronger environmental regulation, and tax incentives that reward sustainable innovation. Some envision a modern *Green Keynesianism*, with governments leading the charge toward a regenerative economy—just as the New Deal reshaped the industrial landscape in the twentieth century. Others call for true cost accounting, requiring companies to disclose the full social and environmental consequences of their operations—so externalities like air pollution or biodiversity depletion are no longer hidden from economic analysis.

Each of these perspectives is essential. We need businesses that embrace purpose beyond profit, finance that fuels sustainable transformation, and governments that create the conditions for long-term change.

And yet, beneath all these systemic solutions lies a simple, often overlooked truth: businesses, financial institutions, and governments are built and led by people. **There can be no ethical business, no responsible finance, no visionary government without conscious, responsible, and visionary individuals behind them.** An economic system that seeks more than profit requires leaders and decision-makers whose purpose transcends self-interest. Likewise, a financial architecture capable of measuring not only risk and return, but also impact, depends on investors willing to look beyond profit alone. Even the most carefully designed policies and incentives will fail if they are not shaped and enacted by people guided by empathy, justice, and responsibility.

Inner work is the missing foundation of economic transformation. It is what nurtures human values, reshapes perception, and expands consciousness.

The great economic transformations of history were never merely technical shifts—they were shifts in consciousness too. The **Agricultural Revolution** marked more than the dawn of farming; it introduced a new way of relating to the earth and to one another. Humanity moved from nomadic, cooperative tribes to settled societies rooted in land ownership, hierarchy, and the idea of surplus—of having more than one needs. Centuries later, during the **Axial Age**, profound philosophical and spiritual awakenings—from Confucianism to Stoicism—reshaped moral understandings of wealth, justice, and human purpose. These emerging worldviews provided ethical foundations that would guide trade, labour, and governance for generations. As the medieval world gave way to the Renaissance, the **Commercial Revolution** brought not only new financial tools like credit and double-entry bookkeeping, but also a shift in human self-perception. The rise of the merchant and the idea of individual agency transformed money into something built on trust and story, rather than just gold or silver. Then came the **Industrial Revolution**, which reimagined nature as raw material and time as something to be measured, optimised, and sold. People became labourers, machines replaced muscle, and growth became the new god. And now, in the **Digital Age**, we are immersed in yet another transformation—where data becomes currency, attention becomes capital, and identity is increasingly shaped by code.

Throughout history, the most profound economic transformations have been rooted in a shift in perception—a transformation of consciousness—that accompanied humanity's greatest turning points. Today, we are called to make that leap once more: to awaken a new consciousness capable of igniting an **Ethical Revolution**—a *conditio sine qua non* for a true **Sustainability Revolution**, and for preserving life on this planet as we know it.

This revolution will not be powered by policy alone. As we strive to build a fairer and more sustainable economy, we must acknowledge that technical solutions, innovation, and economic reform—though essential—are not enough.

Pope Francis repeatedly warned that economic and political systems cannot stand on their own. In his teaching, economics divorced from ethics becomes destructive, and genuine transformation requires an inner conversion—a change of heart that precedes structural change. His message was clear: without moral grounding, no economic model can truly serve human dignity or the common good.

For me, inner work is the foundation of any meaningful economic transformation. At the heart of stakeholder capitalism, purpose-driven business, impact investing, and the 2030 Agenda lies something deeper: the inner work that shapes the integrity, discernment, and responsibility of those who lead the change.

Inner work allows us to see ourselves, and by extension the world, more clearly. Without self-awareness, we remain caught in habitual patterns, driven by unconscious fears, desires, and inherited assumptions. Inner work brings these patterns into the light, giving us the freedom to respond consciously rather than react automatically. It reveals that we are not isolated individuals, but waves within the same vast ocean, deeply interconnected with one another.

Nikole Bozza Ansoleaga

When this awareness takes root, life begins to change. We may not be able to transform the world on our own, but we can transform the one thing fully within our control: ourselves. And when enough people do so, becoming beacons of wisdom, compassion, and integrity, change begins to ripple outward. A new way of being emerges, and with it, the possibility of a more just and sustainable world.

Personal transformation is the soil from which systemic change grows. It is perhaps the least discussed, yet most essential condition for ensuring that outer change is real and lasting.

Marie Curie, the pioneering scientist and two-time Nobel laureate, often reflected on the inseparable link between personal growth and collective progress. She believed that a better world must begin with the moral and intellectual development of individuals. Each of us, she argued, carries both a shared responsibility toward humanity and a personal duty to contribute where our abilities can be most useful.

The world outside is a reflection of the world within. The conflicts, inequalities, and environmental crises we witness today are rooted in inner states of fear, greed, and disconnection. Conversely, peace, justice, and sustainability arise from inner qualities of love, empathy, and moral clarity. Inner work lays the foundation for meaningful and lasting contribution to the world.

Socrates: The Father of Inner Work

When I think about inner work, the first person who comes to mind is Socrates. When asked to summarise all philosophical commandments, Socrates replied: *know yourself.*

> ***"Know yourself"*** **–Delphic maxim, widely cited in ancient sources and reported by Plato**

For Socrates, self-examination was not an abstract exercise but the foundation of a meaningful life. He believed that wealth, status, and reputation were fleeting, while the soul—the inner essence of who we are—was what truly mattered.

> ***"An unexamined life is not worth living."*** **–Socrates, as reported by Plato, Apology 38a (English translation in the public domain, e.g. Benjamin Jowett)**

To live without reflection, he believed, was to live a diminished life. Self-knowledge marked the beginning of wisdom and the cornerstone of ethical responsibility. Caring for the soul was not optional; it was our highest duty.

A similar insight appears in Eastern thought. Confucius taught that social harmony begins with self-cultivation. Order in the world, he believed, cannot be imposed from the outside. It must grow outward from an ordered heart.

> ***"To put the world in order, we must first put the nation in order.***
> ***To put the nation in order, we must first put the family in order.***
> ***To put the family in order, we must first cultivate our personal life.***
> ***To cultivate our personal life, we must first set our hearts right."***
> **–Confucius, The Great Learning, trans.**
> **James Legge (nineteenth century, public domain)**

These ancient teachings remind us that inner work is not just about personal growth—it is the foundation of a just and harmonious society.
My Ode to Inner Work

Inner work to make the unconscious, conscious. Inner work to think critically, to reflect upon the ideas we are exposed to, and the values we have inherited Inner work to transcend the materialistic, technocratic world we live in, reconnecting with our true essence, with others, with nature. Inner work to free ourselves from the mental, emotional, and cultural chains that imprison us. Inner work to create meaning through our life choices, embracing our freedom and the responsibility that comes with it. Inner work to discover our Ikigai, and put it at the service of humanity. Inner work to stop the endless pursuit of more, to reduce anxiety, depression, and stress, to understand that the quality of our lives depends upon the quality of our thoughts. Inner work to acquire the wisdom and integrity needed to become true leaders, so that we can restore ethics to our economy and to its most powerful tool—finance. Inner work, for outer change to be real and lasting. Inner work, as the foundation for reimagining capitalism.

6

Beyond the *HOW*, Embracing the *WHY* and *WHO*

As a global community, we have articulated a shared vision for a better future. The 2030 Agenda for Sustainable Development offers a powerful blueprint for peace, prosperity, and planetary well-being. At its heart are the Sustainable Development Goals, calling for an end to poverty, the protection of our planet, and the assurance that all people can live with dignity.

The SDGs matter because they remind us of something essential: no one should be left behind. They reflect a collective aspiration to thrive in a world that respects both people and the Earth that sustains us.

And yet, in our pursuit of these goals, we have become overwhelmingly focused on the HOW.

We ask how to deploy technology, how to scale innovation, how to decarbonise economies, optimise supply chains, capture carbon, automate efficiency, and measure impact. The HOW is indispensable. Science, innovation, and technological progress give us extraordinary tools. They give me hope.

But tools alone do not tell us why we should use them, nor who we must become in order to use them wisely.

We are entering an age in which artificial intelligence can master technical domains with breathtaking speed—coding, analysing, predicting, optimising. It can refine the HOW with extraordinary precision. But it cannot answer what the HOW is for. It cannot tell us who we ought to be as we wield such power. Knowledge is not wisdom. Efficiency is not conscience. A machine can calculate outcomes, but it cannot assume responsibility for them. That burden remains human. The deeper questions remain.

P. Ansoleaga Abascal, *Philosophy and Finance: A Love Story*,
https://doi.org/10.1007/978-3-032-22218-3_6

Why do future generations, whom we will never meet, have a right to a liveable planet?
Why should dignity not depend on where one is born, on gender, or on circumstance?
Why should peace, education, and health be considered fundamental rather than optional?

As Simon Sinek reminds us, the WHY is where purpose lives. It is what sustains commitment when progress is slow and trade-offs are hard. Without a clear WHY, the HOW risks becoming efficient yet hollow, sophisticated yet directionless.

The Sustainable Development Goals cannot be sustained by innovation alone. They require conviction. The conviction that every human life has equal worth. That dignity is inherent, not earned. That we are not separate from one another, nor from the natural systems on which we depend.

Yet even the WHY is not enough. Before asking why we act, we must ask who we are becoming as we act.

Who are we as investors, as entrepreneurs, as consumers, as voters, as leaders, as parents?
What values shape our decisions when no one is watching?
What trade-offs are we willing to accept, and which ones are we not?

The transformation we seek in our systems cannot exceed the maturity of the people who design, govern, and operate them.

This insight is not new. Across cultures and centuries, wisdom traditions have converged on the same understanding: lasting change begins with self-mastery and moral responsibility. From ancient philosophy to modern psychology, the message is consistent. Power over the external world without mastery of the inner one leads to imbalance, distortion, and harm.

"An unexamined life is not worth living."
–Socrates, as reported by Plato, Apology (38a)
"Yesterday I was clever, so I wanted to change the world. Today I am wise, so I am changing myself."
–Jalāl ad-Dīn Rumi, Masnavi (attributed poetic translation)

In the twentieth century, Carl Jung described how individuals often project meaning, blame, or salvation outward, rather than taking responsibility for their inner lives. Yet transformation, he argued, begins when attention turns inward, when consciousness expands, and when we integrate what we find within ourselves.

A just society cannot emerge from unjust hearts.

A sustainable world cannot be built by those unwilling to sustain their own inner lives.

This work begins quietly. In reflection. In the progressive alignment between our values and our actions. Not in the pursuit of perfection, but in the cultivation of awareness, responsibility, and care.

The future will not be shaped only by what we do. It will be shaped by who we become while doing it.

And it is from this place—from the integration of HOW, WHY, and WHO—that a truly sustainable, dignified, and humane world can begin to take form.

7

My Humble Experience

Philosophy—with a capital P—did not merely change how I think; it changed how I live. It reshaped my relationship with time, with beauty, with suffering, and with joy. What it has given me is so precious that keeping it to myself would feel profoundly selfish. I share it with you, my dear reader, in the hope that this ancient path might offer you a deeper way of inhabiting your life as well.

Philosophy transformed what Socrates would have called my once "unexamined life" into one filled with curiosity, purpose, and poetry. It helped me recognise and gently face what Martin Heidegger described as the *anxiety of nothingness* beneath modern life: the unease that arises when we lose contact with meaning, when we drift through our days absorbed in *doing*, disconnected from *being* itself. What once felt like a vague restlessness, a sense of emptiness I could not name, slowly became an invitation—to reflect, to discipline my attention, and to rediscover wonder.

Thanks to Philosophy, I no longer take beauty for granted. I am grateful for every breath, for every encounter. I focus on what I can control and allow the rest to unfold, trusting that each unfolding—whether gift or challenge—holds something to learn from. I find as much joy in silence and solitude as I do in laughter and conversation. I try to learn from my mistakes with humility, to love with greater presence, and to live fully—right here, right now.

But it has not always been this way.

When I chose to embrace Philosophy as a way of life and began the inner journey of self-cultivation, the path was anything but easy. It still is not. But it is deeply worth it.

P. Ansoleaga Abascal, *Philosophy and Finance: A Love Story*,
https://doi.org/10.1007/978-3-032-22218-3_7

At first, it was uncomfortable, even frustrating. My logical, scientific mind craved measurable results—the kind you get from work or a workout. Introspection, meditation, contemplation offered nothing immediate, nothing tangible to grasp. No quick wins. No clear markers of progress. And life was moving fast. I had a demanding job, two wonderful daughters who needed love and attention, a devoted husband, ageing parents back in Spain, a vibrant circle of friends, and ongoing commitments with Alice for Children. I was also involved in Inclusive Finance, a small think tank I had co-founded with a friend. My mind was spinning at full speed, caught in a perpetual state of urgency and responsibility.

I was deeply conditioned by the belief that I must always be doing something useful. Sitting alone with my thoughts, simply breathing, felt indulgent—almost selfish. Every moment of silence seemed stolen from work, from my daughters, or from caring for others. I felt I was not contributing to what society deemed valuable.

And yet, I persisted.

I persisted for three reasons.

First, I trusted the wisdom of my teachers—figures like Epictetus and the contemporary thinker Daniel Lumera—who had guided me this far. I trusted their conviction that cultivating a compassionate soul and a disciplined mind was essential for inner tranquillity and growth.

Second, I trusted my intuition—my unconscious, and above all, my heart. I knew, deep down, that life was more than achievements, to-do lists, and endless appointments.

And finally, I carried with me a childhood memory of my father. As a child, I would watch him meditate in his armchair, perfectly still. My brother and I thought he was sleeping upright. We would sneak up to tickle him, and when he did not flinch, we laughed until our bellies ached. Nearly forty years later, he still reminds me to meditate—to meet life's pressures with grace and fortitude.

So I persisted.

In doing so, I confronted a difficult truth. Until then, my path had been largely intellectual. I had immersed myself in the writings of the great thinkers, filling myself with moments of insight and beauty, yet struggling to live what I had learned. Both ancient wisdom and modern science praised the benefits of meditation. Still, instead of practising, I kept reading—delaying action with the excuse that I needed to know more.

Friends, both religious and non-religious, but further along on their own inner journeys, would gently tell me, "Paule, you know the theory. It's time to put it into practice." I knew they were right. I sensed that if I nurtured my soul—the very essence of who I am—those fleeting moments of peace could expand into entire days. Days into weeks. Weeks into years.

I trusted that theory would eventually become practice. That progress might be slow, but steady. That what matters most is the path, not the destination. I kept moving, one step at a time, even when the way ahead was unclear. I held on to the wisdom of Lao Tzu:

> ***"A good traveller has no fixed plans and is not intent on arriving."* –Lao Tzu, Tao Te Ching (traditional translation)**

I welcomed failure as a teacher. And slowly, life began to unfold with greater ease and beauty. I felt more deeply connected—to others, to nature, to the vastness of existence itself.

I began to realise that doing things merely as a means to an end strips them of their wonder. So I learned to study, to meditate, to journal simply for their own sake—to savour them—without chasing outcomes. Like Eliahu planting date palms without expecting to taste their fruit.

When I stopped chasing future rewards, I learned how to live in the present. I stopped running after goals and became fully immersed in each moment. I began to recognise the extraordinary hidden within the ordinary. This is why I define Philosophy as the most useless—and yet the most transformative—of all disciplines. Because it is the one that restores magic to life.

I also came to understand that caring for my soul is not an act of selfishness, but one of generosity. What good would I be to my daughters if I were depleted? What calm could I offer others if I were anxious? What wisdom could I share if I did not first embody it?

Over time, Philosophy became for my soul what painting is for the eyes, and poetry for the ears—pure, boundless beauty.

Why am I sharing this?

Because as we grow more aware of our inner world, we begin to make choices that reflect our deepest values—values we hold even when it would be easier to compromise them. Because if we do not guide our thoughts, others will do it for us. Self-sufficiency in thought is essential to self-sufficiency in life.

Epicurus understood this deeply. For him, peace of mind arose from inner clarity, freedom from unnecessary desires, and independence from the crowd's opinions. True happiness, he believed, comes from cultivating this inner autonomy.

As we heal and evolve, we do not just connect more deeply with ourselves—we feel a stronger bond with others and with the world around us. Compassion grows naturally. Values. Thought. Connection.

Whether through mindfulness, spirituality, therapy, religion, or Philosophy—with a capital P—the path of inner work is a lifelong journey. It shapes how we live, how we invest, how we build companies, and how we care for one another. It creates a ripple effect that extends far beyond us.

Outer change begins within.
Reimagining capitalism begins within.
Impact investing begins within.
Purposeful entrepreneurship begins within.
A better world begins within.

8

Why I Am Writing This Book

I am writing this book because I wholeheartedly believe that our greatest crisis is not environmental, social, or geopolitical—it is ethical. And I believe that Philosophy—the love of wisdom—has the power to save us. It can serve as an inner moral compass, helping us reconnect with ourselves, with each other, and with nature. It can bring the clarity we need to face root causes—not just the symptoms—of our problems, and to build a future guided by wisdom, integrity, and care.

In other words, this book is an attempt to weave together inner work and systemic transformation. Rare though it may be, it matters deeply.

In our fast-paced, hyper-connected world, it is all too easy to lose touch with the essence of existence. We become consumed by work, responsibilities, and fleeting distractions—our endless to-do lists, social media scrolls, and surface-level engagements. In the relentless race of **doing**, we leave little room for deeper reflection, for **being**. The profound sense of wonder and meaning that accompanies life often gets buried.

Without wonder, life risks becoming mechanical. Efficient, perhaps—but empty. Wonder is what awakens us. It pulls us out of autopilot and reminds us that existence itself is extraordinary. When wonder disappears, we stop noticing beauty. We stop asking questions. We grow numb to the mystery woven into everyday life. With wonder, life becomes luminous again.

This loss of wonder—this **oblivion of being**—is not new. But it has become more acute in a culture that celebrates materialism, hyper-individualism, and constant productivity. We mistake motion for progress, price for value, profit for purpose, results for meaning, and knowledge for wisdom. In doing

P. Ansoleaga Abascal, *Philosophy and Finance: A Love Story*,
https://doi.org/10.1007/978-3-032-22218-3_8

so, we neglect the inner spaces where insight, fulfilment, and ethical clarity are born.

Philosophy has the power to save us because it restores those inner spaces. It opens the door to wonder, virtue, and connection. It helps us transcend a purely material understanding of life and reconnect with our deeper essence. In doing so, it makes us less self-centred, more whole, and ultimately, more fulfilled.

Ancient wisdom reminds us that when virtue leads the way, each step becomes steadier and more secure. This is one of Philosophy's great paradoxes: by looking back, we learn how to move forward. By recovering what has been forgotten, we gain orientation in the present.

When I speak of Philosophy—the Queen of the Sciences, as Immanuel Kant once called it—I do not mean Philosophy as a purely academic discipline. I mean Ancient Philosophy and Virtue Ethics: Philosophy as a way of life. A daily practice of reflection, discernment, and ethical attention. This distinction is central to the spirit of this book.

Philosophy and Finance: An Unexpected Intersection

This book was born from a longing to bring back together what we have for too long kept apart: capital and conscience, system and soul, the art of doing and the grace of being.

Finance powers the outer world—innovation, ambition, growth. Philosophy nourishes the inner one. At first glance, they may seem worlds apart, yet they are deeply intertwined. Finance shapes economies, livelihoods, and futures. Philosophy asks the questions that give those forces direction and meaning:

What is a life worth living?
What is value?
What is justice?
What is the purpose of capital?

These questions are not abstract. They are embedded in every financial decision we make—as investors, savers, entrepreneurs, or policymakers. Our choices ripple across societies, shaping collective realities and future possibilities.

Finance moves us forward. Philosophy reminds us where we are meant to go. Like the palm and the back of a hand—distinct yet inseparable—our inner and outer worlds travel together. For too long, Finance has been severed from its ethical roots. This book is an attempt to reweave that bond.

By grounding financial decision-making in virtue and values, we can rediscover Finance's transformative potential—not merely to create wealth, but to serve human flourishing and protect the planet. Economics and Finance are never just about numbers. They are about people, communities, and the living systems we all depend on.

An Invitation, Not a Prescription

I am writing this book because, in our relentless pursuit of *doing* and **having**, we have neglected the importance of *being*. We have underestimated the need for a moral compass strong enough to guide power, capital, and ambition. Inner work is not a luxury. It is the ethical foundation without which no system—financial or otherwise—can truly serve life.

This book is an invitation. An invitation to reflect, to question, and to ask better questions about who we are, what we value, and the world we wish to create.

Pablo Picasso once remarked that computers are useless because they only provide answers. His point was not to dismiss answers, but to celebrate the uniquely human power of questions. Socrates understood this deeply. Through questioning, he dismantled assumptions and invited reflection, reminding us that wisdom is living and evolving with us.

Beyond Transactions: Toward Transformation

This book will offer more questions than answers—and that is intentional. Questions awaken curiosity, unsettle complacency, and open new horizons. They allow us to imagine what does not yet exist: a financial system, and a society, shaped not only by efficiency, but by meaning.

By integrating ethical reflection into economic thinking, we can move beyond growth alone to include well-being, sustainability, and justice. We can expand our financial lens from risk and return to a broader triad: risk, return, and impact—intentional, measurable, positive impact.

We can move from transactions to contributions. From accumulation to responsibility. From short-term gain to long-term stewardship. Guided by the wisdom of the ages, we can design systems that balance personal freedom with collective care.

The Wisdom of the Ages

Ultimately, this book is an invitation to move beyond mere existence toward a more conscious and meaningful life.

When applied to Finance, this wisdom encourages us to invest not only for profit, but for purpose. Inner work ensures that our outer actions are coherent, ethical, and lasting.

The reward is not perfection, nor certainty, but something more precious: a truly **eudaemonic life**—one rooted in meaning rather than outcomes, in integrity rather than accumulation. It is not easy. But it is worth it.

And that, quite simply, is why I am writing this book.

9

Why Philosophy? Treating Root Causes, Not Just Symptoms

Many of us are deeply concerned about the state of the world. Climate change is accelerating—fires, droughts, floods, and extreme weather events are becoming more frequent and more disruptive. Insurers are struggling to keep pace with escalating risks. Economic inequality has reached staggering levels; recent analyses suggest that the richest 1% now own more wealth than the bottom 95% combined. Wildlife populations have plummeted by 73% since 1970, with freshwater species declining by 85%. Coral reefs—vital to at least 25% of marine species—are suffering catastrophic losses. The Amazon and the Arctic are approaching dangerous tipping points.

Compounding these crises is a rise in authoritarianism—a pattern history has seen before. In times of perceived crisis, when people feel abandoned by the system, strongmen emerge, exploiting fear, uncertainty, and resentment. They claim to be the only ones capable of restoring dignity, stability, or national greatness. But these movements rarely address the root causes of systemic failure. Instead, they scapegoat marginalised groups, suppress dissent, and consolidate power—allowing underlying problems to fester.

On our current path, the world is still heading toward warming of around 3°C under current policies—hardly a bright trajectory for humanity.

P. Ansoleaga Abascal, *Philosophy and Finance: A Love Story*,
https://doi.org/10.1007/978-3-032-22218-3_9

This Is Why Philosophy Matters

Most of us want to contribute to a better world. In our efforts to fight climate change, inequality, and injustice, we often turn to scientific and technological solutions. As rational beings, we believe that human ingenuity will save us—that innovation will fix it all.

And yes, science and technology are essential. They will play a leading role in shaping the future. But if we are to truly steer humanity onto a sustainable and just path, we need more than isolated fixes for individual crises. We must examine the deeper forces that brought us here. We must question the values, assumptions, and narratives that have shaped our civilization—ideas that have given rise to a mechanistic, individualistic, disenchanted, and fragmented world.

Just as anxiolytics or antidepressants can relieve symptoms without addressing the underlying emotional or psychological pain, we are treating global crises—climate change, war, poverty—without confronting the root causes that drive them.

Yes, we face overlapping and urgent global emergencies. But beneath these lies a deeper problem: the erosion of human values in favour of market values, and the disappearance of a profound sense of connection and belonging—to each other, to the Earth, to something greater than ourselves.

The greatest crisis of our time is ethical. It is the foundation of all the others. It is a crisis of values—those we've inherited, those we've unconsciously adopted, those we rarely question. A false sense of **separation** has taken hold—separation from each other, from nature, from every other being. An extreme **individualism** has eroded community, prioritizing self-interest over collective well-being. A purely **hedonistic** view of happiness has led us to chase wealth, status, power, pleasure, and comfort without seeking deeper meaning. And the fading of any **spiritual dimension** in life has left a void—one often filled by consumerism or distraction.

Only when we challenge our inherited, unquestioned assumptions can we begin to imagine new perspectives and lay the groundwork for a future that is not merely a technologically advanced extension of the present, but something fundamentally wiser, more just, and more sustainable.

From EGO-System to ECO-System Values

In an age dominated by technocratic solutions, Philosophy dares us to go deeper. It challenges us to question the narratives that divide us and allows us to reimagine a fairer, more harmonious world. It urges us to think beyond ourselves, to reflect on the ethical implications of our actions, and to embrace our shared, interconnected humanity.

I know—it is easy to lose faith in kindness, generosity, and hope when division, greed and conflict seem to dominate. But it is precisely in these times that they are needed most.

Philosophy can help us nurture the values we so urgently need. It can help us weaken what I call *EGO-system* values—market values like self-interest, wealth, power, and status—and strengthen *ECO-system* values—human values such as inclusion, justice, compassion, kindness, empathy, and collaboration. The love of wisdom can guide us in cultivating the kind of love needed to make this shift—from *EGO* to *ECO*. It can help us balance external achievement with inner fulfilment, illuminating the path toward a flourishing, eudaemonic life.

A cultural transformation rooted in *ECO-system* values would allow our society to flourish—not through competition and conflict, but through wisdom, kindness, and cooperation. Our economy would thrive—not on exploitation and dominion, but on fairness, inclusion, and mutual care. Finance would no longer serve only profit maximization but would be redirected toward impact, ensuring that capital flows where it is needed most. Investing would no longer be a choice between profit and purpose—all investing would be impact investing. The climate crisis would no longer loom over our future, because we would have restored ecosystems, replenished biodiversity, and built regenerative, circular economies that heal rather than harm.

In this transformed world, our children would grow up surrounded by beauty and equality of opportunity. Their dreams would no longer be constrained by fear or scarcity but ignited by hope, purpose, and the shared pursuit of a flourishing future for all.

I know this may sound utopian. But as Michelangelo once said:

> ***"The greater danger for most of us lies not in setting our aim too high and falling short, but in setting our aim too low and achieving our mark." –attributed to Michelangelo***

If we are to build a better world, we must dare to imagine it first.

Philosophy as a Force for Transformation: Personal, Societal, and Economic Change

A classical philosophical education, centred on the cultivation of virtue, can restore balance—personally, socially, economically, financially. It can bridge the divide between facts and values, reconcile individual interests with the collective good, and nurture harmony between Self and Other, market values and human values, *EGO* and *ECO*. True balance does not require rejecting self-interest or freedom, but rather integrating them into a broader ethical framework—one where entrepreneurial creativity and innovation flourish alongside a deep commitment to justice, inclusion, and sustainability.

This is not an abstract ideal. It is a vision of a world where prosperity does not come at the planet's expense, where the vulnerable are not left behind, where relationships are genuine, and where business and finance are guided by integrity and responsibility.

The wisdom of ancient philosophers—those who sought truth for the service of humanity—offers us timeless guidance. Their teachings remain profoundly relevant in an age that has drifted from ethical reflection.

Philosophy teaches us to cultivate inner wisdom, emotional mastery, and resilience. It does not reject the advancements of modernity—science, technology, or innovation—but enriches them, adding the moral depth needed to prevent these forces from becoming hollow or destructive.

That's why Philosophy. Because it offers us a beacon of hope. Because by embracing it as a way of life, we can exchange anxiety, loneliness, and inner emptiness for a life of meaning and connection. We can restore the moral foundations of society. We can redefine success—not as accumulation, but as contribution. We can shift finance from a tool of extraction to a force for regeneration. We can build an economy rooted in values that serve both humanity and the Earth.

This is the world I believe in—a world where wisdom, kindness, and justice are guiding principles. A world where finance fuels true progress—not just economic, but ethical and human. A world where Philosophy and Finance walk hand in hand as allies in building a flourishing future for all.

10

Why Finance

I hope that as we journey through these pages, the ***WHY*** behind Ancient Philosophy shines brightly. But why finance?

Because in a capitalist system, capital is the lifeblood that nourishes every part of the economy. Finance wields tremendous power—and with great power comes great responsibility. And great opportunity.

The Role of Finance

By Finance I mean the system by which capital—money and other financial resources—is mobilised, allocated, and directed toward productive use. It connects savers and investors to individuals, businesses, and governments in need of capital. In this way, finance has become the backbone of modern economies, sustaining governments, enterprises, households, and global trade. Like blood coursing through the body, capital fuels growth, innovation, and ambition. A single financial decision can ripple across continents, affecting lives far beyond its point of origin—for better or worse.

Throughout this book, I often pair Economics with Finance. To me, they are two sides of the same coin—two social sciences that shape and influence each other. Much like strategy and tactics, economics provides the broader picture, examining resource allocation, societal behaviour, and policy impacts. Finance, in turn, offers the tools to manage those resources, particularly money. One enables strategic vision; the other facilitates practical execution.

P. Ansoleaga Abascal, *Philosophy and Finance: A Love Story*,
https://doi.org/10.1007/978-3-032-22218-3_10

Finance as One of the Architects of Civilisation

Long before markets and monetary systems, human communities survived through subsistence and defence. If a group lacked resources, it secured them as best it could. Cooperation existed within tribes, but between tribes, survival was fragile and often contested.

Over time, exchange began to replace seizure. Trade allowed communities to obtain what they lacked without resorting to force. The emergence of structured exchange was not merely economic progress; it was a civilisational shift. Agreements began to substitute violence. Trust began to extend beyond kinship.

From this transformation emerged finance—the organised exchange of value across time. And with finance came one of humanity's greatest inventions: writing.

The earliest known writing system, cuneiform, appeared in Mesopotamia around 3100 BCE. Its earliest uses were administrative and economic. Clay tablets recorded quantities of grain, livestock, silver, and labour obligations. These were not poems or myths. They were accounts.

The earliest known recorded name in history—found on proto-cuneiform tablets from Uruk, dating to approximately 3400–3000 BCE—is "Kushim."

One tablet records:"29,086 measures of barley, 37 months—Kushim."

Scholars still debate whether Kushim was an individual, an office-holder, or an institution. What is clear is that **the earliest preserved written words in human history relate to economic transactions.**

Before writing, agreements depended on memory and oral testimony. As trade networks expanded and obligations extended over seasons and distances, societies required durable records. **Writing emerged in part from the need to document credit, debt, taxation, and stored goods.** And then, from accounting grew administration. From administration grew law.

The Code of Hammurabi in Babylon regulated contracts, lending, interest rates, and commercial disputes. Egyptian state granaries functioned as stabilising institutions in times of scarcity. Phoenician merchants developed expansive maritime trade networks across the Mediterranean. In classical Athens, the widespread use of coinage—including the silver drachma—facilitated commerce in a society that simultaneously witnessed the rise of democratic institutions and philosophical inquiry.

Where exchange became reliable and enforceable, societies gained stability. And with stability came surplus time and surplus thought.

Finance did not create philosophy, democracy, or mathematics on its own. But by structuring exchange and reducing uncertainty, it helped

create the conditions in which they could flourish. Mathematics advanced alongside accounting. Law matured alongside contracts. Political institutions evolved alongside commercial complexity.

Finance helped move human societies from episodic survival to organised cooperation. It replaced immediate taking with negotiated obligation. It extended trust beyond the tribe. In that sense, **finance has been one of the architects of civilization.**

This is why finance is not merely an industry. It is infrastructure—moral and institutional infrastructure. And like all powerful infrastructure, it can either support human flourishing or undermine it.

Finance Is Not Neutral

Contrary to what many of us were taught at university, finance is not inherently value-neutral. Capital, as a tool, may be neutral—but the way we allocate it reflects the values we choose to uphold. Finance can support companies that give more than they take—those committed to sustainability, equity, and planetary health. Or it can fuel business models that extract value at the expense of people and the Earth—driving deforestation, fossil-fuel expansion, biodiversity loss, or child labour.

When aligned with justice and sustainability, finance becomes one of the most powerful levers for positive change we possess. When governed by short-termism and greed, it does the opposite: it deepens inequality, accelerates environmental degradation, and locks us into systems that undermine our collective future.

This is why finance matters. Where science explains, Philosophy guides, business builds, and finance powers. The question is: *what kind of world do we want our industry to power? What values will we choose? What legacy will we leave?*

History shows us what happens when financial power loses its moral compass—and what is possible when it finds it again.

When Finance Fails: Lessons from History

The Global Financial Crisis of 2008 exposed what happens when finance is driven by short-termism. A complex derivatives market built on subprime mortgages collapsed, plunging the world into recession. Governments stepped in with massive bailouts, but the damage was already done. I remember September 2008 vividly—I was in London, watching colleagues laid off overnight. Entire sectors unravelled. Families lost their homes. It was a stark reminder of what happens when finance loses its moral compass.

The Eurozone Debt Crisis of 2010–2012 showed how financial systems can magnify structural vulnerabilities. In Greece, financial engineering helped obscure national debt, triggering harsh austerity measures and widespread suffering. In Spain, reckless real-estate speculation—fuelled by cheap credit—led to a housing bubble whose collapse pushed the country into crisis.

Black Wednesday in 1992 illustrated the power of individual market actors. George Soros's speculative bet against the British pound forced the UK out of the Exchange Rate Mechanism, earning him over $1 billion in profit and destabilising currency markets. It revealed how concentrated financial power, when detached from broader responsibility, can unsettle entire nations.

Across these episodes, finance prioritised short-term gain over long-term resilience. The result was human suffering. History reminds us that when finance is not rooted in accountability and the common good, it serves the few at the expense of the many.

When Finance Thrives: Capital Aligned with Morality

But when guided by justice, equity, and responsibility, finance can become a powerful force for good.

In the 1980s, global divestment campaigns helped dismantle apartheid. Universities, pension funds, churches, and institutional investors withdrew capital from companies operating in South Africa. Banks severed credit lines. This coordinated economic pressure helped accelerate the collapse of an unjust regime—demonstrating that finance aligned with conscience can drive social change.

Today, finance is also playing a growing role in the fight against climate change. Since the first green bond was issued in 2007, cumulative green bond issuance has surpassed $3 trillion. When combined with social, sustainability, and sustainability-linked bonds, cumulative issuance exceeds $5 trillion. Capital is increasingly flowing into clean energy, resilient infrastructure, and climate-adaptation solutions. In this case, finance is not merely responding to change—it is helping drive it.

Even Joseph Stiglitz, a frequent critic of financial excess, has acknowledged that well-functioning financial systems play a vital role in economic development, noting that financial instruments can "lubricate economic activity."

Financing the SDGs: The $7.7 Trillion Question

To realise the Sustainable Development Goals (SDGs), the world needs three things: finance, finance, and finance. This phrase, often attributed to Amina J. Mohammed, UN Deputy Secretary-General, captures the reality. Addressing poverty, inequality, disease, and climate change requires trillions in investment. The numbers are daunting: $4.2 trillion annually to meet the SDGs and $3.5 trillion each year for clean energy alone.

Governments and philanthropy can not close this gap. OECD nations are already stretched, with debt-to-GDP ratios averaging 110%. Public aid and donations fall far short.

The good news? Private capital is abundant. Global markets manage over $300 trillion—more than triple global GDP. These funds represent more than financial assets. They reflect influence, direction, and possibility. Those who manage them hold immense power to shape the future.

When Finance Speaks, Business Listens

Investors hold extraordinary influence over companies. Publicly listed companies rely on shareholders and bondholders to fund their operations and growth. Shareholders vote on key issues and help shape the direction of the business; bondholders influence terms and expectations. Privately owned companies—whether backed by private equity, venture capital, or families—are no different. In the end, those who provide the capital have the greatest say in how a company is run.

When investors set social and environmental goals, they empower companies to serve more than shareholders. They drive fair wages, ethical supply chains, and sustainable practices—creating shared value for people and planet. And let's not forget: the private sector generates 70% of GDP across OECD countries. It is the engine of global growth.

This is why finance matters. It fuels business. It powers systems. It can extract—or it can uplift. When aligned with purpose, it becomes an extraordinary force for regeneration.

Finance holds the power to reshape industries, societies, and futures. But it does not act on its own. People do. Investors do. We do.

The choice is ours.

11

Why Philosophy and Finance, Together

Throughout history, every era has been defined by its social and economic systems—shaped by politics, power structures, and the forces that unified societies. Philosophy, values, beliefs, and religions offered meaning and served as moral compasses, guiding communities toward a shared sense of purpose. Meanwhile, finance—capital in general, and money in particular—became the lifeblood sustaining these systems, providing the resources needed for innovation, entrepreneurship, and growth.

If our socio-economic system were a car, businesses would be its engine, converting resources and creativity into innovation and progress. Finance, in turn, would be the fuel powering this engine, providing the energy needed to move forward.

Energy, motion, and direction—Finance, Business, and Philosophy—can work in harmony to lead us toward a more just and sustainable future. Of course, governments, regulators, NGOs, and civil society also play vital roles. Central banks, for instance, act like gears—allowing the engine to accelerate through low interest rates, or slow down through higher ones. But for simplicity's sake, let us focus on the car's engine—business; its fuel—finance; its GPS—philosophy. And, of course, the driver: us, human beings.

Without finance, the engine of business would stall, and the car would fail to move. Without Philosophy, even the most efficient engine (business), powered by ample fuel (finance), risks driving aimlessly—or worse, heading straight toward disaster. A disaster like the looming threat of a 3°C rise above pre-industrial temperatures. Only **when these three forces align can we build systems that are not only efficient but also equitable, deeply rooted in human values, and environmentally sustainable.**

P. Ansoleaga Abascal, *Philosophy and Finance: A Love Story*,
https://doi.org/10.1007/978-3-032-22218-3_11

Philosophy as Our Guide

Moral Philosophy—especially Philosophy as a way of life—can inspire us, the drivers of our economic systems, to reintroduce human values into business and finance. It can help us reconnect facts with values, reminding us that numbers are never neutral: they always carry meaning, intention, and consequence. Philosophy invites us to question the role and purpose of capital, urging us to see it not merely as a means to profit, but as a force that can serve the common good.

Philosophy also helps dismantle the myth of ***Homo Oeconomicus***—the idea that we are rational actors driven purely by self-interest, competition, and the relentless pursuit of profit. Ancient Philosophy and modern psychology alike tell a different story. We are far more complex—and far more relational—than this reductionist model suggests. Much closer to Aristotle's ***zoon politikon***: social beings capable of empathy, cooperation, and self-transcendence, motivated not only by material gain but by a deep longing for meaning, connection, and contribution.

Recognising this fuller, richer dimension of what it means to be human challenges us to reimagine our economic and financial systems accordingly—systems aligned not with our lowest impulses, but with our highest potential. Philosophy opens the door to this wider horizon.

But Philosophy offers more than values. It cultivates judgment. In finance, uncertainty is constant. Markets fluctuate, technologies disrupt and incentives collide. Rules alone are not enough. We must distinguish risk from recklessness, growth from excess, innovation from speculation. Philosophy strengthens that discernment. It trains what Aristotle called ***phronesis***—practical wisdom—the capacity to choose well when formulas fall short.

Philosophy nurtures creativity. Philosophy encourages us to think across time, disciplines, and traditions. It teaches us to connect ideas that appear unrelated: ethics with economics, science with responsibility, profit with purpose. Creativity is pattern recognition grounded in meaning. Many paradigm shifts occur not because new information appears, but because existing knowledge is seen differently.

And Philosophy fosters systems thinking. The great philosophical traditions always began with first principles: What is justice? What is nature? What is the good life? These questions require us to step back and see the whole before acting on the part. In a world of interconnected financial markets, global supply chains, and planetary boundaries, this ability to hold complexity without losing clarity is indispensable. Philosophy anchors progress within a wider horizon.

A Roadmap to a Brighter Future

This is why I write about Philosophy and Finance together.

The roadmap to a better future cannot rely solely on the dynamism of financial markets powering science, industry, and innovation. These forces are essential. They are the engine of our socio-economic car—generating movement, scale, and momentum. But an engine alone is not enough. Without direction, speed can become dangerous. Power without orientation can take us further away from where we truly want to go.

Philosophy can provide that orientation. It can be our inner compass—our GPS—linking the power of what we do to the wisdom of why we do it. It helps us discern direction when the road is uncertain, reminding us not only how to move forward, but toward what.

> ***I dream of a world where science explains, entrepreneurship creates, governments facilitate, art inspires, finance powers—and Philosophy guides.***

Philosophy—the love of wisdom—can ensure that our actions remain authentic, purposeful, and aligned with what truly matters. The *Queen of the Sciences* reminds us that progress is not just about moving forward; it's about moving forward in the right direction. When Finance, Business, and Philosophy unite, we can build a future that is not only prosperous, but also ethical, sustainable, and deeply meaningful.

12

Thales of Miletus: First Philosopher, and First Financier

We often think of economics as beginning with Xenophon (c. 430–354 BCE) and Aristotle (384–322 BCE), with their reflections on ***oikonomike***—the art of managing a household or city-state. These early philosophers saw economic life as embedded in ethics and politics, concerned not merely with wealth, but with the good life.

Yet centuries before formal economic thought emerged in classical Greece, the first philosopher of the Western tradition also appeared as one of the earliest individual financiers. Thales of Miletus (c. 624–546 BCE), often hailed as the father of Western philosophy, is best remembered for his rational inquiry into the nature of existence, the cosmos, and the principle of unity behind all things. But Thales also understood the practical world—and the power of foresight.

Thales was a man of extraordinary intellect, yet his contemporaries often mocked him for his apparent lack of worldly success. What good was wisdom, they asked, if it did not bring wealth? What use was Philosophy if it could not fill one's coffers?

But Thales, far from being oblivious to practical affairs, saw beyond the surface of things. He understood that knowledge was not merely for accumulation but for illumination. And so, as if to silence his critics with a single stroke of insight, he devised a masterful demonstration.

Observing the heavens and studying the cycles of nature, he discerned that the coming year would bring an abundant olive harvest. Acting swiftly—while the trees were still bare and no one else saw opportunity—he placed deposits on every available olive press in Miletus and Chios, securing them at a low price before demand arose.

P. Ansoleaga Abascal, *Philosophy and Finance: A Love Story*,
https://doi.org/10.1007/978-3-032-22218-3_12

Nikole Bozza Ansoleaga

When the harvest arrived, the abundance was as he had foreseen. Farmers and merchants, caught unprepared, found themselves in dire need of olive presses, and Thales, holding the key to their necessity, leased them at a premium. His wealth multiplied overnight.

But Thales had no interest in riches. He had not done this out of greed, nor for power, but for proof. Aristotle tells us in Politics (Book I, Chapter 11) that Thales undertook this venture not to amass wealth, but to show that a philosopher could succeed in business if he so desired. His lack of riches, then, was not a sign of incapacity. It was a choice.

"There is the anecdote of Thales the Milesian and his financial device, which involves a principle of universal application, but is attributed to him on account of his reputation for wisdom. He was reproached for his poverty, which was supposed to show that philosophy was of no use.
According to the story, he knew by his skill in the stars while it was yet winter that there would be a great harvest of olives in the coming year; so, having a little money, he gave deposits for the use of all the olive-presses in Chios and Miletus, which he hired at a low price because no one bid against him. When the harvest-time came, and many were wanted all at once and of a sudden, he let them out at any rate which he pleased, and made a quantity of money. Thus he showed the world that philosophers can easily be rich if they like, but that their ambition is of another sort." **–Aristotle, Politics, Book I, ch. 11 (1259a), trans. Benjamin Jowett (1885).**

Aristotle presents this as proof that poverty is not due to a philosopher's inability to make money, but rather to his disinterest in it. Wealth, to Thales, was not an end but a means—a tool to illustrate a greater truth.

Thales' view aligns seamlessly with my dear Stoics, who saw wealth as a preferred indifferent—neither inherently good nor bad, but something that could be used virtuously or viciously. Thales did not reject money, nor did he worship it. He wielded it as one wields a brush upon a canvas, demonstrating that wealth is only as valuable as the purpose behind it.

From the very beginning, Philosophy and finance were siblings, born of the same human impulse—the search for order, wisdom, and the mastery of life's resources.

If Philosophy and finance once walked together, it is because wealth was never meant to stand alone. It was never meant to be hoarded in isolation, but woven into the fabric of human flourishing. It was meant to be cultivated with discernment, directed with integrity, and used in service of something greater than itself.[]

Thales' story is a reminder that these two disciplines, which seem so estranged today, once worked in harmony. And if they did in the past, they can do so again.

For Thales, as for the Stoics, wealth was never the goal. It was a *preferred indifferent*, neither good nor evil in itself, but a tool—one that could serve wisdom or folly, virtue or vice. He understood its potential but refused to be enslaved by it. And in doing so, he offered a lesson that would resonate through the ages.

In an age where financial gain is often mistaken for meaning, his lesson endures: mastery over money is not about possession but **perception**. Those who chase wealth without wisdom may find themselves enslaved by it. But those who understand its nature—who see it as a tool rather than a treasure—remain free.

To me, wealth, in its highest form, is not the accumulation of numbers, but the ability to shape the world with purpose. It is not the master, but the servant, of a well-lived life. When guided by wisdom, it builds, heals, and uplifts. When severed from virtue, it corrodes, consumes, and corrupts.

The reunion is not only possible—it is necessary. And it begins not with systems, but with souls. With the understanding that wealth, like all things external, is only as meaningful as the wisdom that wields it.

The ancients knew this. It is time we remember.

13

Diogenes, Alexander the Great, and the Value of Values

Once upon a time, in ancient Greece, there lived a philosopher named Diogenes, a prominent figure of the Cynic school of thought. Known for his wisdom and unconventional lifestyle, Diogenes rejected social norms and material possessions, choosing instead to live in a large ceramic jar. His Philosophy emphasized living in accordance with nature, embracing simplicity, and finding contentment in what is essential.

Meanwhile, Alexander the Great, a Macedonian king and one of history's most successful conquerors, had built an empire stretching from Greece to Egypt and as far as modern-day Pakistan and India. Despite his extraordinary achievements, Alexander was curious about the famous philosopher who lived without wealth or ambition, yet seemed entirely at peace.

One day, Alexander visited Diogenes. He found the philosopher sitting in the sun and, intrigued by his simple lifestyle, asked:

"Is there anything I can do for you?"

Diogenes looked up and replied with bluntness:

"Yes, stand out of my sunlight."

This bold response struck Alexander deeply. He had come expecting a request for wealth, power, or status—things that most would eagerly seize if offered by the ruler of the known world. But Diogenes, true to his values, wanted nothing more than to continue enjoying the warmth of the sun. His rejection of material gain was a reflection of his unshakable principles.

Impressed by Diogenes' courage and indifference to wealth and power, Alexander reportedly remarked:

P. Ansoleaga Abascal, *Philosophy and Finance: A Love Story*,
https://doi.org/10.1007/978-3-032-22218-3_13

"If I were not Alexander, I would wish to be Diogenes."

Nikole Bozza Ansoleaga

This encounter highlights a profound truth: **our values shape not only our actions but also the way we inspire others.**

Diogenes valued simplicity, authenticity, and freedom. His austere lifestyle reflected these principles. He sought nothing beyond the natural sunlight and the joy of living unencumbered by material possessions. The opportunity to ask for riches or power was in front of him, yet he dismissed it without hesitation—because to accept would have been to betray his own Philosophy.

Alexander's values, in contrast, were grounded in power, ambition, and conquest, driving him to create one of the largest empires in history. And yet, despite their vastly different priorities, the two men shared one crucial value: **courage**.

Diogenes had the courage to live in absolute alignment with his beliefs, to reject the expectations of society, and to speak truth to power without fear. Alexander had the courage to lead armies, to risk everything in battle, and to pursue his grand vision relentlessly.

It is perhaps this shared courage that led Alexander to admire the philosopher so deeply. He recognised in Diogenes a fearlessness that rivalled his own—not on the battlefield, but in the unwavering commitment to his chosen path.

In the end, whether we are building empires or basking in the sunlight, it is our values that shape our thoughts, influence our words, define our actions, and ultimately determine who we are and the legacy we leave behind.

Values: The Deepest Leverage for Change

I told this story to highlight the value of values. The first and most critical step in any meaningful transformation—be it social, economic, or environmental—is values.

Why? Because values shape purpose. And purpose drives action.

To me, values are the deepest leverage for change. When individuals, businesses, and institutions embrace values that serve the greater good, their actions naturally align with those principles. If sustainability is a core value for an entrepreneur, she might establish a social enterprise to accelerate the green transition. If justice is a core value for an organization, it will prioritize fair wages, ethical supply chains, and inclusion. If altruism is a core value for a community, it will cultivate a culture of mutual care and support.

Without values, purpose risks becoming hollow—just another mission statement without real action behind it.

Albert Einstein always insisted that human knowledge and skills alone cannot lead us to a happy and dignified future, and that we should place the proclaimers of high moral standards and values above the discoverers of objective truth.

> ***"Concern for man himself and his fate must always form the chief interest of all technical endeavours.***
> ***Never forget this in the midst of your diagrams and equations."***
> **–Albert Einstein, "Science and Religion" (1939)**

We are the great-grandchildren of the Scientific Revolution and the Enlightenment. As heirs of the Age of Reason, we have inherited a world shaped by rationality, individualism, and economic efficiency. This legacy has brought remarkable progress—longer lifespans, medical breakthroughs, technological marvels—but it has also reinforced a mindset of **separation** and **dominion.**

We have been conditioned to see ourselves as separate: separate from one another, separate from nature, and separate from the future generations who will inherit the consequences of our actions. This **illusion of separation** lies at the heart of many of our greatest challenges—climate change, inequality, economic instability, and social fragmentation.

Alongside this illusion is **the legacy of dominion**: the belief that humans are entitled to exploit the Earth's resources indefinitely. Rooted in ancient texts and later reinforced by Enlightenment thinkers like **Francis Bacon** and **René Descartes**, this worldview cast nature as a machine to be mastered and subdued—its purpose reduced to human utility. Bacon spoke of enlarging "the bounds of human empire" over nature, while Descartes envisioned humans as "masters and possessors" of the natural world. This mechanistic, extractive logic underpinned the rise of modern science, industrial capitalism, and colonial expansion—and continues to echo in today's economic systems.

These inherited worldviews have shaped our modern world, influencing how we live, work, invest, and consume. But they are not immutable. They are human constructs—and like all constructs, they can be questioned, reimagined, and transformed.

The antidote to ego-system thinking lies in embracing eco-system values: human values like love, unity, empathy, kindness, care, collaboration, interdependence, and sustainability. These values remind us that we are not isolated individuals, but part of a vast, interconnected web of life. Our well-being is inseparable from the well-being of others and of the planet.

Ancient philosophies—both Western and Eastern—championed these values. Indigenous wisdom did too. Across cultures and centuries, they understood the interconnectedness of all beings and the importance of living in harmony with nature.

It is not too late to remember what they knew—and to build anew from that ancient, enduring wisdom. Marcus Aurelius (Meditations, VI.38): "***What brings no benefit to the hive brings none to the bee.***" A perfect Stoic reminder that individual well-being is inseparable from the collective.

The future we build will be determined by our values and worldviews. If we choose to reintroduce human values into our personal and societal decisions—as our ancestors and Indigenous communities have long done—we will unlock transformative change. As individuals, we will choose sustainable lifestyles that honour the planet. As investors, we will align capital with impact, ensuring that our money supports businesses contributing to long-term well-being. As voters, we will demand policies that prioritise the collective good.

Values are the foundation of systemic change. They shape purpose. And purpose drives action. And action determines the future we create. Einstein was right—values must take precedence over technical knowledge if humanity is to find true happiness and dignity. **By embracing our human values we can dismantle the myths of separation and dominion that have defined our world for centuries. We can cultivate a society that prioritises care**

over competition, regeneration over exploitation, and wisdom over short-term gain.

The road ahead is not easy, but the choice is ours—to remain passive spectators of decline, or to become architects of renewal. The seeds we plant today will grow into the forests that shelter future generations, the rivers that nourish them, the air they will breathe. Let us walk this path together—not as isolated individuals, but as a chorus of dreamers, thinkers, and doers, turning hope into action, vision into reality, and the love of wisdom into the wisdom of love.

Part 2

Ancient Philosophy

Philosophy offers us a beauty that is not fleeting, not bound to appearances. It is a beauty that radiates from within—shining through the clarity of our thought, the light in our eyes, the warmth of our heart, and the boundless power to make the world better for all.

In this second part of the book, we bring Philosophy down from the ivory towers of abstraction and return it to its truest form: not a subject to be studied, but a way of living. A way of seeing the world—and ourselves—with greater clarity. A daily discipline of attention, presence, and moral purpose.

Here, Philosophy—with a capital P—means something larger than academic thought. It means the lived pursuit of wisdom: a practice of inner freedom and ethical action, capable of transforming both the individual and the world around them.

We will explore how the ancients turned this pursuit into practice through spiritual exercises—timeless disciplines for clarity, peace, and meaning. Together, we will walk beside those who made Philosophy a path to freedom, resilience, and joy. From Socrates to Epictetus, from Seneca to Marcus Aurelius, their words reveal a life anchored in simplicity, strength, wisdom, and virtue.

Among the ancient schools of thought, Stoicism will take centre stage—not as a rigid mask of emotional detachment, but as a profoundly human, joyful, and liberating way of life.

Above all, this part of the book is a celebration of the philosophical life—not as perfection, but as progress. As a daily return to what matters most. A call to awaken, to dream, and to live with courage. A reminder that the pursuit of virtue is the greatest journey we can undertake—not only for our own flourishing, but for the flourishing of all.

This love for Philosophy is one of the greatest gifts my mother ever gave me. Now, I feel a deep responsibility to offer it back to the world—and especially to the world of finance, where I have worked for many years.

I do not write as an expert. I write as a fellow traveller—a *prokoptousa*, one who is making progress. My only wish is that something in these pages may shed light on your path, as Philosophy continues to illuminate mine.

14

Philosophy in Modern Times

If we were to ask ChatGPT, What is philosophy?, we might receive an answer like this:

> ***"Philosophy is the study of fundamental questions concerning existence, knowledge, values, reason, mind, and language. It engages in critical analysis, systematic argumentation, and the exploration of abstract concepts. Philosophy is traditionally divided into several branches: Metaphysics (the study of the nature of reality and existence), Epistemology (the investigation of knowledge, its limits, and its sources), Ethics (the examination of moral values and principles), Logic (the study of reasoning and the structure of arguments), Aesthetics (the exploration of beauty, art, and taste), and Political Philosophy (the study of government, justice, rights, and the state). Philosophers employ various methods—logical analysis, critical discussion, and thought experiments—to explore these profound questions and develop enduring theories."***
> (ChatGPT, 2025)

This definition captures the modern, academic understanding of philosophy—an intellectual discipline devoted to theoretical exploration and conceptual analysis.

Prominent philosophers of the twentieth century, such as Bertrand Russell and Ludwig Wittgenstein, embodied this approach. Russell viewed philosophy as the pursuit of the fundamental questions of human existence, using rigorous logic to seek reliable answers. Wittgenstein, in contrast, believed that philosophy's task was not to provide definitive solutions but to clarify our thoughts and sharpen our perception of the world.

P. Ansoleaga Abascal, *Philosophy and Finance: A Love Story*,
https://doi.org/10.1007/978-3-032-22218-3_14

Though their perspectives differed, both treated philosophy as a cerebral exercise—concerned with reason, logic, and abstract inquiry, often detached from the urgent struggles of daily life.

For much of my own life, I saw philosophy in the same way. Having studied science in high school, earned an engineering degree, and later completed an MBA, philosophy seemed to belong to an entirely different realm—an admirable but impractical pursuit, reserved for bearded thinkers lost in debates over irresolvable paradoxes. Something for ivory towers, not for someone waking up at 6 a.m. to fight in the arena of early 2000s financial London. Not for someone navigating the frenetic trading floors, where decisions were made in split seconds, where adrenaline and competition ruled the day.

I struggled to see how it could be relevant to someone like me—immersed in the work-hard, play-hard ethos of my late twenties, in the most competitive environment I had ever known.

If only I had known then what I know now.

That was how I saw philosophy—until Epictetus found his way into my hands (thanks again, Mum). Until I encountered something far more transformative, far more beautiful. Until I discovered that Philosophy—with a capital P—was not merely a field of study, but a way of life. Not just an intellectual pursuit but nourishment for the soul.

Ancient Philosophy, in particular, revealed itself to me as a compass: a guide to living with clarity, intention, inner peace, and joy. A living tradition—one that offers practical tools for resilience, wisdom, and meaning.

I feel profoundly fortunate to have stumbled upon this unexpected treasure. In fact, I feel profoundly fortunate to be alive in this era—an era where we have unprecedented access to an intellectual inheritance built by those who came before us. As Isaac Newton wrote to Robert Hooke in 1675:

> ***"If I have seen further, it is by standing on the shoulders of giants."***
>
> (Letter from Isaac Newton to Robert Hooke, 5 February 1675, Royal Society Archives)

We can indeed stand on their shoulders—on the shoulders of intellectual and moral giants like Socrates, Plato, Aristotle, Seneca, Epictetus, and Marcus Aurelius. They can continue to guide us, to challenge us, to illuminate our paths. They transcend their own lifetimes. They are, in a profound sense, still alive in their ideas. And through Philosophy, so can we be.

Through Philosophy, we can honour their legacy and join them in the same timeless quest for truth, virtue, and wisdom.

As Seneca reminds us in On the Shortness of Life (De Brevitate Vitae):

"Of all men they alone are at leisure who take time for philosophy; they alone really live.
For they do not merely attend carefully to their own lifetime, but they annex every age to it; all the years that have passed before them are added to their store."
Seneca, On the Shortness of Life, trans. Aubrey Stewart (1889).

With ancient wisdom, we can connect with the past, lighten our present, and find a guide for our future. We can carry the wisdom of all time within us.

15

Philosophy as a Way of Life

Once upon a time, in the candle-lit courtyards of Ancient Greece, there was ***philosophia***—the love of wisdom. But to those who practised it, it was far more than an intellectual pursuit; it was a way of being, a lifelong journey of transformation, a path that sought not only to understand the nature of reality but to shape the soul in harmony with it. Philosophy was a compass for living, guiding one's steps toward wisdom, virtue, and inner peace.

From the very beginning, this longing for understanding moved between the cosmic and the intimate. The earliest philosophers, known as the Presocratics, looked outward. Thales saw divinity in water, Heraclitus found meaning in change, and Anaximander sought the infinite—marvelling at the hidden order of nature and the mysterious unity behind its ever-shifting forms. Their questions were bold, their answers tentative, but their wonder lit the first sparks of a tradition that would never cease asking: ***what is this world, and what is our place in it?***

Then came Socrates, and with him, Philosophy took a different turn. He brought the gaze inward, away from the stars and into the soul. He asked how one ought to live, and he answered not with theories but with questions. He taught that wisdom begins in recognising one's ignorance, and that the ***examined life***—the ongoing, courageous effort to understand oneself, one's values, and one's actions—is the only life worthy of a human being. To him, Philosophy was not something to study, but something to practise—with humility, rigour, determination and courage.

Plato, his student, wove these questions into a magnificent vision, seeing Philosophy as a bridge between the visible world and the eternal truths that lie beyond it. For him, the Good, the True, and the Beautiful were not

P. Ansoleaga Abascal, *Philosophy and Finance: A Love Story*,
https://doi.org/10.1007/978-3-032-22218-3_15

abstract ideals, but real forces—calling us to rise beyond appearances and live in alignment with a deeper reality. Aristotle, in turn, brought Philosophy back to earth. He taught that virtue is a habit, cultivated through daily practice, practical wisdom, and thoughtful action. To flourish, he said, is to fulfil one's potential in accordance with reason—and this requires character.

In the centuries that followed, Philosophy blossomed into many branches, but its essence remained the same. It became a tree with many limbs, rooted in the soil of shared human questions. The Stoics taught that virtue is the only true good, and that serenity comes when our will is in harmony with nature and reason. The Epicureans reminded us that peace can be found in simplicity, friendship, and the absence of fear. The Sceptics counselled humility, urging us to suspend judgment and find freedom in not needing to control what cannot be known. The Cynics practised radical authenticity, stripping life to its bare essentials and challenging society's illusions. And the Platonists continued to seek harmony between soul and cosmos, affirming that the journey to truth was also a return to what we already are.

They debated, disagreed, and diverged—but beneath the surface, they were walking toward the same summit. They all believed that life is not something that simply happens to us, but something we shape through our choices, our attention, and our inner discipline. They were united by a vision of human flourishing—***eudaimonia*** (a state of lasting well-being, fulfilment, and inner harmony)—not as fleeting pleasure or external success, but as a way of being rooted in virtue and guided by wisdom. To me, the differences among the schools were like variations of the same melody: different ways of pursuing a life of presence, freedom, meaning, and joy. Lasting joy. Each school offered a doorway to the same house of wisdom.

This is the Philosophy I cherish—Philosophy with a capital P—the kind that fills the pages of this book. My hope is that, as you read, it will touch you as deeply as it touches me—a flame passed from one seeker of wisdom to another, illuminating the path ahead.

Pierre Hadot, one of the great scholars of ancient thought, resurrected this lost vision of Philosophy. Few have captured its essence as he did. In Philosophy as a Way of Life, he reminds us that, for the ancients, Philosophy was not a mere academic exercise but a way of being—a discipline of the mind, a practice of the soul, a commitment to living wisely, virtuously, and in harmony with the natural order.

Hadot shows that these ancient schools were not merely systems of thought but complete ways of life. They offered spiritual exercises designed to shape the human soul. Reasoning and logical argument were not ends in themselves but tools for transformation—for cultivating resilience, sharpening perception, and refining character. For them, Philosophy was a daily practice of becoming—more just, more patient, more honest, more free.

This is why Hadot's work matters. It is not just history; it is a call to awaken. And if this book carries any hope, it is precisely this: to help awaken that ancient, still-living flame within us.

Because we live in a world that hungers for clear minds, generous hearts, and courageous souls. If we—investors, entrepreneurs, parents, policymakers, and citizens—make decisions from a place of fear, ego, or confusion, our actions will reflect that inner disorder. But if we reclaim our mental clarity, our moral compass, and our spiritual strength, we can begin to shape systems that mirror wisdom instead of ambition, care instead of mere efficiency, truth instead of appearance. Our ancestors remind us that a better world begins ***within***. The world is crying out for such wisdom again. And Philosophy, when lived sincerely, still holds the power to answer.

16

Virtue Ethics—A Philosophy of Being

At the heart of every ancient school lay the same conviction: **a good life must be rooted in virtue.**

Virtue was the inner architecture of a flourishing human life—the structure that allows us to live with clarity, harmony, and moral strength.

Virtue Ethics is the oldest moral tradition of the Western world, and to me, the most deeply human. It does not begin with rules to obey or consequences to calculate, but with a more intimate question: ***Who are we becoming?***

It invites us into a lifelong work of self-cultivation and inner clarity—a process through which our choices flow naturally from our character, and our character slowly grows toward wisdom. This is the kind of Philosophy I cherish, and love.

Although Virtue Ethics is the oldest moral tradition, it is not the only one. Later centuries introduced two other great ethical frameworks: **Consequentialism**, which judges actions by their outcomes, and **Deontology**, which grounds morality in universal duties. I have deep admiration for both, especially for Immanuel Kant's categorical imperative, with its luminous call to act only according to principles we would want to become universal laws. His moral vision rises above self-interest and invites us into coherence, responsibility, and integrity.

And yet, in a world that prizes autonomy and freedom, Virtue Ethics feels both more suitable and more hopeful. It does not impose commandments from above, nor does it ask us to calculate every consequence. Instead, it invites us to cultivate a character so grounded in wisdom, justice, courage,

P. Ansoleaga Abascal, *Philosophy and Finance: A Love Story*,
https://doi.org/10.1007/978-3-032-22218-3_16

and temperance that good actions flow naturally from who we are. In this way, the virtuous life becomes a path toward Immanuel Kant's ideal—not through external obligation, but through inner transformation. We grow into the kind of people who would want their actions to become universal laws.

A Tradition Rooted in the Soul

Virtue Ethics found one of its most luminous expressions in Ancient Greece. Yet its essence—that the good life depends on the quality of our character—appears across cultures. Confucianism, for instance, also places moral cultivation and harmony at the centre of a meaningful human life.

Wherever it emerges, the question at its heart is always the same: *What makes a life worth living?* For the Greeks, the answer was ***eudaimonia***—a state of flourishing, excellence (***aretē***), and deep, enduring fulfilment.

Virtue Ethics begins with **Socrates**, who turned Philosophy inward. He taught that virtue begins in the soul, through dialogue, reflection, humility, and relentless self-examination. For him, virtue was inseparable from wisdom: to know the good was to do the good. Ignorance was the root of wrongdoing. The examined life was, therefore, the only path to moral excellence.

Plato expanded this insight into a grand and luminous vision. For him, virtue was harmony—an inner order of the soul reflecting a deeper order of reality itself. He understood the human being as a tension between reason, spirit, and desire, and taught that justice arises when each part finds its proper place under the guidance of reason. Wisdom, courage, moderation, and justice were living forces: ways in which the soul aligns itself with truth, the Good, and the Beautiful. A just soul, in Plato's view, was the foundation of a just society. Without inner order, no outer order could endure.

It was **Aristotle** who gave Virtue Ethics its most practical shape. In the ***Nicomachean Ethics***, he described virtue as something cultivated through repeated action. In other words, we become what we repeatedly do. Excellence is not a single act, but a habit slowly formed over time, guided by practical wisdom.

Habits are the invisible architects of our lives. They shape us in ways we barely notice—until one day, our character has taken form.

Virtue as a Habit

For Aristotle, we grow into virtue by ***doing*** virtuous acts:

> **"It is by doing just acts that we become just, and by doing temperate acts that we become temperate, and by doing brave acts that we become brave." – Aristotle, Nicomachean Ethics, Book II, trans. W. D. Ross (1908).**

At first, practising virtue can feel as awkward as learning to surf, skate, or play the violin. It is uncomfortable, unfamiliar, and sometimes discouraging. But with patience and perseverance, what once felt strained becomes natural. What once required effort becomes ease.

Virtue becomes a way of moving through the world.

Aristotle also taught that each virtue lives as a **golden mean** between two extremes. Courage stands between recklessness and cowardice. Generosity lies between wastefulness and stinginess. Honesty lives between blunt harshness and manipulative silence.

The virtuous person is not someone who never errs, but someone who learns, through practice, to navigate these living balances with wisdom and grace.

The Stoics later embraced and refined this virtue tradition, placing the four cardinal virtues—wisdom (***phronēsis***), courage (***andreía***), justice (***dikaiosýnē***), and temperance (***sōphrosýnē***)—at the heart of their philosophy. These virtues were not moral ornaments; they were the pillars of inner freedom, resilience, and **eudaimonia**. In the next chapter, we will walk more closely with them.

Goodness: The Highest Form of Intelligence

What I love most about our Greek and Roman thinkers is their conviction that goodness is the highest form of intelligence. For them, wisdom and virtue were inseparable. The truly wise person—the ***sophos***—was one who understood the good and lived in accordance with it. Intelligence was not simply the ability to reason or strategize. It was the capacity to live well: to act with integrity, insight, courage, and care.

How distant this vision feels from our world today, where cleverness so often eclipses honesty, and strategy is admired more than sincerity. We celebrate calculation, optimisation, and "winning," even when those victories come at the expense of others. Yet the ancients remind us of a deeper truth: cleverness without virtue is not wisdom at all—it is simply a more refined form of blindness.

I find myself in complete agreement with them. To me, true intelligence is ethical.

True intelligence is humane.
True intelligence is good.

The Transformative Power of Virtue Ethics

Virtue Ethics calls us to moral excellence. It invites us to focus not only on what we do, but on who we are becoming as we do it. Where other ethical systems analyse actions, Virtue Ethics transforms the moral agent.

When we cultivate virtue, our actions naturally begin to reflect that inner work.

Virtue is a practice—a rhythm of learning, failing, and beginning again. It is the slow, steady alignment of our being with what is true and good. And as we change, so does the world we create.

Every act of patience, every moment of courage, every choice to be honest when dishonesty would be easier—these are the brushstrokes in the painting of a good life.

We all have so much to gain from this path.

17

Stoicism: A Path to Eudaemonia

We live in a *sálvese quien pueda* world—a world where everyone scrambles to take as much as possible from a finite pie. The mindset is clear: the more, the merrier—for me and my inner circle. But in doing so, we often avert our gaze from what's left for others, choosing not to see the inequity so that we do not feel the weight of our actions. Yet, deep inside, we long for something different. We wish for a world where kindness and trust are not rare commodities, where we do not have to guard ourselves against one another, where our interactions are marked by genuine connection.

Our days are filled with relentless busyness, yet we crave stillness. We chase titles and wealth, yet we long for meaning. We surround ourselves with people, online and offline, yet loneliness lingers in our hearts. If the ancient Stoics could see us today, they would say that our fatigue, our sense of emptiness, our constant dissatisfaction, all stem from the same source: a detachment from virtue and the abandonment of its pursuit. We have neglected the essential task of building a moral character.

If Seneca, Epictetus, or Marcus Aurelius were alive today, they would remind us that the path to fulfilment, connection, and inner peace begins with virtue. They would show us that virtue is the key to a meaningful life.

To me, Stoicism is a way of being in the world. It teaches us that virtue is the only true good—the foundation of ***eudaimonia***, a flourishing and well-lived life. To achieve this marvellous state, we are called to live in harmony with nature, embracing both our **rational** minds and our deeply **social** nature. We can survive alone, yes, but we thrive in community. We thrive when

P. Ansoleaga Abascal, *Philosophy and Finance: A Love Story*,
https://doi.org/10.1007/978-3-032-22218-3_17

we align our actions with reason, when we focus on what lies within our control, and when we let go of what does not.

To live by Stoicism is to know ourselves deeply. It is to forge an intimate connection with our inner world, to define the values and principles that shape our existence. In doing so, we build a moral compass—one that stays steady through the chaos of life, guiding us through uncertainty, hardship, and temptation. This pursuit of self-awareness is a lifelong practice of self-improvement, a daily discipline of reflection, examination, and moral refinement. The Stoics called this the cultivation of character—the relentless effort to align our actions with virtue.

Their message is clear: **we can be sculptors of our own souls, shaping ourselves with each thought, each choice, each act of integrity.**

It is this encouragement to become better human beings that makes me love Stoicism so deeply. It offers moral clarity and purpose without asking us to abandon reason (*logos*). It serves as a compass, guiding us toward wise choices, meaningful pursuits, and a noble way of living. And it is fully compatible with both religious and secular lives.

To me, it is pure nourishment for the soul.

I love Stoicism because it offers wisdom for both personal and spiritual growth. It is a philosophy of progress, not perfection. A philosophy of mindful reflection, deliberate action, and a steadfast commitment to our duties within the larger human community. It is a steady, unwavering journey toward self-mastery and inner peace.

As with any journey, there will be moments of doubt—moments when we feel lost. But Stoicism gives us two enduring guideposts: the **Four Cardinal Virtues** and **the Dichotomy of Control.**

Marcus Aurelius, reflecting on the guiding principles of life, wrote:

> "If thou findest in human life anything better than justice, truth, temperance, and courage, anything better than a mind which is satisfied with itself in the things which it is allowed to do, and in the things which it is not allowed to do is satisfied with submission, I say, if thou findest anything better than this, turn to it with thy whole soul, and enjoy that which thou hast found to be the best." –Marcus Aurelius, Meditations, Book III, 6, trans. George Long (1862).

The Stoics never found anything better than wisdom, courage, temperance and justice. To me, there is only one thing greater: **Love**. Selfless, unconditional love—a force that, I believe, lives within each of these cardinal virtues.

Practical Wisdom (**phronēsis**) is the ability to discern what is truly good, what is harmful, and what is indifferent, and to act accordingly. As Seneca reminds us, ***"Philosophy teaches us to act, not to speak."- Seneca, Moral***

Letters, 20.2, trans. Richard M. Gummere (1917). Courage (**andreía**) is the strength to face adversity with grace, to stand by our values, and to do what is right—even when it is difficult. Especially when it is difficult. Justice (**dikaiosýnē**) is the unwavering commitment to fairness, compassion, and kindness in how we relate to others and to the world. Temperance (**sōphrosýnē**) is the discipline to seek balance, to practise restraint, and to live in harmony with ourselves, others, and nature.

Love is not separate from these virtues—it is the spirit that animates them. It is what makes wisdom compassionate, courage noble, justice humane, and temperance gentle. To cultivate virtue is to love ourselves and others.

The Stoics also teach us a powerful truth: some things are within our control, while others are not. This is the **Dichotomy of Control**—the distinction that can set us free.

Epictetus opens his Enchiridion with this luminous principle:

> ***"Some things are in our control and others are not. Things in our control are opinion, pursuit, desire, aversion, and, in a word, whatever are our own actions. Things not in our control are body, property, reputation, command, and, in a word, whatever are not our own actions."***
> **–Epictetus, Enchiridion 1, trans. Elizabeth Carter (1758)**

When we focus on what is within our power—our thoughts, emotions, and actions—we cultivate resilience, inner strength, and freedom. When we fixate on what lies beyond our control, we invite frustration, dependence, and unnecessary suffering.

Stoicism teaches us that transformation begins within. That justice begins with our own actions. That peace is not found in external comforts, but in mastering our own minds. That a meaningful life is one lived with integrity, courage, and compassion.

And perhaps most importantly: to pursue virtue is to pursue the highest version of ourselves. And in doing so, we do not just transform our own lives—we transform the world around us.

From Greece to Rome

The Evolution of a Timeless Philosophy

Stoicism, one of the most influential schools of Hellenistic Philosophy, began with Zeno of Citium (334–262 BCE) and gradually unfolded into one of humanity's most enduring moral frameworks. What started beneath the painted colonnades of Athens grew into a spiritual and ethical tradition capable of guiding emperors and slaves, merchants and scholars, through the trials of life. From the beautiful porches of the Athenian agora to the vast courts of the Roman Empire, Stoicism transformed itself from a small circle of seekers into a Philosophy of living—clear, steady, and profoundly humane.

Across the centuries, this tradition passed through three great movements, each adding new depth and colour.

The **Early Stoa**—Zeno, then Cleanthes, and finally Chrysippus—laid the intellectual and ethical foundations.

The **Middle Stoa**, shaped by Panaetius and Posidonius, carried Stoicism beyond Greece and adapted it to a broader cultural world.

And in the **Roman Stoa**, the Philosophy came fully alive through Musonius Rufus, Seneca, Epictetus, and Marcus Aurelius, who transformed Stoicism from a theoretical system into a practical art of living.

Together, these thinkers shaped a Philosophy for the mind and the soul—offering a wise, steady guide to the human condition across centuries.

Zeno of Citium: The Founder of Stoicism

Zeno's story begins with a shipwreck. Born in Citium (on the island of Cyprus), he was a wealthy Phoenician merchant until fate intervened, wrecking his ship and leaving him stranded in Athens. Seeking shelter in a bookshop, he began reading Xenophon's Memorabilia, and something powerful awakened in him. Inspired, he sought out philosophers, first studying under Crates the Cynic. But Cynicism, with its radical rejection of social norms, felt too austere and inflexible.

So Zeno began shaping a new path—blending Socratic ethics, Cynic simplicity, and Platonic depth into something balanced and humane. Eventually, he began teaching at the Stoa Poikilē, the Painted Porch in the Athenian agora. From that humble porch, Stoicism was born.

Zeno taught that the key to wisdom lay in living "according to nature," meaning in harmony with reason (**logos**) and the rational order of the cosmos. He saw Philosophy as a seamless unity of three disciplines: **logic** (the art of thinking), **physics** (the structure of the universe), and **ethics** (the cultivation of virtue). His ideas formed the roots of a tradition that would guide human beings for millennia.

Cleanthes and Chrysippus: The Systematisers

Zeno's successor, **Cleanthes**, infused Stoicism with spiritual depth. A former boxer and water-carrier who studied Philosophy at night, he brought extraordinary devotion to the school. His ***Hymn to Zeus*** is one of the most beautiful affirmations of Stoic cosmology—a celebration of a universe governed by divine reason and permeated by order and harmony.

But it was **Chrysippus of Soli** who truly built Stoicism into a structured, formidable system. Often called the second founder of Stoicism, he wrote hundreds of works—so many that later ancient authors joked that without Chrysippus, there would be no Stoa.

He refined Stoic logic, strengthened its ethical doctrine, and articulated the Stoic understanding of fate and determinism. He argued that the wise person attains ***apatheia***—freedom from the tyranny of destructive emotions—not by suppressing feelings but by correcting the judgments that give rise to them.

Under **Chrysippus**, Stoicism became a complete philosophical architecture. Yet it was still largely a theoretical system—a philosophy of lectures, disputations, and treatises.

The Romans would transform it into a lived experience.

Roman Stoicism: Practical Wisdom for Life

By the first century BCE, Stoicism had crossed the Mediterranean and entered the beating heart of a very different world. In Rome, a city of power and ambition, of splendour and chaos, the Philosophy shed much of its abstract Hellenistic complexity. It became something more grounded, more intimate, more deeply human. It became a guide for living.

Roman culture valued action, duty, and moral strength. Stoicism found fertile soil there, transforming from a rigorous Greek system into a practical art of life. It became a companion for rulers and rebels, for merchants and mothers, for slaves seeking dignity and emperors seeking humility.

Its spirit came to life through four remarkable voices: Musonius Rufus, Seneca, Epictetus, and Marcus Aurelius—each carrying the flame in their own way, each making Stoicism liveable.

Musonius Rufus: Wisdom for Everyone

At the dawn of this Roman flowering stands **Musonius Rufus** (c. 25–95 CE), a philosopher so devoted to virtue that he was called "the Roman Socrates."

He taught in marketplaces and courtyards, to women and men, aristocrats and slaves alike, insisting that wisdom belongs to all who hunger for it. His lessons were simple, direct, profoundly ethical. Philosophy was a daily practice. A life of simplicity, self-mastery, and service.

His greatest legacy may be his student—Epictetus, who transformed Musonius' teachings into one of history's most powerful visions of inner freedom.

Seneca: The Philosopher-Statesman

Seneca the Younger (4 BCE–65 CE) brought Stoicism into the corridors of power. A playwright, statesman, and adviser to Nero, he lived at the heart of the empire—yet sought clarity amid its noise. His *Letters to Lucilius* and essays, such as *On the Shortness of Life*, transformed Stoic thought into luminous reflections on time, virtue, adversity, and the art of choosing wisely.

For Seneca, Philosophy was "medicine for the soul." It was meant to be applied when life became most difficult.

> *"It is not that we have a short space of time, but that we waste much of it." –Seneca, On the Shortness of Life, trans. Aubrey Stewart (1889).*
> *"We suffer more often in imagination than in reality." –Seneca, Moral Letters, 13.4, trans. Aubrey Stewart (1889).*

His voice remains startlingly modern—clear, compassionate, uncompromising. Through him, Stoicism becomes intimate: a dialogue between friends seeking to become better human beings.

Epictetus: Freedom Begins Within

Born into slavery in Phrygia, Epictetus (50–135 CE) became one of the most influential moral teachers in history. He owned nothing—no wealth, no property, not even his own body—yet he taught a Philosophy of radical freedom. To him, true liberty is always within reach, because it lies not in circumstances but in judgment.

His Discourses and Enchiridion capture his central insight with unmatched clarity:

> *"Some things are in our control and others are not."*
>
> *–Epictetus, Enchiridion 1*

Focus on what is yours—your thoughts, choices, and character—and no setback can break you. Worry about what is not yours—fortune, reputation, the behaviour of others—and you surrender your peace.

Epictetus taught that freedom is not a political condition but a spiritual art. His teachings, preserved by his student Arrian, became a compass for generations—and still illuminate millions of lives today.

There is so much more to say about him—and later in this part of the book, we will return to Epictetus more fully, because his teachings have shaped my own journey more than any other Stoic. His voice has been my companion for years, a steady and kind reminder that **freedom begins within.**

Marcus Aurelius: The Philosopher-King

At the height of Roman power stands Marcus Aurelius (121–180 CE), emperor of the known world and devoted student of the Stoic path. Amid wars, plagues, betrayals, and the crushing weight of imperial responsibility, he wrote the Meditations—a private notebook of reflections never meant for publication. A conversation with himself.

Here was a man who held absolute power, yet chose humility. Who commanded vast armies, yet wrestled—like all of us—with impatience, fear, and anger. Who reminded himself, day after day, that virtue is the only true wealth.

> *"Waste no more time arguing what a good man should be. Be one."*
> *–Marcus Aurelius, Meditations, Book X, 16, trans. George Long (1862).*

Marcus did not write to persuade or to impress. He wrote to endure. His words reveal a human being committed to progress—striving, every day, to return to what is good.

A Philosophy for the Soul and for Society

With the Romans, Stoicism became something new. Less concerned with physics and logic, more devoted to resilience, clarity, and moral character. Less about the structure of the universe, more about the architecture of the soul.

From Zeno of Citium's shipwreck to Seneca's letters, from Epictetus' humble school to Marcus Aurelius' battlefield reflections, Stoicism evolved into a Philosophy for real life—for mornings marked by fear, for nights of doubt, for moments that demand choice.

It became what it remains today: a guide to inner freedom. A companion in times of turmoil. A moral compass for those who wish to live with integrity, courage, and love.

We cannot control the world. But we can always choose how we respond to it. And in that choice, we discover our strength.

18

The First Cognitive Scientists: How the Stoics Mastered the Mind

Stoicism embodies the values I cherish most—the ones I nurture and aspire to embody: empathy, joy, mental clarity, integrity, freedom, authenticity, generosity, and wisdom. Perhaps wisdom encapsulates them all in a single word—a kind of practical knowledge at the service of the good, in the ancient sense of the term. The *Head* at the service of the *Heart*.

Stoicism is profoundly practical, deeply empowering, and utterly optimistic. Contrary to common misconceptions, it does not suppress emotions—it refines them. It helps us cultivate life-enhancing emotions such as gratitude and joy while reducing unnecessary suffering. Stoicism teaches us to recognise our emotions, reflect on them, and—most importantly—accept them. Through that acceptance, pain can become growth, and emotion can become wisdom.

The Stoics were pioneers of psychology—keen observers of the human mind who, had they lived today, might well hold PhDs in cognitive science. Long before modern psychology, they understood that our suffering does not stem from external events, but from the judgments we form about them. They realised that by learning to examine and reshape our thoughts, we could transform our emotional responses—an insight that would much later reappear in Cognitive Behavioural Therapy.

This is precisely the point that William B. Irvine brings to life in *A Guide to the Good Life*. Irvine explains that the Stoics understood a simple truth: a life dominated by emotions such as anger, fear, anxiety, grief, or envy cannot be a good life. For this reason, they became careful and disciplined observers of the mind. They studied how emotions arise, how

P. Ansoleaga Abascal, *Philosophy and Finance: A Love Story*,
https://doi.org/10.1007/978-3-032-22218-3_18

they gain power over us, and how they can be gently intercepted before taking root—or weakened once they do. In doing so, the Stoics anticipated many of the core insights of modern psychology, offering tools for understanding emotions, transforming them, and ultimately reclaiming inner freedom.

To protect the mind from being overwhelmed, the Stoics developed practices to steady themselves in the face of adversity. Through **premeditatio malorum**, they prepared for misfortune before it arrived. Through **reflection**, they examined their thoughts with honesty. Through **attention**, they softened impulsive reactions and cultivated the ability to pause. We will dig into these exercises later in the block, exploring how they shaped ancient lives and how they can shape ours. Their aim was **ataraxia**—a calm, stable inner state that no external storm could easily disturb.

In a world obsessed with external achievements, fleeting pleasures, and constant distractions, Stoicism presents a liberating truth: true peace is found in needing less, in appreciating what we have, in practicing gratitude.

This wisdom remains strikingly relevant today, in an age where consumerism and instant gratification often leave us restless and dissatisfied. **Psychiatrist Dr. Anna Lembke, in Dopamine Nation: Finding Balance in the Age of Indulgence**, explores how modern life exploits our vulnerabilities to pleasure and pain, trapping us in cycles of dependence. She explains that our brains are wired for dopamine-driven reward-seeking behaviour, which once helped our ancestors survive but now makes us susceptible to overindulgence—whether through social media, food, shopping, or even work. In an era of constant stimulation, we become addicted to short-term pleasures while losing our ability to experience deep, lasting fulfilment. Over time, this imbalance makes us more anxious, distracted, and dissatisfied.

Stoicism, with its emphasis on self-mastery, rational discernment, and moderation, offers a way out—a path to genuine freedom. By learning to regulate our desires rather than be ruled by them, we reclaim control over our minds and cultivate a more stable and enduring sense of well-being. Which, by the way, is not only much better for ourselves but also for the planet, since consumerism is exhausting our resources.

True happiness, the Stoics remind us, does not come from chasing external rewards but from mastering ourselves, living with purpose, and contributing meaningfully to the world. This path is not easy, but it is deeply rewarding.

Inner Freedom—Releasing Attachment to Outcomes

One of the most transformative lessons in Stoicism is learning to release attachment to outcomes. To me, this is the essence of inner freedom, especially in a world where our sense of worth is so often tied to external results.

Life rarely unfolds according to plan. While we are busy organizing, striving, and projecting ourselves into the future, reality moves in its own direction, gently reminding us how little control we truly have, and how much of our worry is unnecessary.

Clinging to outcomes is a reliable path to disappointment. Detachment, however, does not mean apathy. It means shifting our attention to what is actually within our control: our choices, our actions, and whether those actions align with our values.

The Stoics teach that self-worth should be rooted in virtue, not results. Success or failure in business, relationships, or any pursuit is secondary. What matters is how we show up—with integrity, courage, and wisdom. When we make this shift from results to values, we free ourselves from the weight of others' opinions and the endless chase for external validation.

Detachment is not about being cold or indifferent. It is about recognizing the impermanence of all things. Success, possessions, even our deepest hopes come and go. By loosening our grip on what is temporary, we become more open to life as it is, moving with change rather than resisting it.

Buddhism calls this non-attachment, and its teaching aligns closely with Stoicism. Both traditions remind us that clinging leads to suffering, while freedom comes through acceptance. For me, this practice is about choosing values over vanity, flow over frustration, and peace over the futile attempt to control what was never ours to command.

Whenever I find myself caught in worry, I imagine Epictetus whispering: **Paule, do your best and let the rest be.**

This simple reminder brings me back to the present, urging me to focus on what I can control—my work, my studies, my preparation—rather than waste energy on uncertainty. It reminds me to trust the process and release my futile attempts to dictate life's outcomes.

Stoicism whispers to us in life's most chaotic moments, reminding us that while we cannot control external circumstances, we can always choose our response. It encourages us to remain steadfast in virtue, to view obstacles as opportunities, and to embrace life with an open, joyful heart.

And you know what? Happiness is the greatest gift we can give to the world. When we are happy, we share our light with others. And that light—like wisdom—is contagious. It sows inspiration, joy, and hope in those around us.

19

The Spirit of the Painted Porch

What I love most about Stoicism is that it is not cold or abstract. It's alive. Yes, it's practical. Yes, it offers tools for clarity and resilience. But it also carries something quieter and deeper: an inner warmth, a sense of companionship, a way of meeting life with a steady mind and an open heart.

Stoicism is joyful, communal, inclusive, and profoundly holistic. It reaches from the smallest details of daily life to the vastness of the cosmos, holding both with the same calm wonder.

The Stoa Poikile, the Painted Porch, was far more than a beautiful place. It was a possibility. A vision. A choice.

In a time when many were excluded, it offered a philosophy open to all. It invited people to step forward with purpose, determination, and grace. It welcomed those willing to trade an ordinary way of seeing—shaped by habit and social conditioning—for a philosophical one that was higher, richer, and freer.

It asked people to stop merely reacting and start truly living. T**o experience the fullness of life without being consumed by its passing storms.** To discover that steadiness does not dull joy. It deepens it.

At its core, Stoicism is an invitation.

To live with courage.
To cultivate gratitude.
To choose integrity.

And to remember that joy and wisdom were always meant to walk hand in hand.

P. Ansoleaga Abascal, *Philosophy and Finance: A Love Story*,
https://doi.org/10.1007/978-3-032-22218-3_19

Joyful

Stoicism invites us to care for our inner life with wisdom and intention. It encourages the cultivation of emotions that illuminate our days—joy, gratitude, awe, and serenity—while gently loosening the grip of those that burden us, such as anger, envy, and anxiety. Stoicism does not ask us to feel less, but to feel more wisely: to replace agitation with calm, entitlement with gratitude, frustration with acceptance, and indifference with wonder.

As William B. Irvine explains in *A Guide to the Good Life*, the Stoics were never opposed to emotion itself. What concerned them were emotions that undermine our peace and clarity. Their aim was not numbness or detachment, but the cultivation of a stable inner tranquillity—one spacious enough for joy, gratitude, and awe to flourish and endure.

We often assume happiness comes from external success—money, status, the perfect life. Yet even when we attain these things, restlessness, anxiety, and dissatisfaction often remain. Think of **Siddhartha Gautama, the Buddha**: he lived in a palace, surrounded by luxury, with a beautiful wife and a newborn son. He had everything the world defines as fulfilment—yet he left it all behind in search of something deeper. The Stoics, too, understood that true happiness is not about what we have, but how we see, think, and live. In other words, who we are.

They developed practical ways to nurture joy:

Marcus Aurelius found gratitude in life's simplest blessings—his breath, the stars, the love of friends. The Stoics practiced the *View from Above* to inspire awe, reminding themselves they were part of something vast and interconnected. They sought inner tranquillity (ataraxia) by letting go of what they could not control, freeing their minds for clarity, serenity, and deep fulfilment. And just as they cultivated positive emotions, they learned to weed out destructive ones.

Seneca, in *On Anger*, reminds us that few things corrode happiness as much as losing mastery over ourselves. We recognise this immediately from our own lives: the moment we surrender to rage, resentment, or irritation, our inner peace dissolves.

Envy is another powerful thief of joy. When we measure our lives against the fortunes of others, dissatisfaction inevitably follows. Seneca observed that much of our suffering arises not from what we lack, but from the habit of comparing our inner state to the external success of those around us. As he writes:

> *"Do you want to know what it is that makes men covetous, ambitious, or fearful? It is because they measure themselves not by their own condition, but by that of others."*

–Seneca, On Tranquillity of Mind (De Tranquillitate Animi), 9.2, trans. Aubrey Stewart (1889).

Peace, Seneca suggests, comes from learning to take our measure from within. True joy is found in needing less. Not in surpassing others, but in becoming wiser, calmer, and more generous than we were yesterday.

Epictetus echoes this insight. Much of what we call anxiety, he teaches, is born not from reality itself but from the stories we tell ourselves about it. We suffer far more in our minds than in the events we face. When we learn to distinguish what is real from what is imagined, a great weight lifts—and with it, the unnecessary suffering we so often impose upon ourselves.

There was a time when a non-promotion, a train delay, a cancelled flight, a critique from my boss, or not being invited to a party would have ruined my day. I would have let it consume my thoughts, turning a temporary moment into hours of frustration or self-doubt.

Now, I see things differently. A missed promotion? An opportunity to grow in ways I had not considered. A delay? Unexpected time to read or reflect. A critique? A chance to learn—or a reminder that I cannot control others' opinions.

Epictetus taught me that every difficulty in life offers an invitation to turn inward and draw upon resources we often forget we have. Trials, rather than breaking us, can introduce us to our own strength.

"Difficulties are things that show what men are." –Epictetus, Discourses, Book I, 24, trans. George Long (1877).

And when criticism comes my way, I no longer feel the need to defend myself. As Epictetus puts it with humour:

"If anyone tells you that such a person speaks ill of you, do not make excuses about what is said of you, but answer: 'He was ignorant of my other faults, else he would not have mentioned these alone.'" –Epictetus, Enchiridion, 33, trans. Elizabeth Carter (1758).

I've learned that I cannot control the actions of others, nor the disruptions of life itself. But I can control my reaction, my mindset, and my ability to find meaning, strength and wisdom in every moment.

A Stoic feels deeply but freely. They marvel at the sunset with gratitude, hold a friend's hand with love, and gaze at the vastness of the universe with awe—all without being burdened by needless fears or resentments. When we master this, **we stop reacting and start truly living.**

Social and Communal

As Professor Massimo Pigliucci beautifully explains in ***How to Be a Stoic***, the Stoics took Aristotle's insight—that we are by nature both rational and social beings—and expanded it into a powerful ethical framework. Aristotle believed the highest purpose of human life was contemplation, the pursuit of wisdom for its own sake. The Stoics, however, shifted the emphasis toward the social, arguing that reason should not remain enclosed within private contemplation but be brought into the world, shaping our relationships, our duties, and the kind of society we help create.

For them, Philosophy was a way of being in the world. To live virtuously was to serve humanity, to contribute to the greater good, to elevate both ourselves and those around us. In doing so, we would not only achieve **ataraxia**—inner peace—but also help create a better world.

Stoicism is deeply social, communal, and empathetic. True happiness is not found in self-centred ambition but in harmonising with nature and working for the well-being of others. At the foundation of Stoic virtue is a profound love for humanity, a recognition of our interconnectedness, and a commitment to justice, wisdom, courage, and temperance—not just for ourselves, but for the whole of society.

The truth about Stoicism—so often misunderstood—is beautifully articulated by Seneca:

> *"No philosophy is kinder or more gentle, none more full of love towards mankind, none more attentive to the common good; its very purpose is to be useful, to give help, and to consider the interests not of itself alone, but of all men, both individually and collectively." –Seneca, On Clemency (De Clementia), 2.5.3, trans. Aubrey Stewart (1889).*

This is the heart of Stoicism: a Philosophy rooted in engagement, grounded in service, and devoted to the flourishing of all. It calls us to meet the world with wisdom, to uplift others through our actions, and to live as responsible citizens of a shared human community.

Inclusive

Before we step into the inclusive spirit of my favourite school of thought, I want to invite you to take a look at the cover of this book—the one you are holding in your hands.

That image, the Stoa Poikilē, the Painted Porch of ancient Athens, is not there by accident. It is the place where Zeno of Citium began teaching Stoicism around 300 BCE: a public space unlike any other. This beautifully colonnaded structure in the Agora, bright with frescoes and sunlight, was a place where anyone could walk in freely to listen, reflect, and learn. There were no gates, no titles, no barriers. Just a colonnade open to the sky and a Philosophy open to everyone.

Open to all, irrespective of status or gender, the Painted Porch welcomed anyone who sought introspection and a virtuous life.

How beautiful—and how humble—that Stoicism was named not after Zeno, but after this public porch. To me, this choice speaks of openness, inclusiveness, and a deep love for humanity. The Stoa Poikilē embodies everything I admire in this Philosophy: its accessibility, its egalitarian spirit, its belief that wisdom is not a private privilege but a shared path.

Stoicism broke many of the social boundaries of its time. It welcomed women, slaves, foreigners, the wealthy, the poor—anyone willing to cultivate reason and virtue. Its central conviction was revolutionary: that every human being carries within them the same spark of logos, the same capacity for wisdom, dignity, and moral excellence.

Nikole Bozza Ansoleaga

My beloved Epictetus—born into slavery and later one of the greatest philosophers of antiquity—is living proof of this. His life is a testament to the Stoic idea that virtue is independent of circumstance.

Women, too, found a home in Stoicism. Their stories are fewer not because their wisdom was lesser, but because history rarely preserved their voices. And yet some shine through the centuries.

Porcia Catonis, daughter of Cato the Younger, was admired in antiquity for her strength of character and philosophical seriousness. Plutarch recounts that, wishing to prove her resilience and her capacity for discretion, she inflicted a wound on her own thigh to test whether she could endure pain without revealing a secret. Whether we read this gesture literally or symbolically, its meaning in ancient literature is clear: it was meant to highlight her moral courage and inner resolve, not to celebrate harm. In a world where women were seldom acknowledged as philosophical equals, Porcia stood as a rare and powerful example of Stoic determination.

Annia Cornificia Faustina Minor, sister of Marcus Aurelius, lived the same virtues her brother reflected upon in his Meditations. Though history remembers him more, she too practiced courage, discipline, and justice with steady constancy.

And then there is **Hypatia of Alexandria**, the brilliant philosopher-scientist of Late Antiquity. Though a Neoplatonist, her devotion to reason, virtue, and cosmic harmony makes her feel—at least to me—like a kindred Stoic spirit: a luminous mind who lived Philosophy bravely and paid for it with her life.

For these women, and for many whose names history never preserved, Stoicism became a source of strength, wisdom, and dignity. Their lives remind us that this Philosophy was always meant to uplift the human spirit—open to anyone who seeks clarity, resilience, and a life shaped by virtue.

Holistic

For the Stoics, true virtue could not be cultivated through ethics alone. It required excellence in reasoning (**logic**) and a deep understanding of the natural world (**physics** and **metaphysics**). **Ethics**, **logic**, and **physics** were not separate branches of study but three strands of a single thread—woven together to shape a life lived in harmony with nature and reason.

The early Stoics—Zeno, Cleanthes, and Chrysippus—insisted on this triadic vision. Understanding the universe (**physics**) helped one think clearly (**logic**), and clear thinking guided right action (**ethics**). Each discipline strengthened and illuminated the others, forming a comprehensive framework for living well.

When Stoicism reached Rome, philosophers like Seneca, Epictetus, and Marcus Aurelius placed a stronger emphasis on **ethics**, offering practical wisdom for navigating the joys and sorrows of daily life. Yet even then, **logic** and **physics** remained essential foundations for moral clarity. Roman Stoicism may have spoken more directly to the heart, but it never forgot that right action must rest upon both right thinking and a right understanding of the world.

This Stoic triad—**knowledge, reasoning**, and **ethics**—resonates deeply with me. Many of the world's most unsustainable behaviours—environmental, social, and economic—arise from neglecting one of these dimensions. Without **knowledge**, we remain blind to the forces shaping our lives and our planet. Without sound **reasoning**, we fall prey to confusion, bias, and fear. Without **ethics**, we risk making choices that elevate short-term desires above long-term flourishing.

To the Stoics, living ethically meant living in agreement with Nature. It meant aligning our actions with universal principles, striving to understand the patterns and truths of the world around us, and acting accordingly with clarity and virtue.

As Epictetus reminds us:

> *"He who has a clear knowledge of good and evil would know how to love; but how could a man who cannot distinguish good from evil, and things indifferent from both, possess the power of loving?" –Epictetus, Discourses, Book II, 22.15, trans. George Long (1877).*

Stoicism is far more than a guide to moral conduct. It is an invitation to cultivate virtue grounded in **knowledge**, sharpened by **reason**, and expressed through **ethical action**—so that we may live in harmony with ourselves, with others, and with the natural world that sustains us.

20

Ancient Spiritual Exercises and the Art of Inner Transformation

Centuries later, within the neoclassical halls of the Collège de France in Paris, the French philosopher Pierre Hadot (1922–2010) would illuminate a forgotten truth: that ancient Philosophy was way more than an intellectual discipline. It was a way of life.

In his seminal work ***Philosophy as a Way of Life (1995)***, Hadot revealed that the great philosophical schools of antiquity—Stoic, Epicurean, Sceptic, Peripatetic, and Platonic—were complete forms of life, woven from daily practices designed to train the soul, refine the character, and calm the passions through continual attention and self-mastery.

He called these practices spiritual exercises: deliberate actions of inner transformation through which reasoning becomes renewal, knowledge becomes wisdom, and life itself becomes Philosophy in motion.

I understand that the word "spiritual" might feel strange or esoteric in our modern world. Contemporary Stoic thinker William B. Irvine prefers the term "psychological techniques," and indeed, many of these practices anticipated contemporary cognitive science. But I remain drawn to Hadot's term. It honours the original truth of ancient Philosophy: that it was meant to nourish the soul, not merely to inform the mind.

Philosophy as Transformation

These exercises were the living core of Philosophy as a way of life—no less essential to the philosopher than training is to the athlete. They were designed to change how one sees, feels, thinks, and acts. And although each

P. Ansoleaga Abascal, *Philosophy and Finance: A Love Story*,
https://doi.org/10.1007/978-3-032-22218-3_20

school emphasised different attitudes—tension for the Stoics, tranquillity for the Epicureans, suspension of judgment for the Sceptics—all pursued the same aim: to help the human being move toward **areté**, the highest expression of excellence, and to attain **eudaimonia**, a life of flourishing, depth, and fulfilment.

Philosophy was not about thinking correctly but about being in the world correctly—a transformation of perception, a re-orientation of one's inner vision, a gradual healing of the soul. Epicurus believed that philosophy was worthless unless it alleviated human suffering.

> *"Empty is the argument of the philosopher which does not relieve any human suffering." –Epicurus, Fragment 221, trans. Cyril Bailey (1926).*

This is why Hadot's work matters to me so deeply. It restores the original, luminous spirit of Philosophy: a path of inner work that calms the mind, strengthens the character, and slowly transforms how we see, how we live, and who we become.

What follows now is an exploration of several ancient spiritual exercises offered as companions for our own inner journey. Each of them carries the power to bring us closer to the life we long for: a life of clarity, courage, serenity, and joy.

Attention to the Present Moment (*Prosoche*)

Among ancient philosophical schools, the exercise of mindful attention was universal. Plato spoke of the care of the soul. Aristotle emphasised reflective self-observation. The Epicureans monitored their desires. The Sceptics examined their judgments.

But the Stoics made of this attention an entire art, giving it a name: **prosoche** (προσοχή).

Prosoche is intentional, ethical attention. It is the vigilant presence that examines our thoughts, emotions, and impulses to remain aligned with reason and virtue. It is the practice of living every moment consciously, deliberately, and freely.

To me, **prosoche** is the foundation of the philosophical life. Self-improvement requires self-awareness, and self-awareness begins with self-observation. Without it, Philosophy remains theory. With it, life itself becomes practice.

A Stoic who cultivates **prosoche** treats each moment as an opportunity for alignment. Every impression (**phantasia**), every impulse (**hormê**), every reaction and judgment is brought into awarenesswith gentle steadiness, as one returns to what truly matters.

When I find myself lamenting the past or fearing the future, **prosoche** becomes my compass.

It redirects my attention to this moment—the only place where life unfolds and where joy is possible.

Epictetus considered **prosoche** the very heart of Philosophy. Without it, he warned, we drift through life half-asleep. With it, we become sovereign over our mind and our moral choices.

He urged his students:

> *"Keep a careful watch over your impressions; for from them arise our impulses, our desires, and our aversions." –Epictetus, Discourses, Book III, 12, trans. George Long (1877).*

This vigilance sharpens perception, dissolves regret about the past and anxieties about the future, and gives what Hadot called "an exact vision of the world."

Prosoche is the beginning of inner freedom—the spark of transformation.

While modern mindfulness often invites us simply to observe, **prosoche** adds an ethical dimension. It asks us not only to notice, but to choose: to align each thought and action with virtue. **It is mindfulness with a compass—presence with purpose.**

Mindful Day-End Reflection

In addition to this constant attention to the present moment, the ancients practised a second form of vigilance: the evening examination of conscience. Seneca describes his own practice in *De Ira* (*On Anger*):

> *"When the light has been removed and my wife, long since acquainted with my habit, has fallen silent, I examine my whole day, and go back over what I have done and said. I hide nothing from myself; I pass nothing by.*
> *For why should I fear any of my faults, when I can say, 'Beware of doing that again; this time I pardon you'?"*
> *–Seneca, On Anger, Book III, 36, trans. Aubrey Stewart (1889).*

I adore this passage. It captures exactly what self-examination is meant to be: gentle truthfulness rather than self-reproach, progress rather than perfection.

Yet in modern life, we rarely engage in this kind of mindful reflection. We track everything—steps, calories, sleep cycles, heartbeats, hydration—but how often do we pause to track our character? Do we ever ask ourselves:

Did I act with wisdom today?
Was I patient?
Did I speak with kindness?
Did I respond with courage?
Did I choose what aligns with the person I want to become?

I often wonder what kind of people we might become if we treated our virtues as carefully as we treat our fitness. If patience were monitored like heart rate, kindness like calories burned, wisdom like daily steps.

To practise **prosoche** throughout the day—and to close the evening with this kind of gentle reckoning—is to cultivate self-awareness, inner steadiness, and moral clarity. It is the art of living deliberately, of accepting what lies beyond our control, and of realigning our will with the flow of nature.

As the ancients knew well, this practice is the cornerstone of the philosophical life.

The Cosmic Perspective

To me, **prosoche**—the ancient form of what we now call mindfulness—is the most essential exercise, because self-improvement, inner growth, always begins with self-awareness. And more than that: joy itself manifests only in the present moment, in the here and now. Yet lasting joy—true **eudaimonia**—requires more than mindfulness and mental clarity. The work of the soul also asks for self-transcendence: the loosening of the **ego**, so that we can rediscover our place within the whole.

So from the anchoring of our attention inward, we now move outward—toward the cosmic perspective, the expansion of our vision. From **within**... to **above**.

The View from Above

Pierre Hadot describes the cosmic perspective, the "view from above", as a way of relativising our private dramas and dissolving the illusions our ego constructs. This exercise invites an imaginative ascent: in our mind, we rise above our room, our street, our city; higher still, until the Earth itself becomes a luminous sphere hanging in silence. From that altitude, our concerns soften, and we see things closer to what they truly are. No longer trapped in the narrow view of the ego, we begin to witness life from the unhurried vantage of the cosmos.

This practice is rooted in Stoic physics and cosmology—the understanding that we are part of an ordered, living universe, woven into something infinitely greater than ourselves. To contemplate the **Whole**—the stars, the infinite expanse of space, the flow of time—is to be lifted beyond our small concerns.

Perspective, Humility, Belonging

The view from above teaches something essential: when we step back, we see things more truly. From that height, a calm awe settles over us. Serenity replaces restlessness. The spirit feels lifted, weightless, at peace.

This cosmic perspective reminds us that we are not the centre of the world, but we are not separate from it either. We are part of the dance—voices in the cosmic song. The Stoic cosmos, permeated by Logos, is a living, rational whole; to see from above is to remember that we belong to it, that we are threads in a vast, living web. And from that remembrance flows an ethical imperative: to play our part well, to live in harmony with the whole.

Marcus Aurelius and the Stoic Practice

When I think of ancient **askēsis**—the disciplined practice of training of the soul—I picture Marcus Aurelius, the philosopher-king and last of the Five Good Emperors, reflecting on the insignificance of human affairs in the vastness of the universe. Practising the view from above allowed him to cultivate a humble kind of leadership—one rooted in duty rather than ego. He often reminded himself that all things are interconnected, and that he was but a part of a magnificent whole:

> *"Frequently consider the connection of all things in the universe and their relation to one another." –Marcus Aurelius, Meditations, Book VII, 47, trans. George Long (1862).*

Despite ruling an empire that stretched from Britain to Egypt, Marcus remained humble. His cosmic vision gave him the strength to meet life's hardships with calm acceptance. And his reign was anything but easy. He spent much of it at war, defending Rome's borders against Germanic tribes and the Parthian Empire. In 165 A.D., the Antonine Plague swept through the empire, killing millions. His personal life was no less turbulent: of the thirteen children he had with Faustina, only a few survived into adulthood. Ancient sources such as Cassius Dio even report rumours of her infidelity—whether true or not, they must have been painful.

And yet, despite war, loss, and betrayal, Marcus did not sink into despair or cynicism. He turned to Philosophy as his guide, and observed how ephemeral and trivial human concerns are:

> *"Consider the rapidity with which all things pass away and are no more: the substances themselves, the accidents attached to them; and reflect how very trivial and contemptible are all things." –Marcus Aurelius, Meditations, Book XII, 36, trans. George Long (1862).*

What kind of world would we live in if today's leaders possessed even a fraction of his humility? If, instead of clinging to power, they saw themselves as temporary stewards—responsible for the well-being of their people, yet ultimately subject to the same universal laws as everyone else? This is what the view from above offers: **perspective**, yes—but more than that: **humility**, peace, and a deep connection that **opens the door to self-transcendence.**

Marcus Aurelius was not the only one practising the cosmic perspective. Epictetus urged his students to "look down from above" as if from the stars, to see human affairs without distortion. Seneca, too, wrote in his *Naturales Quaestiones* that contemplating the immensity of the cosmos frees us from the pettiness of our troubles. For the Stoics, this ascent was never an escape from the world, but a way to return to it with clearer judgment and greater love.

A Childhood Memory: A Very Powerful Helicopter

I first met this practice at home. My mother, a psychologist, sociologist, and lover of ancient philosophy, taught it to me long before I read the Stoics. As a teenager, I often had panic attacks before exams, because I had enjoyed myself until the end and always studied at the last minute. She would come to my room and ask me to close my eyes and take "a helicopter view"—to picture myself from above: first our apartment, then our city of Bilbao, then Spain, then Europe, then Earth, and finally the immense sweep of the galaxy. By the time I reached the Earth, my anxiety had melted away. The exam's importance shrank; the panic felt absurd. And then I could study—still last-minute, but with a calm mind. Looking back, I realise it must have been a very powerful helicopter—one that could reach the stars.

Nikole Bozza Ansoleaga

Let Us Watch the Stars

The next time we feel overwhelmed, we can pause. Close our eyes. Rise. See our life from the stars. We can recall Marcus Aurelius' words:

> *"Look round at the courses of the stars, as if you were running with them; and constantly consider the changes of the elements into one another; for such thoughts purge away the filth of the earth." –Marcus Aurelius, Meditations, Book VII, 47, trans. George Long (1862).*

Many translators render the spirit of this passage as: "Watch the stars, and see yourself running with them." I love this image. I close my eyes. I watch the stars, and I see myself running with them.

Premeditatio Malorum and Melete Thanatou

Beyond attention to the present and the cosmic view, the Stoics also practised exercises that at first sound stark, even unsettling. They asked us to picture adversity before it arrives, and to keep death itself in mind. These practices may seem severe, yet they carry so much wisdom: by facing what we fear most, we strip it of its power and learn to live with greater gratitude, presence, and love. Let us dig into them.

Premeditation of Adversity (Premeditatio Malorum)

This Stoic exercise invites us to imagine misfortunes before they happen—not to dwell in fear, but to rehearse responding with wisdom and calm. At first, it may sound like a paradox. But by vividly picturing loss, illness, conflict, or hardship, we rob these events of their power if and when they ever arrive. More than that, we learn to cherish what we have here and now, and free ourselves from the endless cycle of desire.

In his *Letters to Lucilius*, Seneca explains that freedom from anxiety begins when we learn to anticipate adversity rather than be shocked by it. As he writes:

> *"He robs present ills of their power who has perceived their coming beforehand." – Seneca, Letters to Lucilius, Letter 107.12, trans. Richard Gummere (1917).*

Premeditatio malorum was a practice for building inner strength by imagining adversity before it arrives. By acknowledging that obstacles and setbacks are inevitable, we rob them of their power to surprise or overwhelm us. And in the moments when hardship has not yet come—or never does—we cultivate deep gratitude. Nothing is taken for granted. Everything becomes a gift.

Imagine we are boarding a train. We remind ourselves it could be delayed. If it is, we remain undisturbed—we knew it could happen. If it is not, we feel grateful. The same applies when we set off on a seaside holiday. Our luggage could be lost; it could rain all week. If it happens, we remain undisturbed—these things happen. If it does not, we feel lucky and appreciative. This is *premeditatio malorum* in action: expecting life's uncertainties so they cannot overwhelm us.

The Stoics saw external "goods" like wealth and health as beyond our control—and therefore indifferent in terms of moral worth. True misfortune is not in what happens to us, but in how we respond. By preparing the mind in advance, we ensure that no hardship can shake our inner virtue.

I love this exercise because the less time we spend complaining, feeling angry, or dwelling on our bad luck, the more time, energy, mental clarity, and emotional strength we have for dreaming, creating, or helping someone in need.

Pierre Hadot describes *premeditatio malorum* as a form of psychological immunisation: through repeated practice, rational knowledge is transformed into deep, instinctive acceptance. When difficulties arise—as they inevitably will—we are not caught off guard.

Meditation on Death (Melete Thanatou)

Drawing on Plato's famous definition of Philosophy as "training for death," Pierre Hadot reminds us that the repeated contemplation of our mortality was a core exercise across ancient schools. Far from being morbid, reflecting on death makes life more precious. It reminds us that each moment is a gift, each encounter fleeting, each embrace irreplaceable.

The Stoics believed that contemplating death was the key to living fully and without fear. Melete Thanatou was a way of becoming more present, of valuing life rather than taking it for granted.

> *"You may leave this life at any moment: let that determine what you do and say and think."*
> *–Marcus Aurelius, Meditations, Book II, 11, trans. George Long (1862).*

At first, I found this exercise unsettling—especially when it involved imagining the mortality of those I love. But as I came to understand its purpose, I realised how profoundly it deepens mindfulness and gratitude.

Now, when I kiss my daughters, I am fully aware that I am embracing two mortal beings. That I, too, could be gone tomorrow. This awareness does not bring sorrow—it brings depth. It fills each moment with appreciation, each embrace with meaning. It reminds me never to take them, or anyone else, for granted.

Epicurus wrote:

> *"Death is nothing to us; for when we exist, death is not present, and when death is present, we do not exist."–Epicurus, Letter to Menoeceus, trans. Cyril Bailey (1926).*

The Stoics, too, insisted that everything is fleeting. The more we accept this, the more we can let go of what does not matter and cherish what does.

By meditating on death, we loosen our grip on ego, ambition, and trivial concerns. We expand beyond ourselves. Mortality frees us to love more deeply and live more fully.

Seneca said it best:

> *"It is not that we have a short time to live, but that we waste much of it." –Seneca, Letters to Lucilius, Letter 101.8, trans. Richard M. Gummere (1917).*

Because **in learning how to die, we finally learn how to live.**

A Vision Worth Embracing: Why These Exercises Matter

There were many more spiritual exercises than the ones I have shared. **Learning** itself was an exercise of the soul. So was **dialogue**, for wisdom had to be spoken, heard, and embodied to become real. **Journaling**, too, was a spiritual practice, as were **physical disciplines like fasting or enduring heat and cold**—each a way of training the body to serve the mind, and the mind to serve the soul.

The ancients also carried **maxims** like pocket-compasses—short sentences to remember and repeat when storms arose. They practised ***premeditatio bonorum***, anticipating the good, cultivating gratitude in advance. They contemplated the lives of sages, asking: *What would Socrates do? How would Cato respond?* They knew that philosophy is communal, and so dialogue itself became an exercise—a way to refine truth together.

Beneath all these practices lay a single, unifying vision: the belief that the cosmos is rationally ordered (**logos**), and that human beings, through reason and virtue, can align themselves with it. The Stoics called this living in accordance with nature. Plato and Aristotle described it as attaining a godlike perspective. Either way, the message was the same: wisdom is a new way of seeing. And **when our vision changes, everything changes.**

Each exercise was a bridge between thought and action, between theory and life. Attention to the present moment arose from a deeper understanding of time. Meditation on death flowed from the recognition of our mortal nature. Indifference to externals—fortune, status, praise, or blame—rested on the insight that these things lie beyond our control and are unworthy of disturbing our peace.

Philosophy was a way of living. Practice and theory were two sides of the same path, guiding the student toward authenticity, resilience, and joy.

Hadot described these disciplines as a kind of spiritual athletic training. Just as the body grows strong through repeated effort, so too does the soul.

With every meditation, every reflection, every act of restraint or courage, the philosopher sculpts herself—slowly, deliberately—into something greater.

And what they gained could not be measured in wealth or status. Their reward was far richer: self-awareness, inner peace, clarity of mind, freedom of spirit, and a happiness that no fortune could bestow or take away.

This is the promise of Philosophy when it is truly lived: to guide us back to our highest potential, to gift us with strength and wisdom—not only to transform our own lives, but to become a source of light, courage, and uplift for others as well.

21

Philo of Alexandria's Forever Festival

We often imagine the Stoics as austere figures tightened by discipline, and the Epicureans as carefree hedonists devoted to pleasure. Yet this caricature misses something essential. Ancient philosophers were not enemies of joy. On the contrary, they cultivated a deep, luminous happiness—one rooted in virtue. Their lives were living celebrations of wisdom.

These philosophers stand as role models. They offer us a vision of what could be—a world in which joy, purpose, and integrity are woven into the fabric of daily life. A world where the good is not an afterthought, but the foundation upon which communities, institutions, cities, and even economies are built.

One of the most beautiful portraits of this way of living comes from **Philo of Alexandria**.

Philo was a Jewish philosopher of the first century CE, born in Hellenistic Alexandria, a crossroads of Greek philosophy, Jewish thought, and Roman power. Steeped in Plato and the Stoics, yet faithful to the Hebrew tradition, he sought to reconcile reason and revelation, ethics and cosmology. In doing so, he became one of antiquity's most original voices on the moral life.

In *On the Special Laws*, Philo describes philosophers as embers of wisdom—quietly preserving the flame of virtue within society, not only for their own time, but for generations to come. His vision is so vivid, so generous, that it deserves to be savoured slowly. I encourage you, if you ever have the opportunity, to read his words in full. They reward attention.

What follows is my own telling of his vision—an attempt to convey the spirit, beauty, and depth of his thought.

P. Ansoleaga Abascal, *Philosophy and Finance: A Love Story*,
https://doi.org/10.1007/978-3-032-22218-3_21

Philo imagines a rare kind of human being: someone who trains for wisdom as a way of living. Such a person does not commit injustice, nor respond to it in kind. They turn away from the noise of empty ambition and the restless agitation of crowds—not out of contempt for others, but out of fidelity to peace, serenity, and moral clarity.

Their attention is expansive. They contemplate nature in all its forms—the earth beneath their feet, the sea in motion, the breath of the air, the vastness of the sky. In thought, they accompany the sun and the moon, the fixed stars and the wandering planets, attuning themselves to the rhythms of a greater order. Though their bodies remain rooted in daily life, their souls learn to rise above the trivial and the fleeting, gaining a wider vision of existence.

For such people, the whole world becomes a city. Its citizens are not defined by borders or origins, but by their devotion to wisdom. Civic belonging is no longer granted by status or law, but by virtue itself. Having cultivated inner excellence, they are no longer disturbed by physical discomfort or external misfortune. They loosen their grip on pleasure and desire, and face the blows of fate with steadiness, having reflected on them in advance.

From this way of living arises a distinctive joy. It does not depend on circumstances It flows from character. Philo calls this joy a festival—a celebration that extends across an entire lifetime.

> *"Those who find their joy in virtue celebrate a festival throughout their whole life."*
> *–Philo of Alexandria, On the Special Laws II.45–46*
> *(translation adapted from public-domain sources)*

Such people are few, he admits. They are like glowing embers within our cities, keeping the possibility of virtue alive for all of humanity.

From this vision, Philo dares to imagine what might be possible if this way of life were more widely embraced. If more people chose wisdom, integrity, and beauty for their own sake, fear and grief would lose their grip on our societies. Life itself would become a continuous celebration—not because suffering had vanished, but because meaning, harmony, and joy had taken root.

Philo's vision offers us a glimpse of what our societies could become if guided by wisdom, compassion, and virtue. This future is within reach—but to build it, we must first dare to imagine it.

The capacity to dream comes naturally to us as children, yet few of us carry that gift into adulthood. Children approach the world with wonder, questioning what others take for granted, their eyes open to the mystery of ordinary life. But routine and responsibility often dull this sensibility, hiding beauty behind the veil of the familiar.

Philosophers refuse to let that flame go out. They preserve a childlike astonishment—a way of seeing that keeps the world vast and alive. They remain open to the unknown, willing to question the known, daring to ask what others overlook. This refusal to stop wondering is the essence of the philosophical spirit.

To dream of a better world is to reconnect with that vision. It is to awaken the philosopher within us—the part that still believes in beauty, still senses meaning, still trusts that wisdom can shape how we live together. And perhaps, by holding onto this spirit, we can begin to shape a future guided by kindness, clarity, compassion, and connection.

22

Epictetus: The Slave Who Taught the World Freedom

Epictetus was born around 50 CE in the Roman province of Phrygia, in what is now Turkey. His life began in chains. As a child, he was taken to Rome and became the property of Epaphroditus, a wealthy freedman and secretary of Emperor Nero—a man of influence, and, like many who held power without wisdom, capable of cruelty.

Nikole Bozza Ansoleaga

P. Ansoleaga Abascal, *Philosophy and Finance: A Love Story*,
https://doi.org/10.1007/978-3-032-22218-3_22

A famous story tells of a moment when Epaphroditus, perhaps to test him, perhaps out of malice, seized Epictetus's leg and twisted it with such force that it snapped. Epictetus did not scream, nor beg, nor curse. He simply said with calm certainty, "You will break my leg." And when the bone gave way: "Did I not tell you so?"

Whether the story is literal or symbolic—as some scholars suggest—it captures the very essence of Epictetus's philosophy. Pain is inevitable, but suffering is optional. He had no command over what his master did to his body, but he had absolute command over his inner world. In that moment, he exercised the only true freedom the Stoics believed in: **the freedom of the will.**

He later expressed this truth in his Discourses:

"Lameness is an impediment to the leg, but not to the will." –Epictetus, Enchiridion 9, trans. George Long (1877).

A wound may limit the body, but it cannot touch the spirit. It cannot force a person to be undignified, unjust, panicked, or cruel. This insight—this unbreakable inner sovereignty—is the heart of Epictetus's thought.

Stoicism existed centuries before him, but Epictetus embodied it more purely than almost anyone. Unlike Seneca, who was a statesman, or Marcus Aurelius, who ruled the mightiest empire on earth, Epictetus had no status, no wealth, no political voice. Born into the lowest condition society could impose, he still emerged freer than most emperors.

From Slave to Philosopher

While still in servitude, Epictetus studied under Musonius Rufus, one of Rome's most respected Stoic teachers. Musonius recognised his extraordinary mind, and Epictetus absorbed his mentor's lessons with hunger and humility. Eventually, he was granted his legal freedom.

But to Epictetus, freedom was not a legal category. Freedom was the mastery of oneself.

Once freed, he devoted his life to Philosophy.

Exile and the School of Nicopolis

In 89 CE, Emperor Domitian—fearful of philosophers who encouraged independent thought and resistance to tyranny—banished all philosophers from Rome. Epictetus, now exiled, left for Nicopolis in northwestern Greece, where he founded a school that became one of the most admired in the ancient world.

He lived with radical simplicity: a lamp, a mat, a cloak. His wealth was his mind. His authority came from coherence—he lived exactly as he taught.

Students travelled across the empire to learn from him because he demanded transformation. He was not interested in producing clever intellectuals; he wanted to form excellent human beings.

For Epictetus, happiness had nothing to do with possessions, social status, or reputation. True contentment came from alignment with virtue, clarity about what *is* and *is not* under our control, the ability to face hardship without losing one's inner balance.

The Legacy of a Man Who Wrote Nothing, and Owned Nothing

Like Socrates before him, Epictetus wrote nothing. His teachings survive because his student Arrian—captivated by their power—transcribed them in two works: **The Discourses**, a detailed collection of his lessons, and **The Enchiridion (The Handbook)**, a concise guide to his philosophy. These texts have shaped thinkers for centuries. Marcus Aurelius carried Epictetus's words with him into battle; modern psychologists draw on them as the foundations of cognitive therapy.

Albert Ellis, one of the founders of **Rational Emotive Behavior Therapy**, openly acknowledged Epictetus as one of his greatest influences. It is astonishing to realise that a lesson forged in antiquity—spoken by a former slave—would one day reappear at the centre of modern therapy. The Stoics understood what psychologists would later confirm: our suffering is so often not caused by what happens, but by the meaning we attach to it. This insight lives at the core of **Cognitive Behavioral Therapy (CBT)**, one of the most widely practised therapeutic approaches today.

> *"It is not things themselves that disturb men, but their judgments about these things." –Epictetus, Enchiridion 5, trans. George Long (1877)*

It is astonishing that a man who began life in chains, who owned almost nothing, who wielded no political authority, would end up shaping emperors, psychologists, philosophers, and leaders across millennia. His life stands as living proof of what he taught: that freedom does not come from circumstances—it comes from within.

A Personal Encounter with Epictetus' Wisdom

Last summer, after a wonderful, exhilarating surfing lesson in my beloved Mar Cantábrico, I found myself standing under a cold shower, rinsing the salt and exhaustion from my skin. My teacher, Miguel, and I had just finished our session. As I stood there, lost in thought, I noticed two young women preparing for their lesson. They were both in wheelchairs, their legs lost to some unknown fate. And yet, they radiated a joy so effortless, so unshaken, that it stopped me in my tracks.

They chatted and laughed, their conversation light and filled with anticipation. There was no hesitation in their movements, no shadow of self-pity—only presence. They were not focused on what was missing. They were focused on what remained.

And in that instant, Epictetus's words came alive before my eyes: ***"Lameness is an impediment to the leg, but not to the will."—Epictetus, Enchiridion 9, trans. George Long (1877).***

I had read these words countless times, but never had I seen them like this. These women embodied his philosophy with every breath. While life had taken much from them, it could not take their spirit, their determination, or their will to embrace the sea, to meet the waves with a dignity no hardship could dim.

I felt small. Humbled. Inspired.

How often do we let far lesser hardships define us? How often do we surrender to self-imposed limitations, mistaking our passing struggles for permanent barriers? That day, I understood what Epictetus meant. Life does not limit us. Only our perception of it does.

I turned off the shower, stepped into the sun, and silently thanked Epictetus. For giving me new eyes to see.

Epictetus' Philosophy

Epictetus' philosophy begins with a simple yet profound insight: some things lie within our control, and some things do not. On this distinction rests his entire vision of freedom, peace, and human dignity.

> *"What are our own are opinion, impulse, desire, aversion—in a word, whatever are our own actions. Not our own are body, property, reputation, office, and, in a word, whatever are not our own actions.*

> *If you concern yourself only with what is your own, you will never be hindered, you will never be compelled, you will never blame or accuse anyone, and you will never act against your own will." –Epictetus, Enchiridion 1.1, trans. George Long (1877)*

This passage, the cornerstone of his Philosophy, outlines the dichotomy of control—a teaching so simple yet so liberating. It reminds us that much of our suffering arises from trying to control the uncontrollable. When we cling to external outcomes—our health, reputation, success, or even the behaviour of others—we set ourselves up for frustration. But if we focus on what is truly within our power—our judgments, choices, and inner state—we discover a profound and unshakable freedom.

We can commit to regular exercise, healthy eating, and rest, but we cannot guarantee perfect health. We can prepare diligently for an interview, but we cannot dictate whether we will be chosen. We can love someone deeply, but we cannot control how they love us back. This realization is deeply empowering. It shifts our focus from what we cannot change to what we can—our own thoughts, responses, and way of being in the world.

To me, Epictetus's writings—or rather, his student Arrian's recordings of his words—are a manual for mental clarity, emotional resilience, and spiritual nourishment. Among all the philosophers I know, he stands out as the most practical within the most practical school of thought.

The *Sage of Hierapolis* urged his students to take the task of living with utmost seriousness—to work tirelessly on themselves. What a generous piece of advice!

For Epictetus, the benefits of Philosophy were twofold.

First, by cultivating virtue and focusing only on what is within our control, we free ourselves from unnecessary distress—the tyranny of external circumstances. This discipline strengthens our character, allowing us to rise above impulsive reactions and move through life with wisdom and serenity.

Second, by embodying Stoic principles, we create a ripple effect. We inspire others through our presence—by becoming living examples of integrity, patience, and resilience. A life well-lived brightens the lives of those around.

This is a crucial point because Epictetus saw Philosophy as a social responsibility—a way of existing in harmony with both our rational and social nature. Philosophy refines our thoughts, and in doing so, it refines our actions, our relationships, and our impact on the world.

Progress, I have come to believe, resembles the work of a gardener. Before anything new can grow, the soil must be turned. Old roots must be loosened.

What is tangled, compacted, or overgrown must be disturbed so that new seeds can finally take hold.

As contemporary Stoic writer Chris Fisher noted, genuine inner progress requires this willingness to unsettle our habitual patterns of thought. Without first breaking the hardened ground of our psyche, no new way of seeing can truly flourish.

Please pause for a moment and read that again. **Progress requires effort. It requires a willingness to disrupt, to unlearn, to break free from inherited patterns that no longer serve us.** Just as a gardener must first loosen the soil before new growth can take root, we too must cultivate our minds—questioning assumptions, discarding false beliefs, and nurturing the seeds of wisdom.

This is what Epictetus challenges us to do. To refine our thinking. To challenge our assumptions. To uproot what is unnecessary. To live with greater awareness, clarity, and purpose.

Like Aristotle, Epictetus believed in commitment—the gradual and disciplined refinement of personal character through daily practice. **For him, virtue was the result of consistent inner work, of showing up every day to the task of becoming better human beings.**

Accepting Fate with Grace: Amor Fati and the Cosmic View

For Epictetus, we are not isolated beings adrift in a chaotic universe—we are part of an ordered, rational whole, governed by divine reason (**logos**). Each of us is a fragment of the cosmic body, interconnected with all that exists.

To resist fate, to reject what happens, is to fight against the natural flow of the universe. It is like a leaf resisting the wind, a wave refusing to merge with the ocean. But when we accept that we are part of something greater—when we align ourselves with the wisdom of the cosmos—we find peace.

> *"Seek not that events should happen as you wish; but wish them to happen as they do happen, and your life will go smoothly." –Epictetus, Discourses 1.12, trans. George Long (1862)*

And yet, this acceptance is not passive. It is not about resigning ourselves to misfortune, but about learning how to respond wisely to whatever life presents us.

Epictetus urged his students to cultivate ***Amor Fati***—the love of one's fate. He saw the universe as a vast, intelligent system, where everything unfolds as it must. If we believe that the cosmos operates according to an intelligence greater than our own, then resisting what happens to us is like arguing with the tide.

True freedom, he taught, is not found in attempting to control the uncontrollable. It is found in surrendering to the flow of life with grace.

To wish for something other than what is—to hope for a different past, to resent the laws of nature, to expect people never to change or disappoint—is to wage war against reality. And what could be more exhausting than that?

Instead, Epictetus urged us to align ourselves with the natural order, to accept whatever life brings with trust. Trust that even hardship has its place in the grand design. He reminds us that nothing is inherently good or bad—it is our judgment that colours reality.

The loss of a loved one is painful. But did we expect them to live forever? The betrayal of a friend wounds us. But did we expect humans to be infallible? A delay, an illness, an obstacle—are these misfortunes? Or are they simply life unfolding as it must? Opportunities to learn and grow?

I know this is not easy. Acceptance is never easy. But what is the alternative? To be furious at life? To wage war against the universe? To be consumed by resentment? By seeing ourselves as small yet meaningful parts of the whole, we stop resisting, stop clinging to how things should be. And in doing so, we gain something far greater—peace, freedom, and the strength to walk forward, no matter what comes.

But there is one more step.

When something undesirable happens, we must stop the instantaneous judgment that this event is bad. Instead, we can ask: How might I use this moment to develop my moral character? Because our choices ripple beyond us. Since we are part of the whole, every response we make—every act of virtue or vice—has an effect on the entire cosmos.

If we think of history's most extraordinary figures—those who left a profound impact on humanity—we see a common thread: **they transformed personal suffering into universal wisdom.** Instead of cursing fate, they embraced it, using it as a tool to deepen their character and uplift the world. **Socrates**, condemned to death for questioning the status quo, met his fate with unwavering calm, proving that integrity of the soul matters more than the body's survival. **Jesus**, persecuted and crucified, responded with forgiveness and love, offering the world a stunning vision of grace and redemption. **Joan of Arc** defied armies and empires, enduring trial and execution with unshakable faith in her divine calling. **Viktor Frankl** not only survived the Holocaust but also illuminated a path for millions, proving that our ultimate freedom lies in choosing our response to suffering. **Nelson Mandela**, after

27 years in prison, emerged determined to unify a fractured nation. **Martin Luther King Jr.**, faced with oppression and violence, chose nonviolent resistance, reshaping the course of history. **Malala Yousafzai**, after surviving an attempt on her life for daring to seek an education, turned her suffering into a global movement, becoming a fearless advocate for girls' education and human rights. None of them had easy lives. But they understood what Epictetus taught: **We cannot control what happens to us. But we can always control how we respond. And sometimes, in choosing the noble response, we can inspire others and change the world.**

In fact, it's all about gratitude. Epictetus's prescription for resilience lies in cultivating gratitude.

> *"Do not seek that the things which happen should happen as you wish; but wish the things which happen to be as they are, and you will have a tranquil flow of life." – Epictetus, Discourses 1.6, trans. George Long (1862)*

How do we learn to **love fate** instead of merely accepting it? By choosing to see every challenge as an opportunity for growth:

My husband wakes up in a bad mood. An opportunity to practice patience. Or better yet, an opportunity to understand what he is going through. My boss is giving me unfair, unreachable targets. An opportunity to stay true to my values, to set boundaries, or to learn resilience. My appointment at the hairdresser was at 9 a.m. It is now 10 a.m., and I am still waiting. An opportunity to breathe, to observe, to be present. My back hurts. An opportunity to remember that I am on this wonderful planet for a finite time, that I need to cherish the miracle of being alive. I am far from reaching my financial return target this year. I am offered an investment opportunity that promises high returns—but it does not align with my values. An opportunity to walk away, to stay true to myself, to honour what I stand for.

What would we do without challenges? We would not have the opportunity to test and improve our character. Every difficulty in life presents us with an opportunity to turn inward—to invoke our own inner resources. We can be grateful to them. The trials we endure can reveal our strengths.

> ***"Difficulties are things that show a person what he is." –Epictetus, Discourses 1.24, trans. George Long (1862)***

This is the great paradox of hardship: it reveals us to ourselves. If we choose to see it this way, then every moment—every delay, every disappointment, every loss—becomes a gift. This is not an easy path. But it is the path to freedom.

Because true freedom, as Epictetus reminds us, is not about controlling what happens. It is about mastering how we respond.

The Three Topoi (Fields of Study)

Epictetus saw Philosophy as a way of living, a discipline to be practiced daily to improve our character. And this improvement, he explained, requires mastery over three essential areas: **desire, action, and assent**. These three ***topoi***—or disciplines—are the pillars upon which a eudaemonic life is built, the foundation for all Stoic practice, guiding us toward excellence not just in thought, but in being.

> ***"There are three things (topics, τόποι) in which a man ought to exercise himself who would be wise and good.***
> *The first concerns desires and aversions, that he may not fail to get what he desires, and that he may not fall into what he would avoid.*
> *The second concerns the movements toward action and the avoidance of action, and generally the things which are duty; that he may act according to order and reason, and not carelessly.*
> *The third concerns freedom from deception and rashness in judgment, and generally whatever belongs to the assenting faculty."*
> *–Epictetus, Discourses 3.2.1–2, trans. George Long (1862)*

These disciplines shape how we navigate the world. The **Discipline of Desire** teaches us to align our wants with what truly matters. The **Discipline of Action** ensures that our behaviour reflects wisdom and virtue. The **Discipline of Assent** trains us to see reality clearly, without deception or impulse. Together, they provide a framework for living with clarity, courage, and purpose.

The Discipline of Desire: Mastering What We Seek

We often believe that happiness lies in the fulfilment of external desires—wealth, reputation, admiration, success. But Epictetus warns that placing our happiness in things beyond our control is the surest path to suffering. True fulfilment comes from refining our character. The only desires we should cultivate are those that lead to virtue, wisdom, and inner peace.

If we desire what is beyond our control, we are at the mercy of fortune. But if we desire only what is within us—our integrity, our resilience, our capacity for justice—then we will never be disappointed.

> *"If you desire nothing but what is in your own power, you will never be hindered, you will never be compelled, you will never lament, you will never blame, you will never flatter any person."*
> *–Epictetus, Enchiridion 1.1, trans. George Long (1877)*

This does not mean we must abandon all external pursuits. It means we should pursue them without attachment, without making our well-being dependent on their outcome. We can work toward health, but we cannot control illness. We can seek meaningful relationships, but we cannot dictate how others will treat us. We can strive for success, but we cannot ensure that fortune will favour us.

If we desire wealth, we may become restless. If we desire wisdom, we will always be fulfilled. This is the first lesson: **happiness lies in desiring only what is truly ours—our choices, our virtues, our soul.**

The Discipline of Action: Living According to Nature

The Discipline of Action reminds us that we are part of something greater—a society, a community, a cosmos. Our duty is not to live for ourselves alone, but to contribute to the whole through justice, kindness, and responsibility.

> *"Remember that you are an actor in a play, of such a kind as the author chooses; if short, then in a short one; if long, then in a long one. If it is his pleasure that you should act a poor man, see that you act it well; or a cripple, or a ruler, or a private person. For this is your business, to act well the given part; but to choose it belongs to another." –Epictetus, Enchiridion 17, trans. George Long (1877)*

We do not choose the circumstances of our life, but we do choose how to act within them. The world is shaped by our small, consistent, daily actions. Every time we choose kindness over cruelty, wisdom over impulse, patience over anger, we refine our character and make the world a little kinder.

This is why **prosochē**—the practice of constant attention to the present moment—is essential. To live with wisdom, we must be vigilant over our desires, impulses, and judgments at all times.

> *"As you walk, eat, and sleep, keep before your eyes the thought: 'I am a student of philosophy. What is it appropriate for me to be doing now?'" –Epictetus, Discourses 4.6.34, trans. George Long (1877)*

No moment is too small to practice virtue. Integrity is built in the discipline of daily life.

The Discipline of Assent: Mastering Our Perception

We do not see the world as it is—we see it as we interpret it.

Two people can face the same storm: one curses the rain; the other sees nourishment for the earth.

Two people can face the same failure: one sees defeat; the other sees an opportunity to grow, to learn, to begin again.

This is why the Discipline of Assent is so crucial in Stoic philosophy. Events themselves are indifferent; it is our judgments about them that make them appear good or bad, desirable or dreadful.

Imagine being stuck in traffic. Many of us feel irritation rise instantly—as if the delay were a personal offence. But the Stoic, practising assent, pauses and reflects: This lies beyond my control. Instead of surrendering to frustration, she chooses how to meet the moment—perhaps by breathing more slowly, observing her thoughts, or using the time to reflect.

Or consider a sudden loss—of a job, a relationship, an opportunity. Rather than collapsing into despair, the discipline of assent invites a gentler, wiser question: Is this event truly harmful in itself, or is it my judgment that makes it so?

By learning to examine our impressions before accepting them as truth, we free ourselves from a great deal of unnecessary suffering. We become less reactive, less enslaved by impulse, and more anchored in reason. With time and practice, sound judgment grows quieter and more natural. Virtuous action begins to flow from clarity.

Let me share a story I love—an **ancient Taoist tale** that echoes the Stoic discipline of assent with remarkable grace. To me, it is striking how often wisdom traditions, born worlds apart, arrive at the same luminous insight.

> Long ago, in a small village near the mountains, there lived an old man who owned a single horse.
>
> One morning, the horse ran away.
>
> The neighbours gathered at his gate, shaking their heads.
>
> "How terrible," they said. "What bad luck."
>
> The old man listened, then calmly replied,
>
> "Maybe. We'll see."
>
> A few days later, the horse returned. Behind it came three wild horses, following it home.
>
> The neighbours rushed back, amazed.
>
> "How wonderful," they said. "What great luck!"
>
> The old man smiled softly.

"Maybe. We'll see."

Soon after, the old man's son tried to ride one of the wild horses. The animal threw him, and the boy broke his leg.

Again the neighbours came.

"How awful," they said. "Such misfortune."

The old man answered, as before,

"Maybe. We'll see."

Not long after that, soldiers passed through the village, conscripting young men for war. When they saw the boy's broken leg, they left him behind.

The neighbours returned one last time.

"How fortunate," they said. "Your son was spared."

The old man looked at them kindly and said,

"Maybe. We'll see."

To me, this is absolutely wonderful.

Two ancient wisdom traditions, born more or less at the same time in history, thousands of kilometres apart, sharing the same insight: the refusal to rush into judgment, the courage to remain open when life has not yet revealed its meaning. The humility of knowing that our perspective is partial, that meaning unfolds over time.

This is the wisdom of meeting each moment as it is, without imprisoning it in labels of good or bad, success or failure.

This is precisely what the Stoics meant by assent: ethical patience, clarity of perception, a suspension of judgment until reason—not impulse—is allowed to speak.

To live this way is to trust that life is still in motion.

That the story is still unfolding.

And that wisdom often begins with a simple, courageous pause.

The Harmony of the Disciplines: The Path of the Prokoptōn

These three disciplines—Desire, Action, Assent—are deeply interconnected. The Discipline of Desire teaches us what to value. The Discipline of Action ensures that we live by those values. The Discipline of Assent trains us to see the world as it truly is. Together, these disciplines shape the path of the **prokoptōn**—or, as the Greeks would say of a woman, the **prokoptousa**—the one who is making progress.

But progress requires constant attention. The practice of **prosochē**, this ever-present *watchfulness*—an unwavering vigilance over our thoughts, desires, and actions. It ensures that we remain on the path of wisdom, preventing us from drifting into complacency or illusion. Like a lantern illuminating the road ahead, **prosochē** keeps us aware, awake, and aligned with our highest ideals.

To follow Epictetus is to commit to this lifelong work. To choose wisdom over ignorance, clarity over illusion, virtue over comfort. It is a demanding path, but it is one worth walking. For in the end, what greater purpose could there be than to live fully, freely, and nobly—not at the mercy of fortune, but in harmony with it?

My Path

For me, Epictetus's teachings have unfolded progressively. They begin with **introspection**: the courage to define, with honesty, the kind of person I wish to become. From there comes **humility**: the willingness to set aside arrogance and embrace life as an unending school, where each day offers something new to learn. And finally, there is **practice**: the steady work of translating ideals into action—starting small, remaining faithful, and allowing virtue to become a daily habit.

This, of course, is my path. Each of us must find our own way of walking with Philosophy, but for me, these steps have been the most enduring.

Let us start with introspection. Self-awareness. Defining clearly the person we want to become.

Epictetus urged his students to begin with a simple but courageous act: to decide who they wished to become. Only once that image was clear, he taught, could their actions begin to align with it. A life, like a craft, must be shaped deliberately—guided by ideals, by exemplars, by a conscious choice of character.

There is so much wisdom in this piece of advice. And yet, how often do we stop to make our values explicit, to reflect on who we truly aspire to be? We carefully plan holidays, weekly agendas, and endless to-do lists—but neglect the most important question of all: *Who do we want to be—for ourselves and for others? What are our deepest ideals? What kind of world do we want to help build?*

To me, the first step toward a meaningful life is recognising the necessity of introspection. It is only by looking inward that we can navigate outward with purpose.

Let us continue with the second step. Humility. Relinquishing self-conceit.

"It is impossible for a man to learn what he thinks he already knows." –Epictetus, Discourses 2.17, trans. George Long (1862)

For Epictetus, humility was the true beginning of wisdom. Progress, he taught, starts with the courage to recognise our own limitations. To learn, we must first admit that we do not yet know. To grow, we must accept that we are unfinished.

Humility opens the door to possibility.

Those who approach Philosophy with sincerity do not rush to correct others or display their cleverness. They turn their attention inward. They begin with the most urgent task of all: examining their own thoughts, their own judgments, their own actions.

Epictetus understood that wisdom is a lifelong discipline to be practised. Philosophy demands vigilance, self-reflection, and the bravery to confront our own illusions. It asks for an open mind, a curious soul, and a heart willing to be reshaped.

And from here naturally arises the third step: commitment. Discipline. Practice.

Or, as Epictetus would surely insist—**practice, practice, practice.**

His Precious Advice

Epictetus' advice remains as relevant today as it was in ancient Rome. From cultivating character to navigating relationships, from choosing whom we associate with to how we conduct ourselves in the world, his teachings offer guidance for every dimension of life. While I cannot possibly share all of his wisdom, I would like to offer the lessons that have shaped me most deeply—in the hope that they may shed some light on your path as well.

I hope they inspire you, dear reader, to live them.

Epictetus' counsel is as practical as it is profound: begin small, but commit wholeheartedly to becoming better human beings. We cannot expect to remain calm in extreme situations—like when someone is twisting our leg, as Epictetus' master once did to him. But we can begin with smaller trials. Staying composed when our child teases us. Remaining patient in heavy traffic. Accepting a delayed train without frustration.

These are the moments where progress reveals itself. With patience and consistency, we train ourselves little by little, strengthening our character through daily practice.

Epictetus understood that virtue is forged in ordinary moments—in how we handle small inconveniences, how we respond to minor irritations, how we hold our ground when gently tested. Each modest victory affirms that we are moving in the right direction. Through discipline, introspection, and sustained attention to our thoughts and actions, we slowly cultivate the right habits—the silent architects of character.

And in time, these habits open the door to deeper realisations. That happiness is found within. That self-mastery begins with self-honesty. That a life of inner serenity is not only possible, but worth pursuing.

But the journey is not always easy. Epictetus warned us to expect criticism—and even ridicule—along the path of self-improvement. If we truly wish to grow, we must accept the risk of being misunderstood, even though foolish. Not everyone will recognise the value of this work, and that is fine. What matters is that we remain faithful to the path and keep walking it.

> *"If you wish to improve, be content to be thought foolish and stupid with regard to external things." –Epictetus, Enchiridion 13, trans. George Long (1862)*

Epictetus also cautioned against grounding our self-worth in the admiration of others. The opinions of the world are unstable, shifting, and beyond our control. Even those who love us may not always understand our choices or share our enthusiasms. To depend on external approval is to surrender our inner freedom. True steadiness comes from living in alignment with our values, not from being applauded for them.

Do Not Take Anything Personally

Epictetus repeatedly reminds us not to take things personally—to resist the impulse to turn every word, gesture, or event into a judgment about who we are. When we observe those who are not easily angered, we often discover a shared quality: an inner maturity, a quiet balance, a deep harmony with themselves. Reaching such a state requires temperance, understanding, and a steady confidence rooted within.

For Epictetus, this inner steadiness is not a gift of fortune or temperament. It is a skill. A discipline. Something we can cultivate through practice, reflection, and careful attention to our judgments.

This insight resonates beautifully with *The Four Agreements* by Don Miguel Ruiz, particularly the Second Agreement: Do not Take Anything Personally. Ruiz explains that when we internalise others' words or actions, we make ourselves vulnerable, allowing their fears, frustrations, and projections to disturb our peace. When we stop taking things personally, we reclaim our freedom. Other people's opinions lose their power, and our well-being is no longer at their mercy.

Both Epictetus and Ruiz illuminate a path toward psychological freedom: cultivating resilience and emotional detachment to protect our inner peace. This is not about becoming indifferent or ignoring others; it's about strengthening ourselves so that others' negativity cannot shake us. Over time, this practice fosters a calm, centred mind that remains unaffected by external judgments or provocations. In a world rife with emotional turmoil, this inner strength is a true superpower.

The Importance of Role Models and Social Circles

Epictetus advises us to be attentive to whom we associate with. He reminds us that the people we spend time with gradually shape who we become. Often without realising it, we begin to adopt their interests, their opinions, their values, and even their ways of interpreting events.

> *"If you live with lame men, you will learn to limp." –Epictetus, Discourses 3.16, trans. George Long (1862)*

For Epictetus, keeping company with those who elevate us is an act of care—for ourselves and for the values we wish to embody.

This is one of my favourite pieces of advice. At first glance, it might seem snobbish. But how could a former slave be snobbish or elitist? Epictetus was not urging us to judge others with arrogance, nor was he advocating exclusivity based on wealth, status, or intellect. His insight sprang from a deep understanding of human nature.

We are social beings. Whether we realise it or not, the people we surround ourselves with shape our character, influence our habits, and mould our thoughts. We absorb their interests, their way of seeing the world, their priorities. And so Epictetus urged us to be mindful of those we allow into our inner circle.

Ever since I embraced Philosophy as a way of life, I have taken this advice seriously. How many times have I found myself at a dinner table, caught up in trivial conversations about expensive restaurants? Or worse, in gossip? I would leave feeling empty, as if I had betrayed myself.

But then there are those luminous moments spent with friends who fill me with butterflies—people whose words and actions inspire me to be kinder, more generous, more authentic, more creative, and more courageous. In their presence, my best self emerges. And in those moments, I remember why Epictetus's advice is so powerful.

If we want to become wiser, more resilient, and more virtuous, we must be intentional about the company we keep. **Surrounding ourselves with people who embody the values we aspire to will inevitably shape our own transformation.** This is why Epictetus urged his students to seek out relationships with those who live with integrity, wisdom, and self-discipline—because **the pursuit of virtue is a shared journey.**

This naturally leads us to the importance of role models—those who show us, through their example, the kind of life that is possible.

Epictetus believed that one of the most powerful ways to shape our character is to look toward exemplary lives. By observing those we admire, recalling their strength, clarity, and integrity, and striving to embody these qualities ourselves, our ideals begin to take form. There is nothing artificial in this process. Each of us carries the seeds of virtue within us; we often need only an image—a living example—to help them grow.

Epictetus frequently pointed to Socrates as the embodiment of philosophical virtue—calm under pressure, unshaken by fear, unwavering in his commitment to truth. He believed that by studying such figures, by allowing their example to work upon us, we could gradually internalise their wisdom and make it our own.

I have so many role models in my life. I do not need to see them; just thinking of them makes me smile. Their presence—real, read or imagined—fills my heart with gratitude, with eagerness to grow, to become a better person, to align myself with the rhythm of the universe.

I am deeply grateful to Epictetus, who opened a window of possibility in my life, and to Socrates, whose courage and unbreakable integrity still light the way. I am grateful to my mother, Belén, for her wisdom and humility, and to my father, the most generous person I know. I am grateful to my brothers, for choosing their own paths fearlessly, regardless of societal expectations.

I give thanks to Daniel Lumera, for dedicating his life to the service of others, and to Begotxu, for her strength and courage. I think, too, of Jed Emerson and Jacqueline Novogratz, whose work reminds us what impact investing is truly about, and of Valentina Cislacchi, who leads Alice for Children with love, empathy, and care.

Each of them, in their own way, awakens in me a deeper longing for purpose. Each of them calls me forward—toward greater wisdom, greater generosity, greater authenticity.

I could speak about Epictetus endlessly, as you can probably tell.

His teachings are not easy—but they are profound. They challenge us to rise above our circumstances, to master our thoughts and emotions, and to live with courage, wisdom, temperance, and justice. They guide us toward a life of virtue.

His wisdom remains as relevant today as it was two millennia ago, offering us a timeless guide to a life of meaning, peace, and freedom.

This is why I love Epictetus so much. Because he has given me new eyes. The cosmic eyes, the eyes of gratitude, the eyes of the Eagle. Yes, new eyes—not just to see differently, but to perceive differently. For not all eyes see the same.

When we look at life through the eyes of competition, envy, and fear, we do not inhabit the same world as when we look through the eyes of love, possibility, and growth. Perception is not passive—it is creative. It shapes the world we experience. This is why Epictetus insisted so strongly on the importance of mastering our impressions.

Two people can gaze at the same sky: one sees storms gathering; the other sees rain that will nourish the earth. Two people can stand at the same threshold: one recoils from the unknown; the other steps forward, curious and open to the journey.

We do not see life as it is; we see life as we are. And so, by gifting me with new eyes, Epictetus has gifted me a new life. I will never thank my mother enough for placing his words in my hands. Now I try to return that gift to anyone willing to read these lines.

For inner peace is not something we chase. It is something we become.

23

From *Ego* to *Eco*: Oikeiôsis, Agape, and the Wisdom of Belonging

Within Ancient Philosophy, there is a Stoic idea so powerful that it has become my absolute favourite. It holds the potential to expand our circles of concern and guide us in the great transition—from *EGO* to *ECO*, from the *road of having* to the *road of being*, from Hakim to Eliahu. It is the concept of **Oikeiôsis.**

In a world increasingly fractured—by borders, beliefs, skin colour, socio-economic status—**Oikeiôsis** offers a powerful antidote. It reminds us that we are not separate. That our well-being is interwoven with the well-being of others. That to care for another is, ultimately, to care for ourselves. For me, **Oikeiôsis** flows naturally into **Agapē**—the selfless, expansive love that embraces all beings and the Earth itself, without judgment and without condition.

But before we can fully explore these wonderful ideas, we must return to the foundation from which they rise: **consciousness**.

Consciousness is so vast it resists definition. It is the breath of awareness that animates our existence. The force that allows us not only to observe the world, but to feel it—to connect, to awaken, to grow.

To me, consciousness arises through introspection, meditation, and contemplation. It is the light that transforms knowledge (with a small k) into Wisdom (with a capital W). It is the subtle awareness of Self, of Others, of the Whole—and of our sacred place within it. It is the foundation upon which ethics are built, where compassion takes root, and from which moral action is born.

But rather than defining such an abstract concept in words, let me illustrate it through a story. Inspired by **Mario Alonso Puig**—one of the most brilliant

P. Ansoleaga Abascal, *Philosophy and Finance: A Love Story*,
https://doi.org/10.1007/978-3-032-22218-3_23

storytellers I have encountered—I have created two characters to bring this idea to life: **Alma** and **Ega**.

Nikole Bozza Ansoleaga

Imagine, Mario said in one of his podcasts, that we are all waves in the ocean.

A wave with a high level of **consciousness** understands that she is not separate from the sea—she is the sea. When she encounters another wave—whether taller or shorter, darker or lighter—she instinctively recognises their shared nature. She cares for this other wave, wishes her well, and would never think of harming her. After all, they are one and the same ocean.

Let me call this wave **Alma**. Alma sees beyond the illusion of separateness.

But what happens if a wave forgets that she is part of the ocean? What if she focuses only on her shape—her skin colour, religion, nationality—and that of the waves closest to her (her family and friends), disregarding all others?

Let me call this wave **Ega**.

Ega is ruled by her ego. She sees no connection to others. She does not care when another wave crashes against the rocks or disappears altogether—unless that wave belongs to her inner circle. Ega embodies the myth of separation, which, to me, is at the root of most of our problems.

Lost in her illusion of independence, Ega believes she is protecting herself by drawing boundaries. But those very boundaries become her prison. She sees competition where there could be collaboration. She sees envy where there could be admiration. She sees fear where there could be trust.

Alma, on the other hand, sees the ocean in every wave. She understands that to harm another is to harm herself. She would never wish misfortune upon another wave, no matter how different or distant it appears.

I believe this little story, better than any definition, illustrates the beauty, depth, and importance of consciousness—the faculty that enables Oikeiôsis to unfold.

Oikeiôsis: Expanding Our Circles of Care

The Stoics, inspired by the Cynics, championed the idea of **cosmopolitanism**—the belief that our moral compass should be guided by what is good for humanity. Epictetus captured this universal perspective in his *Discourses*:

> *"If a man has once accepted the doctrine that he is a citizen of the universe, and that he is not merely a citizen of this or that city, how can he fail to be ready for whatever happens?"*
>
> *–Epictetus, Discourses 1.9, trans. George Long (1862)*

This worldview was not just an abstract notion; it was a way of living rooted in **philanthrōpia**—the **love of humanity**. The Stoics saw themselves as citizens of the cosmopolis, a universal city that included all human beings. In this interconnected world—in Alma's ocean—the well-being of each person was inseparable from the well-being of the whole.

At the heart of this philosophy lies one of my favourite Stoic ideas: **Oikeiôsis.**

Derived from the Greek word **oikeios** (meaning "belonging," "affinity," or "appropriation"), Oikeiôsis describes the natural process by which individuals come to recognise their intrinsic connection to others and to the wider cosmos. The Stoic philosopher **Hierocles** used the metaphor of widening circles to illustrate this process.

At the centre lies the self. Surrounding it are successive circles representing family, friends, community, fellow citizens, all of humanity, and finally the entire natural world. We begin with self-awareness and self-care. From there, we extend our concern to those closest to us—our family and loved ones. Gradually, as our moral awareness expands, our circle of care widens to embrace our community, our nation, and ultimately all human beings and the Earth itself.

Epictetus reminds us that becoming our best selves is inseparable from caring for others. Our ethical responsibility does not stop with those closest to us, nor with the powerful, the wealthy, or the educated. It extends to all human beings, simply because they are human. To live well, for the Stoics, was to recognise ourselves as participants in a shared moral community—a human family bound by dignity.

> *"He is a citizen of the universe who recognises that he is bound by nature to all men." –Epictetus, Discourses (idea drawn from 1.9; trans. George Long, 1862)*

If financial markets were designed around oikeiôsis, the very purpose of capital would shift—from accumulation to regeneration, from extraction to shared flourishing.

Agape: The Culmination of Oikeiôsis

To me, **Oikeiôsis** naturally flows into **Agapē**—the selfless, unconditional love that embraces all beings simply because they are part of the Whole. If Oikeiôsis invites us to expand our circles of concern through rational understanding, Agapē elevates this expansion into the realm of pure, altruistic love. It widens our hearts as much as our minds.

When we live both Oikeiôsis and Agapē, we move from *EGO* to *ECO*. We honour the bonds that unite us. We act with kindness, compassion, and moral imagination—not only toward those closest to us, but toward strangers, communities, future generations, and the Earth itself. We begin to live as citizens of the Cosmopolis.

In an age increasingly marked by fragmentation, hyper-individualism, and fear of the other, these ancient concepts offer a luminous, transformative path forward. They remind us that virtue is its own reward, and that our greatest strength lies in connection.

And this is the choice before us: To live as isolated waves—or as part of the ocean. To build financial systems that serve only a few—or to shape economies that uplift all.

24

Choosing a Philosophy of Life

In the end, what our beloved Greco-Roman ancestors teach us is that true happiness lies in transcending an *EGO*-centred life in favour of an *ECO*-centred one—an existence that recognises our profound interconnectedness with others, with nature, and with life itself. This intuition echoes across the ancient world: in Buddhism's insight into interdependence and compassion, in Taoism's invitation to live in harmony with the Tao, in Confucianism's relational ethics grounded in self-cultivation and social harmony, and in Indigenous cosmologies that understand the human being as inseparable from land, ancestors, and future generations.

As Aristotle understood, and as his legacy reminds us, life is about being good and helping others. Rather than prescribing a single "correct" Philosophy, the ancient schools offered different paths toward the same horizon: a life of wisdom, inner peace, and harmony with the cosmos. Their aim was not merely to refine the individual, but to elevate humanity as a whole—the Cosmopolis.

They also remind us of something deeply counterintuitive in today's world: that **self-realisation is only possible through self-transcendence**. That we discover our fullest expression by loosening the grip of the *ego*, by expanding our perspective until the illusion of separateness gives way to relationship—with others, with nature, with the whole.

Much like Eastern traditions, the Greco-Roman practice of care of the Self—cultivated through spiritual exercises—was never intended as a solitary pursuit. It was a means to something greater, a bridge between the individual

P. Ansoleaga Abascal, *Philosophy and Finance: A Love Story*,
https://doi.org/10.1007/978-3-032-22218-3_24

and the universal, moving us beyond the narrow confines of self-interest into a life woven into the fabric of a larger, harmonious whole.

I have already shared how ancient wisdom has reshaped my life—how it has shifted my perception of reality. There are infinite ways to see the world, and **Philosophy has gifted me with new eyes—the eyes of possibility, connection, and hope.**

I see more deeply now. I sleep more peacefully. I laugh more freely. I judge less—far less. I choose my friends carefully, and I spend more time alone, in silence, and whenever possible, immersed in nature. I strive, always, to be fully present. Not that I always succeed, but I always try.

I consume less—far less than before—and I read more, much more. I connect with others on a deeper, more meaningful level. I find myself filled with gratitude. And ultimately, I am happier.

I have fallen in love with all that cannot be bought or measured—sunsets, smiles, authenticity, music, children, animals, trees, and the fleeting, beautiful encounters that make life rich. Anxiety, once a heavy presence in my chest, has disappeared. That is not to say I never feel sadness or anger—of course, I do. Especially when I witness injustice, violence, or our self-inflicted harm as human beings.

But even anger feels different now. When it arises, I no longer let it take hold of me. I recognise it, observe it, accept it—truly accept it—and let it go. I remember Epictetus' warning that whoever provokes our anger gains power over us:

> *"Remember that it is not he who reviles you or strikes you who insults you, but your opinion that these things are insulting. When, therefore, any man irritates you, be assured that it is your own opinion which has irritated you." –Epictetus, Enchiridion 20, trans. George Long (1862)*

The most beautiful part of this journey, however, is knowing that I am still only at the beginning of this wonderful philosophical path. Perhaps that is why I do not call myself a Stoic. I am, above all, a lover and seeker of wisdom. I am a ***Prokoptousa***—one who is making progress.

Or perhaps it is because labels—Stoic, Cynic, Buddhist—can sometimes create separation, while what I feel instead is belonging. I feel like Alma, in Alma's ocean, living within our shared Cosmopolis.

Being a beginner, a ***Prokoptousa***, fills me with joy and excitement. There is still so much to discover—more wisdom, more resilience, more gratitude, more peace. And there are still so many kindred spirits to meet along the way.

The best is yet to come.

Sometimes friends ask me how they might step off the never-ending *hedonic treadmill*—how to free themselves from anxiety without resorting to pills, how to begin their own inner journey, how to feed their *Eagles*.

Their question always humbles me because, truthfully, I do not have the answer. I am not a spiritual leader, a philosopher or a psychologist—just a lifelong student. A lover and seeker of wisdom who stumbles, fails, and tries again, over and over.

I have always been drawn to those who are wiser, older, brighter, and more insightful than I am—people whose very presence inspires me to be kinder, more generous, more humble. So my reflections are never prescriptive. They are simply what has worked for me so far. And to me, the only true prerequisites for becoming a lover and seeker of wisdom are: **Wonder, Integrity, and Determination.**

Wonder, Integrity, and Determination

Wonder: The Spark That Awakens the Soul

> *Philosophy clears the fog of convention and lets us see with new eyes. And what we see then, if we are honest, is astonishing. –Paule Ansoleaga Abascal*

Jostein Gaarder once observed in ***Sophie's World*** that only philosophers and small children look at the world with astonishment. What a tragedy that most of us lose this ability as we grow older.

Without wonder, life becomes mechanical, disenchanted. Days blur into routine, stripped of their magic. We move through the world blind to its strangeness, convinced we've already seen what it has to offer. We call this maturity. But in truth, it is a form of walking asleep, on autopilot. We are physically awake, but inwardly dulled.

Wonder is the antidote. It unsettles us, cracks open our certainty, shakes us out of passive acceptance, and forces us to look again. It makes us question the truths we inherited and the assumptions we barely notice. Wonder invites us to reach beyond easy answers and to embrace the unfamiliar.

To me, wonder is an invitation—to wake up, to remain curious, to seek wisdom. With wonder as our guide, reading and reflection become living practices—ways to dream, refine our moral character, awaken our soul, and reimagine our place in the vast, unfolding mystery of existence.

Integrity: The Courage to Stay True to Ourselves

If wonder is the beginning of a philosophical life, integrity is its test. Life will inevitably place us in situations where compromise seems like the easiest path—where following the crowd, bending our values, or choosing convenience over truth feels like the safer choice.

But **Philosophy without integrity is meaningless.**

Integrity means staying true to ourselves, even when life tempts us to derail or pressures us to conform. It means choosing what is right over what is easy, what is true over what is popular.

Socrates believed that the highest good lay in inner harmony—remaining faithful to oneself even in the face of opposition. He chose integrity over reputation, and truth over life itself

Integrity ensures that our actions align with our values—that we do not merely admire wisdom but embody it. Socrates, Jesus, and Epictetus are among history's most inspiring figures because of their unwavering integrity. Their steadfast commitment to principle left an indelible mark on philosophical, religious, and ethical thought, inspiring and shaping entire communities across millennia.

Determination: Walking the Path with Purpose

If wonder awakens us and integrity grounds us, determination carries us forward. It is the inner strength that keeps us walking the path, step by step.

Determination does not mean striving for perfection. It is not rigid discipline, nor an exhausting checklist of self-improvement. Rather, it is the art of approaching life with a spirit of exploration—a journey of small, loving, daily practices that, over time, shape us into wiser, calmer, more resilient human beings.

We begin simply. Perhaps by embracing the Epicurean habit of savouring life's small joys—a quiet morning with a cup of coffee, the golden light of a sunset, the laughter of a child. Instead of chasing excess, we learn to be present. ***Prosochē***—the practice of constant attention—becomes our guide, helping us notice not only the world around us but also the subtle transformations within.

When we listen deeply, when we observe ourselves without judgment, when we remain true to what gives meaning, we begin to live more intentionally, more freely, more fully. And so, we continue—step by step, moment by moment—until wisdom is no longer something we seek, but something we embody.

Because ultimately, Philosophy is not just about understanding life. It is about living it well.

An Eclectic "T" Approach to Philosophy

One way to approach Philosophy is through the famous "T" approach to learning. The horizontal line of the T represents breadth—exploring a wide range of traditions, thinkers, and ideas across different eras and cultures: classical and modern, Western and Eastern. This broad foundation allows us to see connections between philosophies, drawing wisdom from multiple sources.

The vertical line of the T represents depth—choosing one philosopher, school of thought, or tradition to explore with focus and commitment.

Seneca was a great defender of this vertical path. In his ***Letters to Lucilius*** he warns against reading superficially, jumping from one book to another, comparing it to wandering endlessly without ever arriving anywhere. To him, to be everywhere meant to be nowhere:

> *"Everywhere means nowhere." –Seneca, Letters to Lucilius 2.2, trans. Richard M. Gummere (1917)*

For Seneca, wisdom required focus, digestion, depth.

> *"You must linger among a limited number of master thinkers, and digest their works, if you would derive ideas which shall win firm hold in your mind." –Seneca, Letters to Lucilius 2.2, trans. Richard M. Gummere (1917)*

And I agree—though my philosophical path has not been confined to Greco-Roman wisdom alone, even if it remains my vertical line. I also feel drawn to explore more widely, to ask how other traditions might illuminate our human, social, economic, and financial lives.

What, for example, would finance look like if guided by Kantian ethics? If every investment decision, every act of tax avoidance, every choice of consumption had to pass the universality test—could we will our behaviour as a law for all? And if not, what, then, is our duty as investors, as CEOs, as policymakers?

These are the kinds of questions that breadth awakens in me. Greco-Roman wisdom remains my current vertical line, and Epictetus its pillar. Epictetus grounds me, but Kant challenges me. ***Is virtue ethics the only way forward?***

And yet, just as we evolve, so too does our vertical line, shifting as we grow, as new questions arise, as different teachings resonate in different moments of our lives.

I began "digging vertically" with Epictetus and the Stoics—perhaps because, at that stage in my life, I needed their clarity, resilience, and discipline. Epictetus grounds the Neoplatonic dreamer in me, bringing abstract ideals down to earth, into action, into practice. He teaches a Philosophy of progress, not perfection.

But the more I practice meditation and yoga, the more I feel drawn toward **Eastern philosophies**, particularly **Indo-Vedic wisdom**—a curiosity sparked by the profound impact meditation is having on me. As I immerse myself in this practice, I find myself eager to explore these traditions more deeply—to see how they might further transform my perspective.

The beauty of Philosophy is that it grows with us—it is not a static doctrine. It is a living journey.

My Spiritual Exercises

As we grow, so too does our philosophical practice. My daily rituals—what Pierre Hadot calls spiritual exercises—reflect this ever-evolving journey.

My mornings do not begin with rational Stoic meditation; they begin with breath, presence, and stillness. Each day I practise breathing meditation—bioenergetic respiration followed by simply sitting still—a ritual I cherish with all my heart. This meditation is a gift I give myself: an oasis of serenity before stepping into the world of action and responsibility.

It restores me to my natural state so that, when life pulls me off course, I know where to return. I know where home is—the peaceful place within that never leaves me.

During meditation, when thoughts arise, I let them pass without following or resisting them. If they return a thousand times, I gently return to the breath a thousand times. Over time, I have learned to recognise that these passing thoughts—these clouds—are not who I am. I am the sky that holds them: vast, steady, open, and blue.

Throughout the day, I cultivate ***prosoche***—the Stoic practice of mindful attention. I observe my emotions, my thoughts, the famous clouds, the clarity or fogginess of my mind. I ask myself: *Am I reliving the past unnecessarily? Am I worrying about the future instead of being present? Am I seeking approval rather than staying true to myself? Am I reacting on impulse instead of recognising another person's suffering or need for attention? Am I allowing fear, anger, resentment, or envy to take root? Or worse—am I escaping into distraction, scrolling mindlessly on my phone, instead of confronting reality?*

Self-examination is essential. Developing emotional intelligence requires emotional resilience. I must notice my emotions, welcome them, and let them pass—neither suppressing them nor allowing them to rule me. I trust that I can always return to my natural state of calm, connection, and joy.

To the sky.

As Marcus Aurelius wrote:

> *"Men seek retreats for themselves in the country, by the sea-side, and in the mountains; and thou too art wont to desire such things very much. But this is altogether a mark of the most common sort of men, for it is in thy power whenever thou shalt choose to retire into thyself. For nowhere either with more quiet or more freedom from troubles does a man retire than into his own soul." –Marcus Aurelius, Meditations 4.3, trans. George Long (1862)*

This is what I mean by retreating into myself—returning to that inner state of peace I did not even know existed when I was younger, caught up in constant movement, always running. A state revealed to me by Philosophy, meditation, and contemplation. And now that I know it, it feels like home. Wherever I am, I can always close my eyes, breathe, and return to myself.

This is the gift of my **morning meditation**: a moment when my body is still, my mind calm, and my heart overflowing with gratitude. A moment when the world feels whole, and I sense myself as a small yet essential part of a vast, intricate, and magnificent web of life.

My evenings close with **Seneca's practice of self-examination**—not as a tool for self-reproach, but as a way to track progress. You may recall his advice from the previous chapter: to end each day by reflecting on our thoughts and actions, recognising where we aligned with our values and where we fell short.

I also practise ***Premeditatio Malorum***—mentally preparing myself for life's uncertainties, training my mind to meet adversity with grace. And when I need perspective, I turn to the ***View from Above***—the **Stoic cosmic exercise**—stepping back to see events from a greater scale, reminding myself what truly matters. I embrace apparent "setbacks" with gratitude, knowing they are fertile ground for growth. I keep my phone notes always at hand, **journaling** like Marcus Aurelius—capturing fleeting insights, questions, impressions, and both my right and wrong turns.

I practise **Vinyasa yoga** as a way to harmonise body and mind. Through movement (**āsana**), breath (**prāṇāyāma**), and moments of meditation, I try to soften the grip of the *ego* and open to something larger than myself. Yoga teaches me to move with intention, to breathe with awareness, and to inhabit my body with balance and care.

And in the final posture, **Śavāsana**, I surrender completely. In stillness, I feel **oikeiôsis**—an embodied recognition that I am not separate, but part of something vast, living, and whole. I close my eyes, and for a moment, I wish time could pause for hours.

Walking Our Own Path

When I was young, my father always encouraged me to think for myself. I remember being eleven or twelve when I asked him if I could spend the summer in England to learn English.

"To learn English?" he repeated, tilting his head. I nodded eagerly.

"Yes, Daddy. You need to speak English to have a bright future, don't you?"

He smiled, but instead of agreeing, he challenged me—as he always did.

"A bright future? So you believe learning English is the key to a bright future? That's why you want to go to England?" He paused. *"You're thinking like the crowd out there."*

I was not surprised. He never gave common responses.

"What about going for a new experience? To gain humility? To open your mind, expand your horizon, and see the world from a new perspective?"

At the time, I was not sure I fully understood, much like I had not understood the three-legged stool he often spoke of—balanced on physical, mental, and spiritual legs. But now, I do. And I am profoundly grateful for the freedom of thought he instilled in me.

A Living Philosophy

To me, there is no single "right" Philosophy, no universal spiritual practice, no fixed blueprint for a good life. The journey is ours to shape. For me, that journey has led to a fusion of Epictetus, Greco-Roman wisdom, and Indo-Vedic inspired meditation. For someone else, the vertical line might be rooted in Buddhism, existentialism, or the Bhagavad Gita.

What matters is that we live our Philosophy. That we find our own way of cultivating wisdom, presence, gratitude, and connection. That we seek not just knowledge, but a way of being that aligns with our deepest values. That we understand that goodness, selflessness, and altruism are the highest forms of wisdom. That virtue is its own reward. That self-realisation requires self-transcendence.

Let us remember Thoreau's words: ***"As if you could kill time without injuring eternity."*** Because in the end, that is what it's all about—building a life that feels truly ours, yet one that serves something greater than ourselves.

To live by choice. To shape each day with awareness. To walk our path with courage, humility, and love. This is Philosophy as a way of life: a call to presence, virtue, and freedom. And above all, a call to remember that in shaping our lives with wisdom, we are also shaping the world around us.

Part 3

Looking Back on Economics and Finance

I Dream of a World Where Science Explains, Entrepreneurship Creates, Governments Facilitate, Art Inspires, Philosophy Guides, and Finance Powers

To move forward wisely, we must first look back with clarity. Part III traces the forgotten moral and philosophical roots of economics and finance—from their origins in ancient virtue ethics to the rise of consumerism, financial abstraction, and systemic crises. By revisiting the evolution of economic thought and the ethical questions that once guided it, we will uncover how we arrived at our current paradigm—and how we might rediscover a more conscious, human-centred path.

Block 3 is a journey through ideas and illusions, through systems built and souls forgotten, and through the lives of those who dared to redefine what it means to be truly wealthy.

25

From Ethics to Equations: The Philosophical Roots of Economics

As Ortega y Gasset would say, life only returns a small degree of transparency in the presence of historical reason. Economics, too, reveals itself in the traces of time, where morality and human ambition once walked hand in hand. For over two millennia, economic thought was not just about wealth; it was about virtue, justice, and the purpose of human existence.

But something changed. By the late eighteenth century, a divorce took shape—one between science and Philosophy. Numbers replaced narratives, equations replaced ethics, and economics became preoccupied with efficiency, rationality, and growth. To understand where we stand today—and where we might go—we can retrace the journey of economic thought, back to an era when wisdom was the guiding light.

Let us start, then.

Once upon a time, in the streets of Athens, the highest currency was wisdom. ***Philosophia***, the love of wisdom, was a way of life, a lifelong pursuit to understand existence, morality, and the principles governing the universe.

The early Greek thinkers, the Pre-Socratics, were obsessed with the cosmos—seeking to understand the stars, the elements, the essence of being. Economics, in the way we think of it today, was not their concern. **Socrates (470–399 BCE)** shifted the focus inward, toward the human condition. For him, wealth was neither good nor evil; it was the wisdom to use it well that mattered. He sought a life of **eudaimonia**—human flourishing—believing that virtue, not gold, was the path to true happiness.

Plato (427–347 BCE), his devoted student, carried this vision forward. In *The Republic*, he painted a compelling portrait of an ideal society in which

P. Ansoleaga Abascal, *Philosophy and Finance: A Love Story*,
https://doi.org/10.1007/978-3-032-22218-3_25

justice reigned supreme and wealth served the common good rather than private excess. He warned that both extremes—great riches and great poverty—corrupt the soul and destabilise society.

> *"Wealth and poverty are the causes of both luxury and idleness, and of meanness and wickedness." –Republic, Book IV, trans. Benjamin Jowett (1871)*

Xenophon (430–354 BCE), a soldier, historian, and thinker, gave us ***Oeconomicus***, one of the first known works on economic principles. His wisdom was simple yet profound: the art of managing one's household—economy in its earliest sense—was about balance, stewardship, and care for the community.

Then came **Aristotle (384–322 BCE)**, who regarded Philosophy as the foundation of all rational knowledge. He divided it into logic, the theoretical sciences, and the practical disciplines—among them ethics, politics, and economics. Aristotle understood what later ages would forget: that wealth is not an end in itself, but a means to a higher end. **Wealth should serve life, not the other way around.**

> *"Wealth is evidently not the good we are seeking; for it is merely useful and for the sake of something else." –Nicomachean Ethics, Book I, 1096a5–6, trans. W. D. Ross (1908)*

Aristotle drew an important distinction between ***oikonomia***—the natural acquisition of goods necessary for life—and ***chrematistics***—the unnatural pursuit of limitless wealth. The latter, he warned, was a dangerous illusion. He despised ***pleonexia***, the insatiable desire for more, and condemned usury, arguing that money, by its very nature, should not beget money. For Aristotle, the economy was to be rooted in life and community, not in boundless profit.

A few generations later, in the marbled halls of Rome and the windswept cliffs of exile, **the Stoics** carried forward a more moderate understanding of wealth. Unlike **the Cynics**—Diogenes of Sinope (412–323 BCE) among them, who lived in a barrel and rejected all material possessions—the Stoics did not advocate renunciation. Instead, they classified wealth as a "preferred indifferent": neither good nor bad in itself, but a resource that could be used either virtuously or destructively, depending on the character of the one who possessed it.

Seneca (4 BCE–65 CE), a philosopher, statesman, and one of the richest men of his time, lived among emperors but warned against the excesses of wealth. He understood that money was not a true measure of success.

"It is not the man who has too little, but the man who craves more, that is poor."
–Seneca, Letters to Lucilius (Epistulae Morales), Letter 2.6, trans. Richard M. Gummere (1917)

For the Stoics, true wealth lay in mastery over desire, in self-control amid abundance, and in the wisdom to use power for the good of others.

Marcus Aurelius (121–180 CE), the philosopher-emperor, embodied this ideal. He ruled the greatest empire of his time yet lived simply, reminding himself daily that power and gold were fleeting. He saw wealth as irrelevant to virtue and warned against allowing it to corrupt the soul:

"Receive wealth or prosperity without arrogance; and be ready to let it go."
–Marcus Aurelius, Meditations, Book VIII, 33, trans. George Long (1862)

As Rome fell, so too did its secular philosophies. A new force took hold: **theology**. The pursuit of economic wisdom became entwined with faith, and for over a millennium, ethical considerations remained at the heart of economic thought.

Saint Augustine of Hippo (354–430 CE) preached that wealth should serve charity, not personal indulgence; in his view, greed was a spiritual disease that corroded both soul and society. Centuries later, **Thomas Aquinas (1225–1274)** merged Aristotle's logic with Christian doctrine, advocating for just prices and fair wages, and insisting that economic exchange must be governed by justice rather than sheer profit. The Islamic world, too, contributed to this discourse—most notably **Ibn Khaldun (1332–1406)**, who saw commerce as a moral endeavour that required regulation to prevent exploitation, anticipating modern ideas of economic cycles and the social foundations of prosperity.

Their voices remind us that economics was once inseparable from ethics. But the tide began to turn.

The Scientific Revolution shattered old ways of knowing and opened new horizons. It is often said to have begun in 1543 with the publication of **Nicolaus Copernicus'** ***De revolutionibus orbium coelestium*** (On the Revolutions of the Celestial Spheres) and to have culminated in **Isaac Newton's** ***Philosophiæ Naturalis Principia Mathematica*** (Mathematical Principles of Natural Philosophy, 1687). By the late seventeenth and early eighteenth centuries, experimental inquiry and mathematical method had gained authority, shaping the intellectual landscape of the Enlightenment.

The transition to modern science was underway.

Galileo Galilei (1564–1642) redefined our vision of the cosmos; Isaac Newton (1643–1727) formulated the laws of motion; and René Descartes (1596–1650) famously declared *cogito, ergo sum*—"I think, therefore I am." Even if everything else could be doubted, the existence of a thinking mind was beyond question.

Yet this new scientific spirit did not limit itself to the heavens or to matter in motion. Economics, too, was swept up in the search for precision, predictability, and universal laws.

As we have seen, for centuries economic thought had been part of moral philosophy. Aristotle, Augustine, and Aquinas all treated wealth as something to be guided by ethical considerations—never an end in itself. But as science reshaped human understanding, thinkers began to search for economic laws as immutable as Newton's laws of motion. Economics ceased to be a question of justice and became a question of efficiency, rationality, and growth: *How do markets function? What are the laws of supply and demand? How can wealth be maximized?*

This shift culminated in the eighteenth century with **Adam Smith (1723–1790)**. In ***An Inquiry into the Nature and Causes of the Wealth of Nations (1776)***, Smith laid the foundation for modern economics as an independent discipline. His concept of the "invisible hand" suggested that individuals, in pursuing their own interests, unintentionally contribute to the common good. He introduced the idea of the division of labour, showing how specialization increased productivity. He championed free trade, rejecting mercantilism's zero-sum vision of wealth.

As Smith famously observed:

> *"It is not from the benevolence of the butcher, the brewer, or the baker, that we expect our dinner, but from their regard to their own interest. We address ourselves, not to their humanity but to their self-love, and never talk to them of our own necessities but of their advantages." –Adam Smith, The Wealth of Nations (1776), Book I, Chapter II*

It was a revolution in thought. No longer did economics ask, What is just?—but rather, What is efficient?

Yet to reduce Smith's ideas to a mere exaltation of selfishness would be a serious oversimplification. In ***The Theory of Moral Sentiments (1759)***, written nearly two decades before ***The Wealth of Nations***, he emphasized that free markets alone could not sustain a just society. Human beings, Smith argued, are bound together by sympathy—the capacity to imagine ourselves in another's situation. Without moral sentiments and social norms, markets risk degenerating into exploitation and instability. And yet it was Smith's later metaphor of the "invisible hand"—the idea that individual self-interest unintentionally generates social order and prosperity—that came to dominate economic thought. His earlier insight, the presence of an "invisible heart," was largely forgotten.

Smith's successors—**David Ricardo (1772–1823), Thomas Robert Malthus (m 1766–1834), Jean-Baptiste Say (1767–1832), and John Stuart Mill (1806–1873)**—shaped the tradition we now call classical economics. They refined and extended Smith's insights, formalizing theories of comparative advantage, population dynamics, and market equilibrium. They did champion free markets and limited government intervention. But to present them as apostles of *laissez-faire* alone would be misleading. Their economics was still deeply entangled with moral philosophy, concerned with justice, responsibility, and the common good.

For the classical economists, markets were not ends in themselves but instruments of human progress. Ricardo grounded his theory of trade in the idea of mutual benefit. Malthus, though remembered for his gloomy predictions of scarcity, sought to warn of the dangers of inequality and overextension. Mill, more than any, kept the ethical thread alive, insisting that liberty was inseparable from responsibility and that economic arrangements should serve human development, not enslave it.

In **Principles of Political Economy (1848)**, **John Stuart Mill** argued that economic growth should not be an end in itself, but a means to human well-being. He recognised the importance of free markets while also acknowledging their limits, advocating for progressive taxation, social welfare policies, women's rights, and even worker cooperatives. He envisioned a future "stationary state" in which economic progress would be measured not by endless accumulation, but by human flourishing.

As Mill wrote:

> *"It is scarcely necessary to remark that a stationary condition of capital and population implies no stationary state of human improvement. There would be as much scope as ever for all kinds of mental culture, and moral and social progress; as much room for improving the Art of Living." –John Stuart Mill, Principles of Political Economy (1848), Book IV, Chapter VI, Section 1, "Of the Stationary State"*

For Mill—and for much of the classical tradition—economics had not yet been severed from moral philosophy. It remained concerned not only with the creation of wealth, but with how wealth should be used to serve human flourishing and social progress.

Karl Marx (1818–1883), writing in the heart of the Industrial Revolution, offered a radical critique of classical economics. While he shared the classical economists' commitment to Philosophy, he rejected their optimism about markets and property. To Marx, capitalism was a moral failure. It alienated the worker and concentrated power in the hands of the few. He exposed the contradictions within classical economics and proposed a new, historically grounded theory of value—one that saw economic systems as stages in a broader, conflict-ridden evolution. Yet despite their disagreements, both Marx and the classical economists still spoke the same philosophical language—concerned with justice, labour, freedom, and the future of humanity.

The real rupture came later. It was not Marx, but the rise of neoclassical economics in the late nineteenth century, that signalled the divorce between economics and Philosophy. While it built upon the insights of classical economics, it introduced a new focus on marginalism—the idea that most decisions are made not in sweeping, all-or-nothing ways, but at the margin, in small, incremental steps. Economists argued that what matters is not the total value of something, but the value of one more unit. Instead of asking only big questions about wealth or justice, they now studied everyday choices: *Should I consume one more loaf of bread? Work one more hour? Save one more coin?*

Economics began to look less like moral philosophy and more like physics—equations replaced ethical inquiry, and curves of supply and demand took the place of questions about justice. With figures like **William Stanley Jevons (1835–1882), Carl Menger (1840–1921), and Léon Walras (1834–1910)**, the discipline shifted toward abstraction, mathematics, and individual utility (the idea that people make choices to maximise personal satisfaction). Marginal analysis, optimisation, and equilibrium (the point where supply and demand balance) replaced ethical inquiry and historical context. Economics began to model itself on physics—aiming for precision and prediction, but often at the cost of meaning and moral depth.

Then came 1929.

The stock market crash of October 1929 triggered the Great Depression, the most devastating economic crisis of the twentieth century. For much of the 1920s, speculative bubbles had driven stock prices to unsustainable heights, fuelled by easy credit, minimal government oversight, and the widespread belief that markets were inherently self-correcting. When the bubble burst, panic selling cascaded into financial collapse. Banks failed. Businesses shut down. Unemployment soared.

The crisis exposed the limits of *laissez-faire* economics. It showed that markets, left entirely to themselves, were not always rational, stable, or self-regulating. Neoclassical economists had assumed that market forces, like the laws of nature, would naturally restore balance. But in 1929 the invisible hand faltered, and the consequences were human: families in breadlines, abandoned farms, shattered livelihoods.

It was in response to this disaster that **John Maynard Keynes (1883–1946)** developed his groundbreaking ideas. Keynes rejected the classical belief that markets would inevitably return to equilibrium after a downturn. In ***The General Theory of Employment, Interest, and Money (1936)***, he argued that in times of crisis governments must intervene—spending money, creating jobs, and actively steering the economy to restore stability.

Keynes was not only an economist but also a moral thinker. His work asked fundamental questions: *How do we reconcile market efficiency with social justice? How do we balance individual freedom with the common good? What is the role of the state in ensuring human flourishing?*

His ideas shaped Franklin D. Roosevelt's New Deal (1933–1939), the rise of the welfare state, and the post-war consensus that emphasized government intervention to prevent economic collapse. Keynes' vision was not simply a technical fix for market failures. It was a reassertion of an older truth: that economics exists to serve people, not the other way around.

For several decades, Keynesian economics defined policy across much of the world. Governments invested in infrastructure, regulated financial markets, and built social safety nets. The result was unprecedented economic growth, expanding middle classes, and sharp reductions in poverty across Europe, North America, and beyond.

But by the late twentieth century, the pendulum swung back. Stagflation in the 1970s—rising prices combined with high unemployment—seemed to undermine Keynesian prescriptions. A revival of free-market fundamentalism followed, led by figures such as Milton Friedman and the Chicago School, and by political leaders like Ronald Reagan and Margaret Thatcher. The emphasis shifted once again toward deregulation, privatisation, and a belief in the primacy of markets.

Friedman (1912–2006) led the charge. He and his contemporaries resurrected neoclassical thought, but this time with a sharper edge. Government was not the solution, they argued—it was the problem. Markets alone should dictate the course of economic life. The role of business, Friedman famously claimed, was not to serve society but to maximize profit. A corporation's sole duty was to its shareholders.

In the decades that followed, economic policy became increasingly fixated on growth. GDP became the measure of success. The pursuit of wealth—endless, accelerating, unquestioned—became the defining goal of modern economies. And in the process, something vital was lost.

Modern economics, once deeply intertwined with philosophy, ethics, and social justice, transformed into something narrower: a science of efficiency. It came to be governed by ***homo economicus***—a reductionist model of the human being.

Homo economicus is rational, self-interested, and always seeking to maximize utility. He has no history, no psychology, no moral dilemmas. He is a perfectly calculating machine.

This way of thinking has reshaped how policymakers, institutions, and financiers perceive human nature. If individuals are rational profit-maximisers, then free markets must be the best way to organize society. If self-interest inevitably produces the best outcomes, then the purpose of economic growth need never be questioned—only pursued. And if efficiency and individual freedom are the highest virtues, then ethics, history, and justice become distractions, rather than essential economic concerns.

This framework has shaped decades of economic thought. It justified deregulation, financial speculation, and globalization in its most ruthless forms. It championed cost-benefit analyses that claimed to measure everything—except dignity, fairness, or well-being. It redefined human progress as nothing more than an increase in consumption and GDP growth.

But not everyone accepted this.

Behavioural economists such as **Daniel Kahneman** (1934–2023) and **Amos Tversky** (1937–1996) shattered the assumption that humans always act rationally. They demonstrated that people are driven by biases, emotions, and imperfect knowledge—often making decisions that contradict the cold logic of homo economicus. **Amartya Sen** (1933–present) challenged the narrow obsession with GDP, arguing that true economic progress must be measured by human capabilities: health, education, freedom, and dignity. **Kate Raworth** (1970–present) proposed a new framework altogether, one that places planetary boundaries and social well-being at the very heart of economic thought.

And yet, despite the 2008 financial crisis exposing the fragility of a paradigm that failed both people and planet, the dominant model remains. Economics still largely operates as if it existed in a vacuum—divorced from history, ethics, psychology, and sociology. The discipline has gained extraordinary precision, developing sophisticated models and statistical techniques that have made markets more predictable, policies more targeted, and businesses more efficient. But in narrowing its scope, economics has also lost its depth, its humility, its sense of purpose. It has lost its willingness to ask higher questions, to think long-term, to take a wider view. It has forgotten the wisdom that once guided it.

I am not an economist. I have never received formal training in economic theory. I am an engineer turned financier—by chance rather than choice. Yet in my two decades of professional life—attending countless economic conferences, reading endless reports, analysing market trends—I have rarely, if ever, heard discussions of ethics or justice in mainstream economic thought. Unless, of course, I went searching for them, in the work of exceptional thinkers like **Amartya Sen.**

I fully acknowledge that the specialisation of economics as a scientific discipline has brought immense progress. Economics has become a great guardian of efficiency, ensuring that the machinery of production, trade, and finance runs as smoothly as possible. But in its narrowing, in its divorce from its philosophical roots, it has lost the courage to ask: Why? Why do we seek growth? Why do we seek efficiency? What are we growing for?

The great debate of the twentieth century—Capitalism versus Communism—did not help either. It became a battle over means: market versus state, private property versus collective ownership. It was framed as a question of control, not of ends. And in doing so, it neglected the deeper question: What is the purpose of economics in the first place? Is it merely about allocating resources? Or is it about cultivating a just, flourishing, meaningful life?

The first economists—**Xenophon, Aristotle, Adam Smith, John Stuart Mill, Karl Marx**—were all philosophers. They thought about human well-being, about justice, about the balance between wealth and virtue. Even **Keynes**, in the wake of the Great Depression, asked philosophical questions: *How do we reconcile freedom and fairness? How do we structure markets to serve society rather than the other way around?*

It is time to ask these questions again. It is time to reunite what was once whole: to bring economics and Philosophy back together. To remember that wealth is not an end but a means—to human flourishing, to ecological healing, to the well-being of future generations.

The world today does not need more equations proving the efficiency of markets or the effectiveness of state intervention. It needs a renewed conversation about purpose. Growth for its own sake is not enough. Wealth without justice is not prosperity. A system that treats people and nature as expendable resources is not sustainable.

Economics can once again become a discipline of values, of ethics, of human flourishing. Not only a study of how markets work, but of what kind of economy we need—one that serves us, future generations, and our beautiful and only home.

26

The Shadows of Consumerism: Plato's Cave and the Illusions of Growth

The Consumerist Ethos: A Self-Perpetuating System of Desire

In the previous chapter, we explored how economics gradually detached itself from Philosophy, transforming from a discipline grounded in ethics into a mechanized, value-neutral science. From **normative**—what ought to be—to **positive**—what is. This shift culminated in the twentieth century's fixation on efficiency, profit maximization, and consumption.

But what if this transformation went beyond mere economics? What if it altered the very way we perceive the world?

The Scientific Revolution, one of humanity's most pivotal intellectual turning points, did more than advance empirical knowledge—it fundamentally reshaped our values. Questions of ***why*** were increasingly replaced with ***how***. Ethics and purpose, once central to human inquiry, gave way to empirical evidence, mechanism, and instrumental rationality. This shift produced remarkable progress, yet it also carried a hidden cost: it **narrowed our perception of what it means to flourish as human beings**. We forgot about our interdependence with one another, and with our beautiful and only home.

Nowhere is this transformation clearer than in economics. The Aristotelian conception of the human being—the ***Zoon Politikon*** (a political, communal animal), embedded in relationships and civic life—gradually faded. In its place emerged ***Homo Oeconomicus***, the rational, self-interested agent driven by utility maximization.

This transition began during the Enlightenment, when **Thomas Hobbes** (1588–1679) and **John Locke** (1632–1704) laid the foundations for individualism and self-interest as primary forces of human nature. Their ideas paved the way for **Adam Smith's (1723–1790) invisible hand**, which framed free

P. Ansoleaga Abascal, *Philosophy and Finance: A Love Story*,
https://doi.org/10.1007/978-3-032-22218-3_26

markets as the ultimate regulators of social well-being. But as we have seen, while Smith himself warned against unchecked self-interest in *The Theory of Moral Sentiments* (1759), later interpretations distilled his work into a doctrine of pure market rationality.

The Industrial Revolution (1760–1840) intensified this shift. Machines replaced artisans, mass production overshadowed local economies, and the worker—once embedded in communities—became a replaceable cog in an impersonal system of labour. Utilitarian thinkers like Jeremy Bentham (1748–1832) and John Stuart Mill (1806–1873) further entrenched this framework, arguing that maximizing pleasure and minimizing pain should be society's guiding principle. Over time, economic rationality replaced ethical reasoning, sidelining justice, virtue, and the common good—so treasured by my marvellous Stoics.

By the late nineteenth century, neoclassical economics had codified these ideas into mathematical models. Humans were reduced to rational utility calculators, and the pursuit of consumption became the defining metric of prosperity.

The twentieth century witnessed the full emergence of the capitalist-consumerist paradigm—a system in which perpetual consumption was no longer just an economic function but an ideological imperative. Mass advertising, branding, and corporate expansion fuelled an insatiable cycle of desire, acquisition, and dissatisfaction.

Economist Edward Cowdrick (1897–1978) described this shift as ***the new economic gospel of consumption.*** The moral language of thrift and necessity was replaced by an ethos of endless acquisition. Advertising campaigns did not merely sell products; they manufactured desires, subtly reshaping societal aspirations. Hazel Kyrk (1886–1957) and Theresa McMahon (1878–1961), pioneers of consumption economics, even argued that social envy was essential to economic growth.

President Herbert Hoover's (1874–1964) 1929 *Report of the President's Committee* on Recent Economic Changes (Recent Economic Changes in the United States) explicitly celebrated mass production, rising consumption, and the continual creation of new wants as signs of progress. The report portrayed economic progress as an ever-expanding cycle of desire, in which new wants were endlessly created and satisfied, only to be replaced by still newer ones. Consumption was no longer framed as a response to need, but as a boundless engine of growth.

We were no longer simply consuming to meet needs—we were consuming as a way of being. As historian **Yuval Noah Harari (b. 1976)** insightfully observes, capitalism and consumerism function as modern belief structures—complete with commandments, promises, and rituals.

In this new ethic, the wealthy are urged to invest endlessly, while the rest of society is encouraged to buy without restraint. Unlike older moral traditions, which demanded discipline, self-restraint, and inner transformation, this ideology asks very little of us—except that we continue to desire and consume. In return, it promises a kind of paradise: happiness, fulfilment, a better life always just one purchase away.

But what if this promise is an illusion? What if fulfilment does not lie in ***having*** more—but in ***being*** more?

Plato's Allegory of the Cave and the Shadows We See

Harari is right. This relentless focus on consumption has created an illusion, much like **Plato's Allegory of the Cave.**

In Plato's timeless story, prisoners are chained inside a dark cave, facing a blank wall. Behind them burns a fire, and between the fire and the prisoners is a walkway where objects pass, casting shadows on the wall. The prisoners, knowing nothing else, mistake these flickering shadows for reality. They believe they understand the world, when in truth, they are only seeing distortions of it.

Now, consider our modern world. Are we, too, prisoners? Are the shadows on the cave wall nothing more than advertisements, media narratives, and cultural scripts that tell us happiness lies in wealth, status, and consumption?

Just like Plato's prisoners, we are conditioned to accept illusions as truth. **The capitalist-consumerist system thrives because it keeps us too preoccupied to question it—too busy chasing the next product, the next upgrade, the next dopamine hit.** But what if we turned around?

William B. Irvine (b. 1952), one of my favourite modern Stoic thinkers, describes a phenomenon that echoes Plato's cave: **the hedonic treadmill.**

Irvine explains that we humans rapidly adapt to both pleasure and pain. Each time we acquire something new—a job, a luxurious item, a lifestyle upgrade—the thrill fades, and we find ourselves chasing the next one. This never-ending pursuit leaves us restless.

The good news is, **the Stoics provide an antidote: awareness, gratitude, and voluntary simplicity.** Instead of endlessly striving for more, they teach us to appreciate what we already have. By shifting our focus **from external**

accumulation to internal richness, we liberate ourselves from the illusions of the cave.

Stepping out of the cave is not easy. It requires questioning the very system that has shaped our desires, values, and ambitions. Plato warns that those who return to the cave to free others are often met with resistance—even hostility.

True freedom lies not in *having* more, but in *being* more.

Perhaps the way forward is not to reject self-interest but to reconcile it with the common good—to integrate entrepreneurship, innovation, and wealth creation into a framework of social and environmental responsibility.

I believe a revival of classical philosophical education—rooted in virtue ethics, wisdom, and holistic human flourishing—can help us restore balance: between self and other, facts and values, efficiency and justice, head and heart. A world where we finally step beyond the shadows and into the light.

Challenging the capitalist–consumerist paradigm requires precisely the kind of inner work I have been describing in this book: the cultivation of character, the recognition that our worth is not measured by material achievement but by inner virtue. It requires embracing a different compass of values—*ECO*-centric rather than *EGO*-centric, collective rather than individualistic, human values rather than market values.

It requires embodying ***Oikeiosis***—Alma's mindset. Honouring our interconnectedness and our interdependence. After all, we cannot be truly happy if we are surrounded by unhappiness.

Like pursuing a philosophical life, stepping into the light is not easy—it requires determination and constant attention. It is not easy, but it is truly worth it. Let us remember Aristotle: ***Virtue is its own reward.***

We will be rewarded with wisdom, inner peace, and true happiness. With better, more authentic friendships. With a life of meaning and purpose—one where, when we look back, we do not regret neglecting what is truly important.

27

Finance Through the Ages: Power, Progress, and Moral Dilemmas

I see modern economics as the study of how societies allocate resources, and finance as the engine that makes this allocation possible. Like strategy and tactics, economics provides the wider vision, while finance delivers the means of execution. As we saw in the previous chapter, economics was once deeply intertwined with Moral Philosophy. Over time, as economic thought evolved, so too did financial systems—fuelling extraordinary innovation but also giving rise to profound moral dilemmas.

Finance has built cities, connected civilizations, and lifted millions out of poverty. But it has also commodified human beings, funded wars, and widened inequality.

To glimpse where finance may be headed, we must first understand where it has been.

Financial ingenuity dates back to antiquity. In **Mesopotamia (c. 3000 BCE)**, temples functioned as proto-banks, storing grain and silver for safekeeping and issuing loans to farmers and traders. These early financial systems facilitated trade, enabled the rise of city-states, and helped structure the first economies. As trade expanded across regions, credit systems soon emerged. Merchants borrowed silver or goods to fund trading expeditions, repaying their debts with interest upon their return. The Code of Hammurabi (c. 1750 BCE)—one of the world's first legal codes—even set out regulations for lending and interest rates, demonstrating how finance was already recognised as both essential and potentially exploitative.

In **Ancient Greece**, financial practices developed alongside philosophical thought. The economy was built on trade, and Athens in particular became a financial hub, with a sophisticated system of moneylending and credit to

P. Ansoleaga Abascal, *Philosophy and Finance: A Love Story*,
https://doi.org/10.1007/978-3-032-22218-3_27

support commerce. Maritime loans were common, allowing merchants to finance voyages with borrowed money that would be repaid upon the successful return of their goods. If the ship sank, the loan was forfeited—a rudimentary form of financial risk-sharing. Wealthy individuals often acted as private lenders, funding trade and infrastructure. Yet lending also became a source of oppression, as many poor citizens fell into servitude to repay their obligations.

One of the earliest examples of financial strategy comes from **Thales of Miletus (c. 624–546 BCE).** According to Aristotle, Thales used his knowledge of astronomy to predict a bountiful olive harvest. Acting on this foresight, he secured exclusive rights to olive presses when demand was low. When the harvest proved abundant, he leased them at a premium, earning a substantial profit. This clever manoeuvre can be considered the first derivative of all time—a contract based on the right to use the presses, whose value fluctuated with future harvest conditions. In essence, Thales monetized time, risk, and foresight—centuries before modern financial markets were born.

Rome's financial systems were even more sophisticated. The **argentarii** (moneylenders and bankers) facilitated loans, managed accounts, and issued credit, enabling massive infrastructure projects such as roads and aqueducts. Wealthy families and the **publicani** (private contractors) invested in public works, war efforts, and long-distance trade. But Roman finance also revealed its darker side—just as it funded roads and aqueducts, it also financed the expansion of slavery. The Roman economy relied heavily on enslaved individuals, who were often bought and sold with borrowed money.

After the fall of Rome, Europe's economy became more agrarian, but financial innovation did not stagnate. The rise of merchant guilds and local markets introduced new forms of trade finance, ensuring fair exchange and quality control. Religious doctrine also shaped medieval finance. Christianity condemned usury (charging excessive interest on loans), leading to creative financial workarounds. Medieval merchants used bills of exchange, which functioned like an early form of cheque—allowing money to be transferred without the physical exchange of gold or silver.

One of the most enduring financial institutions of this period was **Banca Monte dei Paschi di Siena**, founded in 1472 in Italy. Originally a charitable institution, it provided loans to farmers and merchants, an early example of finance serving both economic and social needs. This era saw the emergence of banking dynasties, such as the **Medici family** in Florence, who pioneered letters of credit, allowing merchants to trade across Europe without carrying large sums of gold. These financial innovations paved the way for modern banking.

By the sixteenth and seventeenth centuries, finance became a global force. The rise of mercantilism led to the formation of joint-stock companies, allowing individuals to pool resources and share risks. Two of the most famous were the **British East India Company (1600) and the Dutch East India Company (VOC, 1602).**

The Dutch East India Company (VOC) is often considered the first modern corporation, as it issued tradable shares and pioneered the first stock exchange in Amsterdam. While these financial innovations fuelled economic expansion, they also enabled exploitation—financing colonialism, monopolising trade, and, most infamously, profiting from the transatlantic slave trade. European banks and investors were deeply involved in financing ships, plantations, and human suffering—a stark reminder that finance has never been morally neutral.

The eighteenth and nineteenth centuries saw the rapid expansion of industrial finance. The development of railroads, factories, and mass global trade required huge amounts of capital, leading to the rise of investment banks and large-scale lending. Families like the **Rothschilds** played a pivotal role in financing governments, wars, and infrastructure, shaping the global financial system. But industrial finance also deepened inequality. Factory owners amassed fortunes, while workers endured harsh conditions, child labour, and poverty wages. Once again, finance proved to be both an engine of progress and a tool of oppression.

The twentieth century brought rapid financial innovation. The expansion of stock markets, the rise of investment banking, and the growth of global capital flows made financial markets more interconnected than ever. However, the increasing complexity of financial products also led to greater risks. **The 1929 Wall Street Crash**, one of the most devastating financial collapses in history, was the result of years of excessive speculation, easy credit, and overconfidence in an ever-rising stock market. In the 1920s, as the economy boomed, investors poured money into stocks, often borrowing heavily to do so—a practice known as *buying on margin*. Banks, eager to capitalise on the boom, lent vast sums to individuals and businesses with little oversight. This created a speculative bubble, where stock prices soared far beyond their real value. When confidence wavered and selling began, the bubble burst.

On **Black Thursday (24 October 1929)**, panic selling set in, with 12.9 million shares traded—more than triple the usual volume. By **Black Tuesday (29 October 1929)**, the market had completely collapsed, wiping out billions of dollars in wealth overnight. Banks that had invested heavily in the market failed, businesses shuttered, and unemployment skyrocketed. What followed was the **Great Depression**, a decade-long economic catastrophe that devastated millions of lives. The financial chaos revealed the dangers of an unregulated market, forcing governments to step in for the first time. In the aftermath, **Keynesian economics** reshaped finance, with central banks taking a more active role in stabilising markets and governments introducing regulations to prevent another disaster of such magnitude.

By the late twentieth century, finance had evolved beyond supporting the real economy. The rise of financial engineering—with instruments like derivatives, securitisation, and high-frequency trading—meant that financial markets were increasingly detached from industries, workers, and production. This phenomenon, known as **financialisation**, meant that profits were increasingly made not from supporting goods or services, but from the financial transactions themselves.

This culminated in the **2008 Global Financial Crisis (GFC)**, which exposed the moral hazards of unchecked speculation—finance without Philosophy. The GFC was an ethical failure, a stark reminder that financial systems cannot function without accountability, long-term thinking, and a sense of responsibility to the societies they shape.

28

Numbers, Greed, and the Price of Blindness: A Story of the Global Financial Crisis

What happens when an entire system is built on momentum, greed, and blind faith in its own logic? What happens when no one stops to ask, why? This is the story of the 2008 financial crisis. And it is also my story.

In the early 2000s, banks in the United States started giving out more and more home loans, even to people who did not have stable jobs or enough savings. These risky loans were called **subprime mortgages.** Normally, banks would not lend to people who could not afford to pay them back, but they believed it was safe because house prices kept going up. If someone could not pay their loan, they could just sell the house for more than they owed and repay their mortgage.

At the same time, something else was happening. Banks were not just giving out risky loans—they were also packaging them together into **mortgage-backed securities (MBS)**. These were giant bundles of thousands of mortgages, sometimes containing over 1,000 loans in a single package. They divided these packages into different layers, or "tranches," based on risk. The safest tranches were paid back first, while the riskiest ones were last in line. This financial engineering made risky loans look safer than they really were. And banks were making money twice—first from lending to risky homeowners, and then from packaging and reselling those loans to institutional investors.

Instead of focusing on the real economy—helping businesses grow and people afford homes—banks were creating complex financial products that existed only to generate profits for themselves.

To make things worse, credit rating agencies—the companies that judged how safe these investments were—often gave the highest ratings (AAA) to these mortgage-backed securities, even though they contained risky loans.

P. Ansoleaga Abascal, *Philosophy and Finance: A Love Story*,
https://doi.org/10.1007/978-3-032-22218-3_28

These agencies were paid by the same banks that created these investments, an obvious conflict of interest. Instead of warning investors about the risk of MBSs, they helped banks sell more bad loans through these structured products.

Since these mortgage-backed securities had high ratings, banks and investors worldwide—including in Europe and Asia—bought them, believing they were safe. The profits were enormous, so banks kept on packaging and selling more and more of these risky loans. Until the bubble burst.

For years, house prices kept rising because banks kept lending more and more money, making it easier for people to buy homes. But by 2007, the cracks began to show. Too many houses were being built, and there were more homes than buyers. People started defaulting on their loans—many homeowners could not afford their payments anymore, and banks had to sell their homes, flooding the market. Then, banks tightened lending. Suddenly, fewer people could get loans, demand collapsed, and house prices began to fall.

By **2008**, the crisis had spiralled out of control. Banks had so many of these bad investments that they ran out of money. The first major collapse was **Bear Stearns**, which was saved by the government and sold to JPMorgan Chase in March 2008. But by September 2008, the unthinkable happened—**Lehman Brothers** collapsed. The bank had too many bad loans and no one wanted to save it.

This was a catastrophe. Banks all over the world had done business with Lehman, and suddenly, they were at risk too. Other major banks began to fall. **Merrill Lynch** was about to fail but was rescued when Bank of America bought it. **Washington Mutual**, the largest savings bank in the U.S., collapsed. **AIG**, one of the biggest insurance companies in the world, had insured many of these bad investments and nearly collapsed too. The U.S. government had to bail it out with $180 billion.

Normally, banks lend money to each other. But now, they were too scared—they did not know which banks were safe and which were about to go under. This led to a credit crunch, meaning businesses and regular people could not borrow money easily anymore. If businesses could not borrow, they could not pay their workers, and many had to shut down. Unemployment soared.

To stop the entire system from collapsing, governments in the U.S. and Europe stepped in. In the U.S., the government created the **Troubled Asset Relief Program (TARP)**, spending **$700 billion to save the banks**. In Europe, governments also bailed out banks and introduced emergency measures.

But this led to a huge ethical debate: Why should taxpayer money be used to save the same banks that had caused the crisis? At the same time, millions of ordinary people were suffering—losing their jobs, homes, and savings. But many bank executives kept their bonuses. At Merrill Lynch, executives received $3.6 billion in bonuses even as the bank was being bailed out. At AIG, the company that needed $180 billion in public money, executives paid themselves $165 million in bonuses—even though their company would have failed without government help.

This sparked public outrage.

Ordinary people were losing their homes while the very bankers who had caused the crisis were still getting massive pay checks. Even though government actions prevented an even bigger disaster, the world entered a deep recession. Millions of people lost their jobs. Entire families struggled to survive.

The crisis did not stay in the U.S.—it spread across Europe. Many European banks had bought risky American investments. Some countries, like Greece, Spain, Italy, Portugal, and Ireland, were hit even harder because their governments had already borrowed huge amounts of money before the crisis. When the financial system collapsed, these countries struggled to pay their debts.

Greece was in the worst shape and nearly went bankrupt. To prevent total economic collapse, the European Union (EU) and the International Monetary Fund (IMF) lent Greece billions—but in exchange, Greece was forced to cut spending massively. Schools, hospitals, and public services were slashed. Ordinary people paid the price for the mistakes of the financial system.

During the Great Recession (2007–2009), the U.S. unemployment rate doubled from under 5% to 10%, leaving millions jobless. In Europe, the impact varied. Latvia's GDP shrank by 25%, with unemployment reaching 22%. Spain and Italy faced deep recessions.

The financial industry's mistakes were paid for by the public.

The financial crisis of 2008 was a failure of perception, a failure of judgment, and a failure of wisdom. It was a system running on momentum, fear, and blind faith in its own logic, unable to see beyond the immediate, unable to recognize the reality beneath the numbers. I know this not because I read it in books or analysed it in hindsight—I lived it. I was there, inside the machine, watching it unravel from the trading floor, breathless and powerless, as the world came crashing down.

From Adrenaline to Awareness: My Reckoning with the System

The fields of economics and finance are often said to attract individuals who prioritise financial security, efficiency, and rational self-interest. That was not me at all. I was a dreamer—romantic, creative, impulsive—a young enthusiast who just happened to be very good at maths (and school in general).

I wanted to study Beaux-Arts or Architecture, but my father, whom I adored, insisted on Engineering. I wanted to make him happy. And I thought, solving problems? That sounds interesting enough. But I never—not even once—thought about making money, securing a stable future, or climbing the ranks of the financial world.

I was too busy partying, travelling, and imagining alternate lives in cosmopolitan environments like London. I was a young, enthusiastic and energetic citizen of the world who wanted to discover it all.

I ended up in finance by chance, not by choice. I wanted to live in London, an expensive city, and in 2006, after finishing an MBA in Paris, I found my way there.

I started at Bloomberg, a less demanding job which allowed free evenings to finish my MBA thesis. Then, a friend told me that Bank of America was looking for an engineer on the structured equity derivatives desk. I hardly knew what a stock or a bond was—let alone a derivative. Not a clue. But they liked my numerical skills, so they hired me.

A structured equity derivatives desk is a highly specialized team within an investment bank that creates, prices, and trades complex financial products linked to the stock market.

Unlike plain-vanilla stocks and bonds, structured derivatives are custom-built instruments, designed to offer investors specific risks and rewards. These instruments can be used to hedge risk, enhance returns, or create exposure to specific market movements in ways that would not be possible with the underlying stocks. In many ways, they echo what Thales of Miletus envisioned millennia ago with his ingenious use of olive presses: the strategic harnessing of foresight and risk to create opportunity.

For example, the desk might structure a product that allows a pension fund to gain exposure to the performance of the S&P 500, but with downside protection—meaning they get the upside if the market rises but are shielded from some of the losses if it falls. Or they might create a basket of stock options with embedded leverage, allowing a hedge fund to amplify potential gains (and losses).

These products are priced using advanced mathematical models—the Black-Scholes model, Monte Carlo simulations, and other quantitative methods that help predict how these complex instruments behave under different market conditions.

At its core, a structured equity derivatives desk is part mathematics, part trading, part sales, and part financial engineering—translating market risk into profit opportunities for banks and their clients. But, as I would later realize, it was also a world of abstraction, where numbers detached from reality became the only thing that mattered.

So there I landed. The following years felt like a film—a whirlwind of adrenaline, intensity, and survival. I only understood it later. At the time, I was too deep inside it to see.

In my first week, my boss told me, with a contemptuous smirk, that I was the oldest intern he had ever met. I was 26, I think. I just smiled in response. Not knowing what else I could say or do.

I started as an equity derivatives junior sales, then moved to equity derivatives structuring a few months later. But regardless of the role, every decision on the trading floor felt urgent, absolute, high-stakes. Prices moved in milliseconds. A miscalculation, a hesitation, a misplaced decimal could cost millions. There was no space for reflection, no time to step back, no margin for error—only action, reaction, execution.

I was terrified to leave my desk, even to go to the ladies' room, because one of the traders would either shout across the floor—*"Paule, where are you?"*—or email the entire team, CC'ing the big boss, just to ask the same question.

A colleague would often lean over and ask me: *"Are you sick?"*

"No," I'd say, confused.

"You look sick," she would insist. Almost every morning.

I was not sick. I was exhausted and terrified.

When I had to prepare a pricing for the traders, I would wake up at 5 a.m., get to the trading floor by 6 a.m., and review the numbers again and again, making sure there was no mistake before my €200 million equity derivative indicative pricing was sent to them, and executed life.

I was scared to death of getting it wrong. The fear of not being good enough, sharp enough, tough enough kept me in a state of constant anxiety.

Then came Lehman Brothers' collapse.

We had assumed we would buy them, but instead, we ended up buying Merrill Lynch. The decision was made over the weekend, but the official bankruptcy filing came on Monday, September 15, 2008. We knew the day would be brutal. We arrived at the trading floor before dawn. We did not drink water. We did not eat. Not until trading hours were over.

At one point, someone handed me a term sheet for a structured derivative with Lehman—a failed counterparty. We needed to swap it immediately, but the problem? I could not recognize the language.

It looked Scandinavian. *Thanks God I have done Erasmus in Copenhagen!* I thought. I started running across the trading floor, shouting: *"Scandinavian speakers! I need Scandinavian speakers!"* A Swedish colleague finally stepped in and helped me translate it.

Nikole Bozza Ansoleaga

After those chaotic days, Human Resources started calling people one by one. They had a few minutes to pack their belongings and leave. It was ruthless.

One day, the phone rang so many times that some of us hid in the bathroom, hoping we would not be found and fired! Not just at Bank of America—this was happening in every bank across London. You could see them in the Underground, carrying boxes, their faces filled with resignation and disbelief. I was transferred to Merrill Lynch, from Canary Wharf to St. Paul's. I had survived—but not because I was good. I had survived because I was cheap.

On my first day at Merrill, my new team members did not speak to me. Not a single word. I was not welcomed.

I found another job internally, moving from equity derivatives to prime brokerage, serving hedge funds. It was just as hectic, relentless, and unforgiving as before. I started changing bosses every six months. And with them, the team's strategy kept changing too. We no longer knew where we were sailing.

> *"If one does not know to what port one is sailing, no wind is favourable." — Seneca, Letters to Lucilius, Letter 71.3, trans. Richard M. Gummere (1917)*

I will never forget when we went on a team-building paintball evening. One of the guys from another bank shot me at point-blank range—so close and so hard that I went home covered in bruises, crying from the pain. The next morning, he sent me a Bloomberg message. He wanted to take me out to dinner—to apologize. I was shocked. I never answered.

Another moment I will never forget: The new boss of the desk—one of the most confident, ambitious, and energetic women I had ever seen, who would run around the trading floor in impossibly high heels—was suddenly fired. Rumours swirled. "She was taking cocaine at work," someone whispered. She was gone. Just like that.

The few personal conversations I had with colleagues were never about ideas, never about meaning, never about purpose. They were about expensive bags, Michelin-starred restaurants, and luxury holidays. I did not fit. I always felt like an outsider under threat. I was constantly in survival mode—trying to prove I was tough enough, smart enough, worthy enough to be there.

In this hectic, high-stakes environment, I was so busy surviving that I could not see beyond the numbers. The financial numbers. And nobody else could either. Everything was abstracted into spreadsheets, models, and Bloomberg screens. Money was not money—it was derivatives, ISIN codes, bid-ask spreads. A derivative had a *bid* and an *ask*—a price for those who wanted to buy, another for those who wanted to sell. There was an underlying share, or a basket of shares, beneath it. But we never thought about them. They were just ISIN codes on a Bloomberg screen—not companies where real people pursued dreams and built futures. Behind those numbers were companies, workers, entire livelihoods—but we did not see them. **The industry was built on a language of abstraction, one that further detached us from the real-world impact of our work. The more complex the financial instrument, the further removed we were from human consequences.**

I was too young, too naive, too weak, too scared, too vulnerable to question all this. In such an environment, there was no time for reflection, no space for meaning, no room for big-picture thinking—only action, reaction, execution. My brain was wired for survival. Deep ethical or philosophical considerations were a luxury I could not afford.

The Normalization of the Absurd

Only when I left that world did I truly take *the view from above*—the Stoic cosmic perspective—and begin to understand what I had been through. I realised that when everyone around you operates the same way, you stop questioning it. The absurdities—working through the night, shouting across the trading floor, measuring success by how much pressure you can endure—become the norm. No one asks *why*, because the system rewards those who keep their heads down and play the game. It is either up or out. Fear and adrenaline trap you in a cycle of reaction rather than reflection. The system ensures you are too busy, too anxious, too addicted to the highs to wonder about the deeper meaning of what you are doing.

It was only when I stepped out—when the noise died down, when the Bloomberg screens went dark, when the pressure lifted, when I moved into the second-league but far kinder Italian financial industry—that I could finally see the whole picture.

Why share this story about my years on the trading floor? Because it matters for systemic change.

I never worked with bad people—not at all. Most had good hearts. We were simply operating from a profoundly dysregulated state. Decisions were driven by urgency, ego, and bonuses—big bonuses—rather than by wisdom, justice, or long-term thinking.

This matters for systemic change because a financial system built on short-term profit maximisation at the cost of long-term sustainability is, in many ways, the outward expression of a collective dysregulated state.

The Connection Between Our Nervous System and Our Decisions

Our somatic state influences our perception and cognition.

When we operate from a dysregulated state—when we are stuck in fight, flight, freeze, or fawn—our perception becomes distorted. We see threats everywhere, we focus on short-term survival, and we struggle with complexity.

Cognition becomes rigid: black-and-white thinking takes over. Curiosity, innovation, and wisdom shrink.

On the other hand, when we operate from a regulated state—when we are calm, engaged, and present—our perception expands. We can hold multiple perspectives, recognize patterns, and respond rather than react. Our thinking becomes flexible. We engage in deep reflection, ethical reasoning, and creative problem-solving.

The Role of Philosophy in Finance

That's why, to me, Philosophy—the love of wisdom—is not a luxury. It is a necessity, especially in the powerful financial industry, where a single decision can destabilize markets, devalue currencies, and shake entire nations. Think of George Soros, whose speculative attack on the British pound in 1992 forced the UK out of the European Exchange Rate Mechanism, sending shockwaves through the economy. One individual, one financial move—an entire nation shaken.

Reclaiming our best state—both individually and collectively—is a prerequisite for systemic transformation. If we aspire to design financial and economic systems that support human flourishing, we need decision-makers who operate from a state of mental clarity, presence, and ethical awareness. A system designed by *EGO*-driven minds will always produce *EGO*-driven outcomes.

But a system designed by wise, clear, and ethical minds can create a better world.

As we have seen with the practice of spiritual exercises, inner work requires time, focus, moments of silence and mental space. Living philosophically demands pause, mindfulness, and moments of reflection—space to step back and see the bigger picture. It requires **Prosoche**—the vigilant attention to our thoughts, emotions, and reactions. Without this space, we remain trapped in the narrow confines of our daily tasks.

If our days are packed with meetings, data analysis, and risk assessments, our minds will be absorbed in market movements, strategies, and economic shifts. We will be unable to see beyond *what is*—to imagine *what could be.* Without stepping back, we cannot design a financial system that deeply considers the lives our investments touch. **That's why finance needs Philosophy.**

29

From Doing *Less* Harm to Doing *More* Good: The Evolution of Ethical Finance

The history of finance reveals its dual nature. From Thales's olive presses to modern high-frequency trading, financial ingenuity has propelled human progress. It has funded empires, built cities, and linked economies across continents. Yet it has also commodified human lives, widened inequality, and plundered the natural world.

In every age, however, there have been voices of conscience—communities and individuals who refused to see finance as merely a machine for wealth accumulation. They understood that money could be more than a means of extraction. It could be a force to uphold justice, protect dignity, and serve the common good.

The story of ethical finance is one of slow, deliberate evolution—from the earliest religious prohibitions against exploitation, the ancient forerunners of what we now call **exclusions**, to the modern rise of **impact investing**, which seeks not only to avoid harm but to actively create positive change.

The Ancient Roots of Ethical Finance: Wealth as Stewardship

Long before the emergence of financial markets, moral traditions across civilizations emphasized fairness in trade, the responsibility of wealth, and the dangers of exploitation.

In Jewish law (c. 1500 BCE), wealth was understood not as absolute ownership but as stewardship. The **Jubilee Year**, described in the Torah, mandated that every 50 years, debts would be forgiven, land would be returned

P. Ansoleaga Abascal, *Philosophy and Finance: A Love Story*,
https://doi.org/10.1007/978-3-032-22218-3_29

to its original stewards, and agricultural activity would cease. This was a deeply ethical and ecological principle, recognizing that wealth should not be hoarded indefinitely and that the Earth itself must be respected. As Leviticus 25:23 states:

> *"The land shall not be sold for ever: for the land is mine; for ye are strangers and sojourners with me." –Leviticus 25:23, King James Version*

A few centuries later, Islamic finance, rooted in the Quran (609–632 CE), established similar principles. The prohibition of riba (usury) reflected a commitment to fairness and shared risk, ensuring that financial transactions served the well-being of all parties involved. Zakat (charitable giving) reinforced the idea that wealth should circulate within society rather than concentrate in the hands of the few.

Christianity, too, viewed finance through a moral lens. One of the most striking moments in the New Testament is **Jesus Christ's cleansing of the temple**. Upon entering the temple courts, he found moneylenders exploiting worshippers, turning a sacred place into a marketplace. In a rare moment of anger, he overturned their tables and drove them out, declaring:

> *"My house shall be called the house of prayer; but ye have made it a den of thieves." – Matthew 21:13, King James Version (1611)*

This act was a direct condemnation of financial corruption. The temple authorities allowed money changers to exploit pilgrims, profiting from inflated exchange rates and unfair practices. Jesus' actions were a bold rejection of an economic system that preyed on the vulnerable instead of serving them.

From Ancient Greece to the ethical teachings of Judaism, Christianity, and Islam, financial exploitation—especially usury—was widely condemned. **Dante's Inferno** even placed usurers in the lowest part of the Seventh Circle of Hell, portraying them as figures who distorted the natural order by using money to generate wealth without labour. **The message was clear across traditions: finance should serve human dignity, not exploit it.**

Ethical finance is not just good business—it is about restoring fairness, responsibility, and moral integrity to economic systems, seeing them holistically as living networks where every decision ripples across people, communities, and the planet.

During the **Middle Ages**, the **Church** maintained a firm stance against usury, condemning it as unnatural—turning money, a medium of exchange, into an instrument of exploitation. In response, **St. Thomas Aquinas** introduced the concept of the "just price," advocating fairness in trade and lending. Meanwhile, **Franciscan monks** in fifteenth-century Italy established **Montes Pietatis** ("Mountains of Piety")—institutions that provided low- or no-interest loans to the poor. These charitable pawnshops were among the first forms of ethical banking, designed to offer an alternative to predatory moneylenders.

The first Monte di Pietà was founded in Perugia in 1462, initiated by **Bernardino da Feltre**, a Franciscan friar. Troubled by the devastating effects of high-interest lending on the poor, Bernardino preached across towns and cities, inspiring the creation of these institutions as acts of mercy and social justice. Citizens donated money to create a pool of funds from which the poor could borrow against small items of value—without falling into cycles of debt. This movement quickly spread across Italy and later into other parts of Europe, blending compassion with finance in a way that felt revolutionary for its time.

Even beyond religious institutions, ethical finance found its place in emerging economic structures. **Guilds**—associations of artisans and merchants—played a crucial role in promoting responsible economic practices. Unlike moneylenders who often exploited desperate borrowers, guilds fostered mutual support, fair pricing, and ethical standards. They upheld the belief that wealth should be created with integrity, ensuring that trade was both profitable and honourable.

The Quakers and the Birth of Ethical Investing

By the seventeenth and eighteenth centuries, a new form of ethical finance emerged.

The Quakers, a religious movement founded in England, were among the first to apply moral principles to investing. They refused to profit from industries they deemed unjust—including the slave trade, weapons manufacturing, and alcohol production. Instead, they directed their money toward businesses that aligned with humanitarian values, investing in industries that promoted education, fair wages, and ethical business practices.

This was a radical departure from the financial norms of the time. In an era when financial gain was rarely questioned on moral grounds, this was revolutionary. The Quakers' principled stance challenged prevailing norms and laid the groundwork for what we now call socially responsible investing.

The Twentieth Century: Ethical Finance Becomes Activism

By the twentieth century, ethical finance was no longer just a personal or religious choice—it had become a political movement.

During the Vietnam War (1955–1975), investors began boycotting the defence industry, refusing to fund companies profiting from war. This led to the creation of the first modern socially responsible mutual fund, the **Pax World Fund (1971)**, which excluded investments in military contractors and polluting industries.

One of my favourite examples of ethical finance in action was the anti-apartheid divestment movement (1980s–1990s). As global outrage over South Africa's apartheid regime grew, investors—including universities, pension funds, and corporations—began divesting from companies that supported the system.

One of the movement's leaders, Leon Sullivan, a Baptist minister and corporate board member of General Motors, introduced the Sullivan Principles, a code of conduct that required U.S. companies in South Africa to treat Black workers fairly. When these principles failed to produce systemic change, Sullivan took a bolder stance, calling for total divestment from apartheid-linked businesses.

By 1990, over 150 institutions, including Harvard and major pension funds, had pulled their investments. The financial isolation of the apartheid regime played a critical role in its collapse, proving that capital could be a weapon for justice.

The Twenty-first Century: From Avoiding Harm to Creating Change

For centuries, ethical finance was defined primarily by what it refused to support—usury, weapons, tobacco, or industries associated with clear social harm. But by the late twentieth and early twenty-first centuries, a deeper question began to surface. If we have the power to avoid the worst companies, why not also choose the best? Why not direct capital toward those actively contributing to human and planetary well-being?

This shift in perspective gave rise to ESG investing—an approach that evaluates companies not only by how much profit they generate, but by how they generate it. ESG stands for Environmental, Social, and Governance criteria.

The environmental dimension asks whether a company protects the planet or depletes it. The social dimension examines how it treats people—employees, customers, and communities. Governance looks at leadership, transparency, accountability, and ethical decision-making.

Investors, often with the support of specialised rating agencies, began assigning scores across these dimensions, seeking to allocate capital to companies that serve a broader range of stakeholders—not only shareholders.

One such example is Johnson & Johnson. In 1943, its chairman Robert Wood Johnson articulated a corporate credo that would later be recognised as a landmark in what we now call stakeholder capitalism. Long before ESG entered the financial lexicon, the company defined its purpose as serving patients, healthcare professionals, employees, communities, and society at large—placing shareholders last, not first.

The credo affirms that business success begins with responsibility. It emphasises delivering high-quality products at fair prices, creating dignified and inclusive workplaces, contributing positively to local communities, and acting as a careful steward of natural resources. Profit, in this vision, is not the ultimate goal but the natural consequence of operating with integrity, innovation, and long-term perspective.

Robert Wood Johnson himself described the credo not as an act of philanthropy, but as a practical blueprint for sustainable business. When companies honour all their stakeholders, he believed, shareholders ultimately benefit as well.

In this sense, the Johnson & Johnson credo captures the essence of what ESG investing seeks to promote: companies that lead not only in market performance, but in responsibility—placing people, planet, and purpose at the heart of profit.

And yet, even ESG proved to be only a first step.

The emergence of impact investing carried this evolution further. Rather than merely avoiding harm or rewarding responsible behaviour, impact investors actively seek opportunities that generate measurable, positive change. These investments are guided by intention.

Impact investing directs capital toward ventures that address real human and environmental challenges: expanding access to clean water, healthcare, education, affordable housing, renewable energy, and ecosystem restoration. Investors ask not only *How much will I earn?* but *What kind of world am I helping to build?*

It is a different understanding of **return on investment**—one that includes not only financial gain, but meaning, justice, resilience, and hope for future generations.

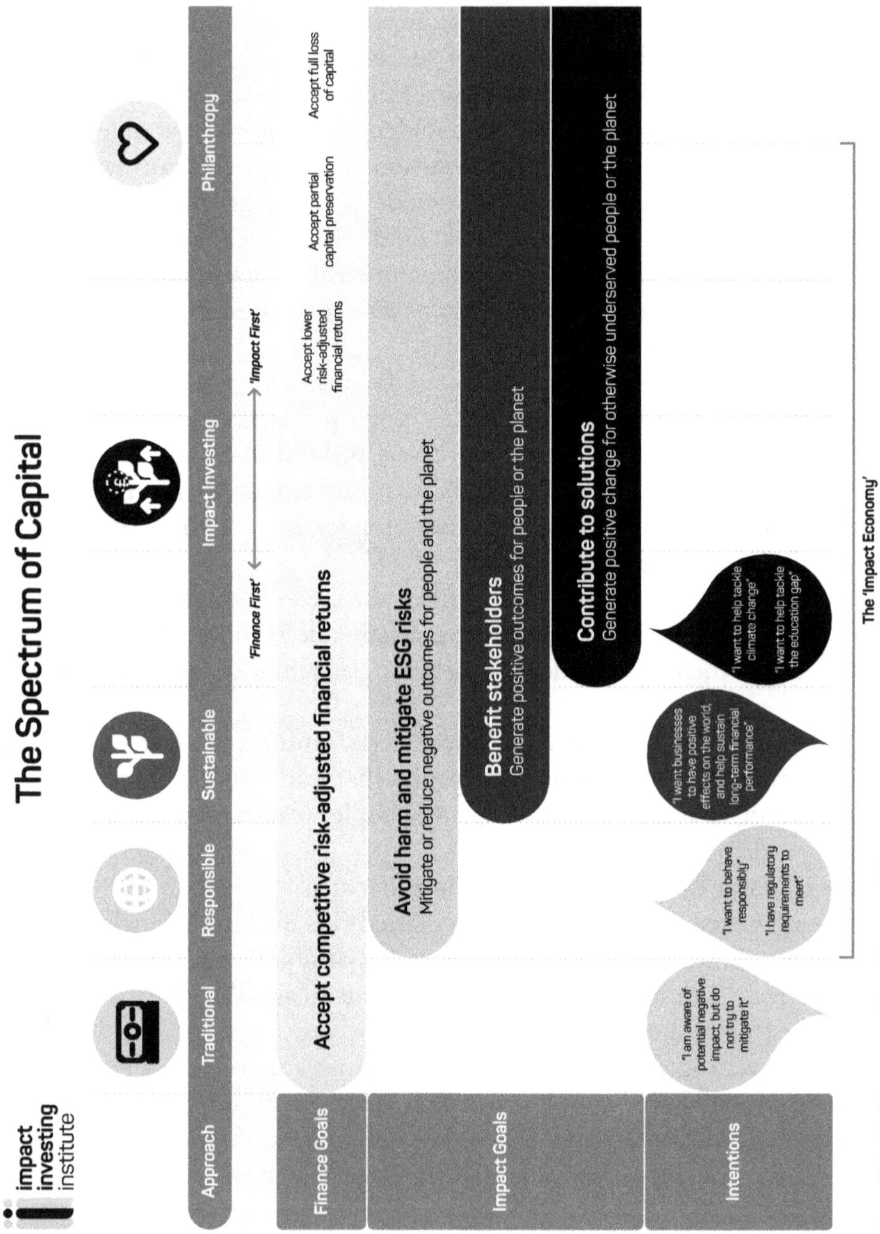

Source: Bridges Fund Management and Impact Management Project.

The Spectrum of Capital

Today, finance exists on a spectrum of values—a continuum that financial practitioners call the **Spectrum of Capital.**

At one end are **traditional investors**, focused purely on maximizing financial returns.

Next come **responsible investors**, who aim to avoid harm. They filter out companies involved in exploitation, environmental destruction, or corruption. This approach, rooted in exclusions, is reminiscent of the Quakers refusing to invest in the slave trade, or the global divestment campaigns that helped bring down apartheid.

Beyond them are **sustainable investors**, the so-called ESG investors. As discussed, ESG stands for Environmental, Social, and Governance—three key areas that can affect a company's long-term performance. ESG investing aligns financial success with responsible business practices, managing risk and rewarding companies that perform well across these dimensions.

At the farthest end of the spectrum are **impact investors**, who aim for measurable, positive change. Impact investing is built on a powerful idea: that capital can be a tool for transformation. It involves investing with the clear intent to generate social or environmental benefit—alongside financial gain. Some impact investors are even willing to accept lower returns (known as concessionary investments) in exchange for meaningful, lasting outcomes.

A defining feature of impact investing is **intentionality**—the deliberate choice to pursue a specific, positive outcome.

Interestingly, **intentionality**—or **prohairesis**—is also a cornerstone of Stoic philosophy. For the Stoics, what defines a good life is not what happens to us, but how we choose to respond. **Outcomes lie beyond our control; what matters is the intention behind our actions.** Much like impact investing, Stoicism places its faith in deliberate, value-aligned action—not in external results. Both recognize that progress, not perfection, is the path to purpose.

Another essential principle of impact investing is **additionality**—the idea that an investment creates an outcome that would not have happened otherwise.

And then there's **measurability**—a commitment to track and report the real-world effects of capital.

These principles come to life through simple, vivid examples:

- **Intentionality**: "I am investing in a renewable energy company because I want to reduce CO_2 emissions and accelerate the transition to clean energy."

- **Additionality**: "My microloan enabled a young woman in Kenya to start her first business—an outcome that wouldn't have occurred without this capital."
- **Measurability**: "Thanks to the investment, 500 homes in a rural region now have access to solar electricity—and we can measure the emissions avoided and lives improved."

While ESG and impact investing are often conflated, they are not the same. ESG evaluates how environmental, social, and governance factors affect a company's financial performance. Impact investing starts from another question: what good can be created through capital? It is investing on purpose, with purpose. All impact investments integrate ESG considerations, but not all ESG strategies aim for intentional, additional, measurable impact beyond financial returns.

At the right-hand side of the Spectrum of Capital—the spectrum of values—lies **philanthropic capital**: capital that does not seek financial return at all, but is fully devoted to social and environmental impact. This includes charitable giving, grants, and donations aimed at alleviating poverty, advancing human rights, supporting education, protecting nature, and more. Philanthropic capital may be the purest expression of altruistic intention—fuelled by a desire to serve the common good.

Taken together, the spectrum of capital reminds us that every deployment of capital carries weight. From pure philanthropy to profit-seeking capital, every financial decision is also a decision about our future.

Where we choose to invest determines which businesses survive, which innovations take root, and what kind of world unfolds. All investments have impact—whether we measure them or not, whether we intend them or not. Finance is never neutral. It either sustains the status quo or shapes what is yet to come.

When aligned with moral clarity, finance becomes a force for justice, sustainability, and regeneration. By recognising the ethical weight of our choices, we reclaim the power of capital to grow wisdom, dignity, and life.

We widen its purpose.
We deepen its meaning.
And we begin to build a future where value is measured not only in returns, but in the flourishing of humanity and the Earth.

There are people who have dared to walk this path—who have shown that capital can serve far more than the purpose of making more capital. This next chapter is a tribute to them: visionaries who proved that finance, guided by purpose, can become a force for dignity, justice, and lasting change.

30

Financial Heroes: People Who Redefined Wealth

There are many financial heroes in history—known, and mostly unknown. Women and men who dared to challenge the status quo, who questioned the moral boundaries of profit, and who pioneered new models of finance rooted in ethics, empathy, and human flourishing. In their stories, we find not only inspiration—but a map of what is possible when money is no longer an end in itself, but a means to serve life. I wish I could name them all. They each deserve to be remembered, for their courage was not always celebrated, their voice not always heard. But their legacy lives on—in the world they helped shape, and in the path they opened for us to walk.

John Woolman (1720–1772): The First Financial Activist

John Woolman was born in 1720 in Rancocas, New Jersey, into a devout Quaker family. From an early age, he was drawn to the principles of justice and compassion—values that would define his life's work as both a preacher and an ethical reformer.

Woolman was one of the earliest financial activists in history. At a time when slavery was an accepted pillar of the global economy, he took an uncompromising stand against it. As a Quaker, he believed all human beings were equal before God, and he argued that profiting from slavery—whether through direct ownership or investments in industries that depended on it—was a moral stain.

P. Ansoleaga Abascal, *Philosophy and Finance: A Love Story*,
https://doi.org/10.1007/978-3-032-22218-3_30

In his famous Journal, he wrote:

> *"The love of ease and gain are the motives in general of keeping slaves." –John Woolman, Journal (c. 1774)*

Woolman not only refused to participate in slavery himself but actively campaigned to persuade fellow Quakers to divest from it. Traveling from town to town, he met with business owners and investors, confronting them with difficult questions about their financial complicity in injustice. His persistence bore fruit: many Quakers freed their slaves and withdrew their capital from the institution of slavery.

His work laid the moral groundwork for future abolitionist movements, introducing a radical idea for its time—that money carries our values. That where we invest our wealth reflects who we are.

Andrew Carnegie (1835–1919): The Gospel of Wealth

Andrew Carnegie's life is the quintessential rags-to-riches story. Born in 1835 in Dunfermline, Scotland, he immigrated to the United States as a child, settling in Pittsburgh. The son of a struggling weaver, he began working at age 13 in a cotton factory. His intelligence and ambition propelled him through the railroad and steel industries, where he built one of the largest fortunes of the Gilded Age. Yet, Carnegie's true legacy is not defined by his wealth—but by how he used it.

In 1889, he published **The Gospel of Wealth**, an essay that laid out a radical vision of the moral responsibility of the wealthy. Its most famous line captured its essence:

> *"The man who dies rich, dies disgraced." –Andrew Carnegie, The Gospel of Wealth (1889)*

Carnegie believed that great wealth came with an obligation—to be reinvested into society for the common good. He dedicated nearly 90% of his fortune to philanthropy, funding over 2,500 public libraries, supporting education through Carnegie Mellon University, and creating foundations that advanced science, the arts, and peace. Unlike traditional charity, which he saw as a bandage for poverty, Carnegie's vision was about long-term empowerment—creating opportunities for people to uplift themselves.

Through his philanthropy, he redefined what finance could be: a poweful tool to uplift others.

Leon Sullivan (1922–2001): The Preacher Who Took on Apartheid

Born in 1922 in Charleston, West Virginia, Leon Sullivan grew up under the harsh realities of racial segregation. Rather than being broken by those constraints, he transformed them into a lifelong commitment to justice. A Baptist minister, civil-rights leader, and moral visionary, Sullivan became one of the most powerful examples of how finance—when guided by conscience—can confront systemic injustice.

Sullivan's most enduring legacy emerged in the 1970s, when he became the first Black man to serve on the board of General Motors. From this position of influence, he became acutely aware that multinational corporations—including American ones—were economically sustaining South Africa's apartheid regime. Capital, he realised, was not neutral. It was either complicit—or capable of resistance.

In response, Sullivan devised what became known as the **Sullivan Principles in 1977**. These principles established a corporate code of conduct for companies operating in South Africa, demanding non-segregation in the workplace, equal pay for equal work, fair employment practices, meaningful training and promotion opportunities for Black South Africans, and an active commitment to improving living conditions beyond the factory gates. More than a checklist, they were an attempt to introduce moral accountability into global business at a time when such language was rare.

The Sullivan Principles (1977)
An ethical framework for corporate responsibility under apartheid

- *Eliminate racial segregation in all workplaces and facilities*
- *Ensure equal and fair employment practices for all employees*
- *Guarantee equal pay for equal or comparable work*
- *Provide education, training, and advancement opportunities for Black and non-white employees*
- *Increase the representation of Black and non-white individuals in management and leadership roles*
- *Contribute to improved living conditions beyond the workplace, including housing, healthcare, education, and transportation*
- *Actively oppose laws and practices that perpetuate racial, social, and economic injustice*

Introduced in 1977 and expanded in 1984

Many U.S. corporations initially adopted the principles. But when progress proved superficial and compliance cosmetic, Sullivan reached a difficult conclusion: ethical guidelines alone were insufficient. Justice required a stronger medicine.

He therefore called for total divestment from companies complicit in apartheid. Universities, pension funds, churches, and institutional investors were urged to withdraw their capital and refuse to profit from oppression. Financial pressure—applied deliberately and collectively—became the instrument of change.

The impact was historic. By the 1980s, more than 150 major institutions, including leading universities such as Harvard, had divested from South Africa. Capital fled. Markets spoke. The apartheid regime, increasingly isolated and economically strained, began to fracture. Finance, wielded with moral clarity, helped alter the course of history.

To me, Leon Sullivan embodies the Stoic virtue of courage in its highest form: the courage to act when compromise is tempting, the courage to accept personal cost in the service of justice, the courage to align means with ends. The phrase often attributed to him—you cannot serve freedom while supporting oppression—could stand as a moral compass for today's financial system.

Too often, we attempt to do both. We speak of sustainability while financing destruction; we praise inclusion while enabling exclusion; we champion transition while funding its opposite. These contradictions are no longer tolerable. Sullivan's legacy reminds us that capital always chooses sides—and that integrity demands we choose wisely.

Esther Afua Ocloo (1919–2002): The Pioneer of Microfinance

Born in 1919 in Peki Dzake, Ghana, Esther Afua Ocloo grew up in a small farming community. Despite the barriers faced by women in colonial Ghana, she became a trailblazer for women's economic empowerment and is widely regarded as one of the pioneers of microfinance.

Ocloo's entrepreneurial journey began with just six shillings, which she used to start a small business producing marmalade and orange juice. Her success awakened a deeper calling: to help other women gain the skills, confidence, and financial means to shape their own futures.

She believed that women were central to the economic and social fabric of their nations—but that potential could only be realised if women were given access to tools: credit, education, and opportunity. In 1958, she co-founded Women's World Banking, a global organisation dedicated to expanding financial services for low-income women.

Through her work, millions of women gained access to capital, built businesses, supported their families, and transformed their communities—demonstrating that small investments, guided by trust and dignity, can generate profound and lasting social change.

Jacqueline Novogratz, Jed Emerson and Sir Ronald Cohen: The Pioneers of Impact Investing

Jacqueline Novogratz, Jed Emerson, and Sir Ronald Cohen are pioneers who helped shape the modern impact investing movement—not just with capital, but with vision, heart, and intellectual leadership.

Novogratz's Acumen redefined what it means to invest in dignity and possibility, and her writing—especially **Manifesto for a Moral Revolution**—offers profound insights on moral leadership.

Emerson's groundbreaking concept of Blended Value challenged the artificial separation between financial return and social impact, laying the philosophical and practical groundwork for how we measure value today. His book **The Purpose of Capital** is a must-read for anyone seeking to rethink the role of money in society.

Sir Ronald Cohen has worked tirelessly to institutionalise impact, developing innovative tools like Social Impact Bonds and tirelessly advocating for transparency and measurable progress. His book **Impact** is a visionary roadmap for building a more just and equitable financial system.

Their work challenges the traditional definition of financial success—proving that investments can generate justice, dignity, and lasting change.

Lives That Inspire Positive Finance

Those we have named in this chapter—Woolman, Carnegie, Sullivan, Ocloo, Novogratz, Emerson, Cohen—and the millions whose names we may never know, remind us of what is possible when money becomes an instrument of virtue. They remind us that the future of finance will not be written solely in numbers, but in values. Not only in returns, but in relationships. Not just in markets, but in meaning.

You may have noticed, as I did, the historical absence of women in financial history. The world of finance has long been shaped by male voices and visions. But this, too, is beginning to change. As sustainable and impact investing have grown, so too has the presence and power of women within finance—perhaps because these forms of investing prioritise what has long been undervalued: long-term thinking, community well-being, environmental stewardship, and social equity. These are values women have carried for centuries, often from the margins—through care, education, activism, philanthropy, and resilience.

This is cause for hope. A new generation of women is stepping into finance not to replicate the old models, but to reimagine them. Feminine wisdom—empathy, intuition, care, collaboration, the courage to nurture life—is shaping a new kind of capital. One that dares to hold people and planet alongside profit. That chooses to ask not only how much we earn, but what kind of world we are earning it in.

Finance, like the world it shapes, is being transformed. And this time, it is listening to voices too long silenced, and learning to speak in a different register—the register of the heart. For only when the feminine is welcomed back into finance will capital truly serve life.

Part 4

Looking Forward

Nikole Bozza Ansoleaga

Philosophy clears the fog of convention and lets us see with new eyes. And what we see then, if we are honest, is astonishing

This final block carries us from inner transformation to systemic change. From education to economics, from finance to the very fabric of our lives, it calls us to reimagine the foundations of our shared future. A vision in which flourishing is measured not by possessions, but by character. In which progress is defined not by speed, but by depth.

Here we will explore how impact investing, systems thinking, and the revival of Paideia can help us build a world that is not only more sustainable, but also more soulful. We will meet the Almas—entrepreneurs and investors who embody a new mindset, blending creative courage with moral purpose.

Block 4 is an act of hope, a vision we shall embody before we build the world we want. A reminder that the future is not something we inherit, but something we create—together, with open eyes, steady hands, and hearts aligned with what truly matters.

The future grows within us—through the values we choose, the courage we cultivate, and the care we extend to others. Long before it becomes visible, it is already waiting to be embodied.

31

A New Vision for the Future: Alma's Ocean

Dear reader, welcome to the final section of this book. It is time to look forward—to imagine what could be. Writing these words reminds me why I embarked on this journey.

I believe Philosophy—especially ancient Philosophy—can serve as a moral compass for finance, guiding markets, investments, and economic systems to operate within ethical boundaries. Economics was born of Philosophy, and it can return to its roots. When the power of finance meets the wisdom of Philosophy, we unlock an extraordinary force—one that can serve justice, nurture equality, and restore beauty to our shared world.

I also believe Philosophy can address the root causes of our greatest challenges: our disordered inner state and the fractures we have created with our true selves, with others, and with nature. It has the power to dissolve the ***oblivion of being*** and the ***false idea of separation*** by inspiring the inner work essential for clarity of mind, steadiness of heart, and awakening of spirit. Philosophy can guide us back to the essence of existence—making us wiser, more peaceful, and more deeply connected human beings.

These two aims—healing within and transforming without—are inseparable. Only by nurturing our highest mental, emotional, and spiritual capacities can we give birth to outer actions worthy of the future. What we carry within inevitably flows outward. Every decision we make—including every investment—is a reflection of our inner world, rippling outward into infinity. Thought shapes action. Emotion fuels decision. Inner and outer are two sides of the same coin: distinct, yet never separate.

Philosophy also teaches us to pause, to reflect, to think critically—a rare luxury in our hurried age, yet essential for freedom, independent thought,

P. Ansoleaga Abascal, *Philosophy and Finance: A Love Story*,
https://doi.org/10.1007/978-3-032-22218-3_31

and creative insight. We live in a world where values, paradigms, and worldviews are constantly handed to us—often without our consent, and almost always without reflection. Philosophy invites us to slow down, to examine what we have inherited, to question what no longer serves us, and to dare to reimagine what could be.

This feels more urgent than ever. **Not only can Philosophy act as a guardian of ethics and wisdom, it can also be a catalyst for creativity, openness, and transformation**. It can widen our horizon, loosen rigid thinking, and help us reframe problems. It can reveal possibilities where we once saw only constraints. And it can remind us that the limits we perceive are often nothing more than the limits of our imagination.

The great philosophers—from **Aristotle** to **Kierkegaard**, from **Lao Tzu** to **Simone Weil**—were not just moral thinkers; they were visionaries who reimagined the human experience. They questioned what seemed inevitable, dismantled old paradigms, and inspired new ways of thinking about value, relationships, and purpose. This is precisely what entrepreneurship and finance need today. We do not just need better metrics, investments, or regulations—we need a deeper imagination. **We need Philosophy not just to guide our decisions but to expand our sense of what is possible.**

In other words, I am writing this book to inspire **a way of thinking—and being—that is less mechanistic and more holistic**. To resist the emptiness of a purely utilitarian existence. To balance external achievement with internal fulfilment. To remind us that true transformation does not begin with metrics, policies, or technologies—it begins within. In the quiet spaces of our soul.

You already know what I believe: the greatest challenge we face today is not artificial intelligence, geopolitical conflict, polarization, climate change, or rising inequality. As urgent and alarming as these crises are, they are symptoms—not root causes.

At the heart of it all lies a deeper fracture: a false idea of separation. Separation from one another, from nature, from meaning itself. This illusion has given rise to hyper-individualism and a culture of domination—of others, of the planet, and even of our own selves. And compounding it is the disappearance of any spiritual dimension from modern life. We live in ***Ega***'s ocean—disconnected, disenchanted, and adrift. People do not go to bed hungry because there is not enough food in the world. They go to bed hungry because there is not enough compassion.

Egoism is the true pandemic of our age; anxiety, depression, loneliness, and fear are its consequences. According to **Gallup's Life Evaluation Index**, as of 2023, only 29% of the global population rated their lives highly enough to be considered thriving. The rest—60%—were struggling, and 12% were suffering. This is heartbreaking.

We are rich in material possessions, yet poor in human values.
We are rich in academic titles, yet poor in wisdom.
We are rich in connections, yet poor in real friendships.
We are rich in technological advances, yet poor in virtuous leadership to ensure they serve us all.

But here is the great news: this ***oblivion of being*** can be reversed. It is not written into the laws of nature. It stems from the values we have inherited, the mindsets we've accepted without question, and the systems we have built upon them. And values, mindsets, and systems can be changed—as our ancestors have shown us time and time again.

Virtue can be nurtured. Practiced again and again, it becomes a habit. And the second piece of great news? Virtue is its own reward. It pays us back with inner peace and lasting joy.

That's why we can look forward with hope. We can imagine what the world might become if we embraced our deepest human values—love, compassion, empathy, beauty, wisdom, and creativity. Values that science confirms lead to greater happiness, longer lives, and deeper fulfilment.

If we embraced our human values, the world would transform. It would become ***Alma***'s ocean—a vast, living tapestry of interconnection and meaning. We would see ourselves as part of something magnificent and whole. Part of the Stoic Cosmopolis resting upon the Logos. Well-being, purpose, and social harmony would take precedence over status and accumulation. Success would no longer be measured by wealth, but by the depth of our relationships, the impact of our contributions, and the fulfilment we find in everyday life. Businesses and economies would prioritise sustainable, inclusive growth—directing capital toward ventures that uplift communities and restore ecosystems. Careers would be built around purpose, creativity, and contribution. Workplaces would nurture autonomy, mastery, and belonging—becoming places that enrich us. Human relationships would deepen, grounded in empathy, authenticity, and presence. Community life would thrive, replacing hyper-individualism with mutual support and shared purpose. Consumerism would loosen its grip as people rediscover joy in simplicity, in nature, in shared experience, in self-discovery. Leisure would no longer be a guilty pleasure, but an essential part of a flourishing, ***eudaimonic*** life. Education would evolve—shifting from producing workers to shaping whole human beings. It would cultivate character, wisdom, resilience, and ethical judgment. Philosophy would return to the classroom, alongside emotional intelligence, ancient wisdom, and civic engagement. Students would be prepared for life.

Alma's ocean is the future I envision. I know it is utopia—but the decision to work toward it will illuminate our path, and it is worth every step.

Daily life will test our commitment. The news will tempt us with despair. The aggression of others will challenge our inner peace. The systems we inhabit will try to bend us toward cynicism. That is why inner work is not a luxury—it is a necessity. It is what will keep us from betraying ourselves. It is what will allow us to see the world through new eyes. It is what will anchor us, again and again, in what truly matters.

32

A New Foundation for Systemic Change: Inner Work

If human values are the greatest lever for change—the roots of the world we want to build—then inner work is the act of planting and strengthening those roots until they grow deep, strong, and unshakable.

This practice is the foundation of the world I envision, because it allows us to see ourselves—and, by extension, the world—more clearly. Without self-awareness, we remain trapped in habitual patterns, driven by unconscious fears, desires, and social conditioning. Inner work brings these patterns to light, giving us the freedom to choose how we respond, rather than being dictated by them.

To me, turning inward through reflection, self-inquiry, mindfulness, meditation, prayer, journaling, or contemplation is to tend to our roots, to nourish our values so that they may flourish. It is to clear away illusion until the soul shines as it was meant to—until we learn to breathe with the universe. Until we dismantle the false barriers of perception and thought we have built over centuries. Until we recognise that we are not isolated fragments, but waves of the same vast ocean—deeply, beautifully interconnected.

There are many ways to cultivate this inner work. Some find their path through meditation, others through prayer, art, or time in nature. For me, the doorway has been the path of wisdom—the discipline we call Philosophy.

The Queen of the Sciences has opened me to reflection, meditation, and contemplation. This is the path I have chosen to walk, and the one I now share with you in the hope that it may enrich your own journey. But inner work is not confined to Ancient Philosophy, nor is there one path for all. What matters is not the form, but the essence—the honesty, the intention, the presence.

P. Ansoleaga Abascal, *Philosophy and Finance: A Love Story*,
https://doi.org/10.1007/978-3-032-22218-3_32

The ancients understood this well. For them, Philosophy was a compass for the soul—a discipline that shapes our character, orders our lives, and guides our actions when we are surrounded by uncertainty. As Seneca reminds us in his *Letters to Lucilius*, without Philosophy we are easily ruled by fear and restlessness; with it, we learn how to live with steadiness, courage, and inner peace.

As we cultivate awareness, we begin to notice the illusions we carry—the false stories we tell about ourselves, others, and the world around us. When these illusions fall away, what remains is a more authentic Self, no longer built on ego, insecurity, or the need for external validation.

From this authenticity grows genuine connection. Freed from the urge to seek approval or act from fear, we meet others with honesty, openness, and presence. We listen more deeply, without the impulse to impose our views. And in recognising our own struggles, we awaken to the shared human experience in others—and with it, a richer empathy, a fuller compassion, a truer sense of connection.

> *"Be kind, for everyone you meet is fighting a hard battle."* –a saying often attributed to ancient wisdom

The Stoics saw this process as part of **oikeiôsis**—the natural expansion of concern from the self to the broader human community. As we grow in self-awareness, we come to see ourselves as interconnected beings. We move from self-absorption to belonging.

Remember the metaphor of the waves—**Alma** and **Ega**? At first, like Ega, we see ourselves as separate. But through inner work, we come to recognize our true nature—as manifestations of the same vast ocean. With this awareness, oikeiôsis, agape, and love for all life naturally lead to a life of purpose and ethical action.

All ancient wisdom traditions tell us that Alma is far happier than Ega. And today, modern neuroscience is confirming what these traditions have long known. Science is catching up with ancient wisdom.

The **Harvard Study of Adult Development**—one of the longest-running studies on human happiness—has tracked participants since 1938. It found that the greatest predictor of happiness and well-being is not wealth, fame, or professional success. It is the quality of our relationships—strong, close connections that provide love, support, and belonging. Loneliness, by contrast, is as harmful to health as smoking or obesity. Warm and supportive bonds reduce stress, build resilience, and foster happiness.

Inner work also reconnects us with the rhythms of **nature**. It reminds us that we, too, are part of it. Just as a tree does not rush its growth, nor does the ocean resist its tides, we learn to embrace presence, patience, and flow. Have you ever seen a stressed surfer or a burned-out mountain climber? Nature quiets the relentless pressure to perform and achieve, allowing us to return to a state of *being* rather than constant *doing*.

Inner Work Helps Nurture Human Values

Human values are not external ideals imposed upon us. They are qualities we cultivate from within. Without inner work, these values remain abstract concepts rather than lived realities.

Wisdom arises from reflection and discernment, which inner work strengthens. **Justice** deepens when we examine our biases and learn to see beyond our limited perspectives. **Courage** grows when we confront our fears and insecurities, rather than being controlled by them. **Temperance** develops as we gain mastery over our impulses and desires, recognizing what truly nourishes us.

Without inner work, these values remain fragile. We might talk about justice but be blinded by our own unconscious biases. We might admire courage but be paralyzed by fear of failure or rejection. Inner work aligns our thoughts, words, and actions with our deepest values, making them integral to who we are.

Inner Work Is Not a Retreat—It's a Prerequisite for Change

There is a misconception that inner work is a retreat from the world, a withdrawal into oneself. In reality, it is the opposite. It is what allows us to engage with the world in a more meaningful, ethical, and impactful way. Without inner work, activism can become reactive, leadership can become ego-driven, and even good intentions can lead to unintended harm.

The transformation we seek in the world—greater justice, sustainability, and human flourishing—must begin within. When we cultivate clarity, resilience, and compassion within ourselves, we naturally bring those qualities into our relationships, communities, and systems. Inner work fosters the mindset shift we need: from hyper-individualism to connection, from mere survival to flourishing.

Inner work is the seed of justice, the soil of compassion, the wellspring of resilience. It is the current that carries us toward Alma's ocean.

33

A New Vision for Education: Paideia

In the future I envision, inner work becomes central to how we educate the next generation. In Alma's ocean, education no longer molds students for productivity alone; it nurtures wholeness. It cultivates not only intelligence but wisdom, not just knowledge but self-awareness, not only technical skills but also character. True education, in this future, nourishes the human spirit—fostering moral clarity, reflection, and a deep sense of interconnected purpose.

This vision draws from ancient wisdom. In Greece, **Paideia** was not merely instruction—it was the formation of character. It wove together philosophy, rhetoric, mathematics, and the arts to cultivate citizens capable of living wisely and well. **Arêtē**—excellence—was not a private ambition but a moral calling, the pursuit of virtue in harmony with the common good. At the centre stood Philosophy, guiding each learner toward self-knowledge and ethical living.

The Romans, in turn, inherited and reimagined this model through their ideal of **humanitas**: education as the cultivation of virtue, dignity, and civic responsibility. Cicero believed that true education shaped not only the intellect but the moral fabric of society—it was the foundation of justice itself.

Today, these classical ideals invite us to reimagine education once more—not as training for employment, but as preparation for life.

Modern education has drifted far from these classical ideals. It prizes technical proficiency and credentials over wisdom and meaning. Children are evaluated for their productivity rather than their potential—measured by what they can perform rather than what they can become, by grades rather than the depth of their thinking, by outcomes rather than the quality of their

P. Ansoleaga Abascal, *Philosophy and Finance: A Love Story*,
https://doi.org/10.1007/978-3-032-22218-3_33

character. From an early age, they are immersed in a system that rewards competition more than cooperation, performance more than presence.

Sociologically, this shift reflects a broader cultural drift: the reduction of human worth to measurable output. Psychologically, it breeds anxiety, perfectionism, and a fragile sense of identity—for **when value is tied to achievement, self-worth becomes conditional**. The result is a generation trained to excel, yet uncertain how to live.

Maria Montessori warned that while we speak endlessly about peace, we rarely educate for it. Education, she argued, too often rewards competition rather than cooperation—forgetting that rivalry is the seed of conflict. True education should cultivate peace—within ourselves and with one another. It should inspire excellence not as domination, but as contribution.

A Paideia-inspired education would restore virtue, empathy, and collaboration to the heart of learning. It would teach that success lies not in surpassing others, but in uplifting them. It would value critical thinking, creativity, and civic engagement as highly as technical proficiency.

Rather than divide science and the humanities, this renewed model would unite them. Science explains how the world works—but Philosophy and the arts remind us why it does, and why it matters. Education must form problem-solvers who are also ethical citizens—stewards of the common good.

Education, then, becomes a lifelong journey—one that embraces the development of mind, body, and soul. As the Stoics remind us, learning how to live is not a finite achievement but a task that lasts as long as life itself. Wisdom, reflection, emotional intelligence, and physical well-being are not extracurricular—they are essential.

Education is the foundation of leadership. In Discourses IV.1, Epictetus reminds us that human nature is fundamentally good—that we are social and affectionate beings, naturally drawn toward justice and what is morally worthy. Children are born aligned with this essence, but society often pulls them away. A holistic, virtue-based education can restore that alignment, guiding the leaders of tomorrow toward wisdom, courage, and purpose.

With Philosophy as our compass and a Paideia-inspired education as our map, we can nurture not only brilliant minds but also noble hearts. This is how we build a future where leadership seeks to serve—and where capital is a means to elevate the human spirit.

34

A New Perspective on Progress: Da Vinci's Systems Thinking

"Study the science of art. Study the art of science. Develop your senses, especially learn how to see. Realize that everything connects to everything else." –Leonardo da Vinci (commonly attributed)

Leonardo da Vinci saw the interconnectedness of all things. He approached the world with boundless curiosity, blending disciplines that others kept apart. For him, art illuminated science, and science enriched art—each revealing patterns and truths hidden to those who had not yet "learned how to see."

Nikole Bozza Ansoleaga

P. Ansoleaga Abascal, *Philosophy and Finance: A Love Story*,
https://doi.org/10.1007/978-3-032-22218-3_34

This vision is no less relevant today than it was in Renaissance Florence. Consider finance and Philosophy—two realms often thought to stand worlds apart. Yet through Leonardo's lens, they are profoundly complementary. Philosophy can illuminate finance, guiding it toward wisdom and ethical progress. Finance, in turn, can enrich Philosophy by grounding its ideals in action and tangible impact.

Together, they offer a way to design systems where prosperity is built on on purpose, humanity, and care for the planet.

All great minds, past and present, embrace systems thinking, a way of seeing that acknowledges the interconnectedness of all things. Long before the term existed, ancient sages understood its power. The Stoics, for example, taught that living well means living in alignment with nature. For them, this meant recognizing that human beings are part of a larger rational and moral order—the cosmos governed by the logos, a universal principle of reason believed to structure and connect all things. Our flourishing, they believed, depends on acting with wisdom, justice, and care for the whole. Concepts such as **oikeiosis**—our natural inclination to care for others—**cosmopolitanism**, and **altruism** reflect a deep awareness of interdependence.

This insight appears across many wisdom traditions. In Buddhism, the principle of interdependence is expressed through the concept of **pratītyasamutpāda**, often translated as dependent origination—the idea that all phenomena arise through relationships and conditions rather than existing independently. In Indigenous worldviews across the Americas, humans are understood as part of a living web that includes animals, rivers, forests, and future generations. Confucian philosophy similarly emphasizes relational harmony, reminding us that individual flourishing is inseparable from the well-being of the community. Different cultures, different languages, yet the same insight emerges again and again: **everything connects.**

Finance today desperately needs this mindset. Too often, it operates in a fragmented way, or as Jed Emerson insightfully describes, in a bifurcated way. In this paradigm, the world is divided: we either invest for profit or for purpose. We either pursue financial gain, or we commit to social or environmental good—as if the two must exist in separate spheres. It's a dichotomy that has shaped modern capitalism, one that reduces value to a single metric: **return on investment.**

But value is not one-dimensional. As Emerson argues, true value is blended. It is not neatly split into financial, social, and environmental silos—it is integrated, interdependent, and holistic. Every investment generates multiple forms of value, whether we acknowledge them or not. Emerson's concept of

Blended Value calls us to recognize this reality—that the financial, social, and environmental dimensions of any enterprise are intrinsically linked.

When we embrace this shift **from bifurcated thinking to blended thinking**, we begin to ask deeper, wiser questions: not just *"What is the financial return?"* but *"What kind of world is this investment creating?"* Not just *"What can I extract?"* but *"What can I contribute?"* We understand that true wealth is measured not only in profits, but in purpose. Not just in numbers, but in lives improved, ecosystems restored, and dignity upheld.

Leonardo da Vinci's way of seeing invites us to break down artificial barriers between disciplines, goals, and values. Just as he sketched flying machines while studying anatomy, and painted masterpieces informed by mathematics, we too can design a financial system that sees the full picture. One that does not fragment reality, but integrates it. One that redefines progress not as growth for its own sake, but as the flourishing of all life. This is the path from bifurcation to wholeness. From separation to synthesis. From ego-system logic to ecosystem awareness. And it begins with learning how to see.

> *"The real voyage of discovery consists not in seeking new landscapes, but in having new eyes."*
> *–Marcel Proust, In Search of Lost Time (À la recherche du temps perdu), vol. 5, La Prisonnière*

Marcel Proust's insight underscores the transformative power of perspective. Our actions are shaped by how we see the world. Finance, when seen through a new lens, is part of a greater whole—a system influenced by historical, cultural, social, and ecological forces. By shifting our perception, we shift our actions, aligning capital with values that sustain humanity and the planet.

35

A New Vision for Economics: Alma's Economy

If we dare to see with new eyes, we might also dare to build with new hands—crafting systems of regeneration. This is where *Alma's Economy* begins.

For decades, we've been told there is no alternative. No alternative to neoclassical orthodoxy, to deregulation, privatization, low taxes, and an unwavering belief in market efficiency—the conviction that prosperity will eventually trickle down and lift all boats. We have built entire systems around a narrow, outdated vision of human nature: ***homo economicus***—a being driven purely by self-interest, rational calculation, and predictable behaviour.

But reality has shattered that illusion. The Global Financial Crisis exposed the fragility of unchecked markets. A pandemic laid bare the human cost of economic inequality. Climate change continues to endanger the most vulnerable. The pursuit of endless growth is pushing us beyond the limits of our planet. The promise of prosperity for all has failed too many. According to Oxfam, the richest 1% now own more wealth than the bottom 95% of the world's population combined. This statistic is morally indefensible. The system has failed the majority.

We need a new vision for economics—one that acknowledges our interdependence and serves both people and planet. An economy not built solely on growth, efficiency, and profit, but also on justice, inclusion, and purpose. We need **Alma's Economy**—the economy that will emerge when we embrace our human values, commit to inner work, and choose to live a philosophical life. An economy shaped by Paideia-inspired education, one that cultivates a new generation of visionary economists, entrepreneurs, investors and teachers. A circular, regenerative, inclusive economy that restores dignity and opportunity to every child, no matter where they are born.

P. Ansoleaga Abascal, *Philosophy and Finance: A Love Story*,
https://doi.org/10.1007/978-3-032-22218-3_35

This vision is not new. It has been given many names: stakeholder capitalism, sustainable economics, inclusive economics, doughnut economics. Let us call it Alma's Economy—to keep it free from ideology and political baggage. Let us name it after the soul of what truly matters.

Alma's Economy Will Open Its Doors

It will open its doors to Philosophy, to History, to the Natural Sciences.
It will open its doors to diversity of thought.
It will open its doors to a richer understanding of the human being, beyond *homo economicus*.
It will open its doors to new metrics, beyond GDP.
It will open its doors to an eudaimonic vision of happiness, beyond the Hedonic Treadmill.
And it will restore to Adam Smith the justice he deserves.

Alma's Economy will open its door to Philosophy. Economics will widen its lens, moving beyond technical efficiency to moral inquiry. Economists will no longer be mere technocrats, fixated on models and productivity, but moral thinkers—asking what kind of society we want to build, what justice demands, and what true prosperity looks like.

Alma's Economy will open its door to History. It will gain both humility and wisdom. It will remember that economic systems are not natural laws, but human creations—imperfect, evolving, and subject to revision. If past models have failed, or if they brought progress but left injustice in their wake, we can—and must—learn from those lessons.

Alma's Economy will open its door to the Natural Sciences. Economics will no longer treat nature as an externality but as its very foundation. Policies will be designed within planetary boundaries, guided by climate science, biodiversity, and the urgent need to regenerate the ecosystems that sustain us. Extractive systems will give way to circular ones, ensuring that prosperity is not built on depletion.

Alma's Economy will open its door to diversity of thought. Like the ancient Stoa Poikile, it will welcome all voices. The most vulnerable must have a seat at the table. By embracing diversity across gender, class, culture, and indigenous wisdom, our economy will serve the cosmopolis—not just the privileged few. An inclusive economy will work toward shared flourishing.

Alma's Economy will open its door to a new understanding of the human being.

For too long, we have accepted a narrow, impoverished vision of human nature—a vision embodied by **Homo Oeconomicus**, the rational, self-interested actor, endlessly optimizing for individual gain. This archetype has shaped our systems—economic, financial, educational—embedding the belief that selfishness is natural, and altruism a rare exception.

But this idea is incomplete. It flattens our complexity and erases our innate capacity for connection. It tells only a sliver of the human story. **In Alma's Economy, we reclaim the full spectrum of our nature.** Psychology, evolutionary biology, and anthropology offer a richer view. Yes, self-interest exists—but so does something far greater. We are not just Homo Oeconomicus. We are **Homo Cooperativus, Homo Empathicus, Homo Ethicus**. We are beings who thrive through trust, compassion, and shared purpose. We are Almas—and we can build Alma's ocean.

Human history is not simply a chronicle of competition; it is a testament to the power of cooperation. Reciprocal altruism, kin selection, and group collaboration have been vital to our survival and flourishing. Mirror neurons allow us to feel the joy and suffering of others as if it were our own. Moral reasoning empowers us to rise above short-term gain and act for the common good. Mutual aid and collective wisdom—not just rivalry—are what built the civilizations we call home.

Aristotle's **Zōon Politikon**—his vision of humans as inherently social and political beings—rings truer than ever. We do not exist in isolation. We create meaning, share resources, and shape futures together. We flourish not in spite of others, but because of them.

By embracing a philosophical life, we begin to see ourselves clearly—as interconnected beings, waves of the same ocean. From that clarity flows transformation. When we remember who we truly are, we redefine what matters. We reimagine what progress means. We see wealth not as accumulation, but as flourishing. Not as power over others, but as harmony with life.

We begin to build Alma's Economy—an economy that honours our highest nature. One rooted not in fear and scarcity, but in trust and abundance. One that sees success not in individual ascent, but in collective well-being.

The Streetlight and the Lost Key

There is an old Sufi parable about a man called Nasrudin. One night Nasrudin is searching for his lost key under a streetlight. A passerby asks whether he lost it there.

"No," Nasrudin replies, "I lost it somewhere in the darkness."

"Then why search here?"

"Because here there is light."

Nikole Bozza Ansoleaga

The story carries a simple but uncomfortable truth: we often search not where the answers lie, but where it is easiest to look. Economics has sometimes fallen into the same trap.

For nearly a century, **Gross Domestic Product (GDP)** has been the world's dominant measure of economic success. It determines policy decisions, shapes financial markets, and influences how we perceive national power and progress. Governments strive to maximise it, and even the slightest fluctuation in GDP growth can trigger financial turmoil. But while our world has evolved, our economic indicators have not kept pace.

GDP is, at best, an incomplete measure. It captures the total value of goods and services produced but tells us little about the quality of life, well-being, or sustainability of that growth. GDP does not account for the things we cherish most—our sense of safety, the beauty of our landscapes, the purity of our water, or the strength of our social fabric. It assigns the same value to €100 spent on weapons as it does to €100 spent on a child's education. It considers environmental destruction invisible. It disregards the unpaid care work that sustains families and communities—work often performed by women. It measures production but ignores the depletion of resources, the erosion of social trust, and the fragility of ecosystems.

Even as a purely economic statistic, GDP is flawed. It focuses on the present while neglecting the future. Today's production can exhaust natural capital, widen inequality, and destabilise societies, yet GDP fails to register these costs. It counts extraction but not depletion, growth but not sustainability, wealth but not its distribution.

Like Nasrudin, modern economics is searching under the streetlight. Philosophy invites us to search where the truth actually lies—and to develop new metrics that measure and safeguard our planet's true wealth.

This is what Alma's economy will do. **Alma's Economy will open its door to new metrics to assess our planet's true wealth.** It will use complimentary metrics that give a more complete picture of our planet's wealth and our well-being. Metrics that capture long-term well-being, environmental health, and social cohesion.

Metrics such as Net Domestic Product (NDP), which improves upon GDP by accounting for depreciation—the wear and tear on infrastructure, machinery, and technology. This helps us assess whether economic growth is genuine or merely consuming existing resources.

Comprehensive Wealth goes even further. Unlike GDP, which focuses on immediate production, Comprehensive Wealth assesses whether a nation is building or depleting its long-term prosperity. It measures not just Produced Capital (factories, roads, machinery), but also:

Human Capital—the education, skills, and health of the workforce.
Natural Capital—forests, minerals, freshwater, biodiversity.
Social Capital—trust, institutions, governance, and social cohesion.

The **Human Development Index (HDI)**, introduced by the United Nations, shifts the focus from production to people, measuring well-being through health, education, and income. The **Genuine Progress Indicator (GPI)** takes this even further. It adjusts for environmental and social costs, ensuring that factors like pollution, inequality, and resource depletion are reflected in economic assessments. The **Inclusive Wealth Index (IWI)** integrates multiple dimensions of wealth—natural, human, and produced capital—to evaluate whether a nation is truly securing prosperity for future generations.

These are just a few examples. **Bhutan's Gross National Happiness index** measures the country's progress based on well-being. Recently, Bhutan introduced the **Gelephu Mindfulness City project**, integrating ecological harmony and spiritual contentment into its economic development strategy.

90 years ago, we lacked the tools to measure these things. Today, we can. Advances in artificial intelligence, big data, satellite remote sensing, drone surveillance, and air quality monitoring now allow us to assess economies in ways that were once unimaginable. AI can track ecosystem degradation, measuring the true value of natural capital and the cost of human impact on the planet. With these tools, Alma's economy moves beyond outdated economic indicators and creates a future where progress is measured not just by how much we produce, but by how well we care for people, nature, and the fabric of our societies.

The **World Happiness Report 2024** proves that economic success alone does not determine well-being. While GDP per capita is one of the indicators, the report also evaluates social support, healthy life expectancy, freedom to make life choices, generosity, and perceptions of corruption—highlighting the broader dimensions of human flourishing. In fact, **the happiest countries—Finland, Denmark, Iceland, Sweden, Norway, and the Netherlands—rank highest not because of their economic strength alone, but because they foster strong communal support, mutual trust, and minimal corruption.** These societies prioritise social cohesion, ensuring that people feel secure, valued, and free to shape their own lives. They are also among the most economically and gender-equal nations in the world.

The United States, the world's wealthiest country, ranks only 23rd in happiness. This challenges the assumption that economic power alone guarantees well-being. While the U.S. has immense financial resources, its wealth is not evenly distributed, and deeper societal challenges—inequality, violence, mental health struggles, weapons proliferation, poor work-life balance, and chronic stress—seem to erode overall happiness. The ranking suggests a profound lesson: money alone does not buy happiness. Economic growth matters, but so do trust, equality, security, and well-being. The happiest countries invest in universal healthcare, education, work-life balance, and social safety nets—prioritising collective stability over pure financial gain.

This is not utopia. **This is the economy we can create. The technical solutions exist. The tools to measure progress beyond GDP are already at our disposal. What we need now is the will to embrace them**, the wisdom to redefine what we value, and the courage to align our policies with what truly enriches life.

The way we define economic success shapes the policies, investments, and structures that govern our lives. And as the saying goes, ***what gets measured***

gets done. If we measure only GDP, we will prioritise production and consumption at the expense of well-being, equality, and environmental sustainability. But if we expand our economic indicators, we can design policies that foster human flourishing, social cohesion, and planetary health. To build Alma's ocean together. This shift is already happening. Countries like New Zealand, Rwanda, and others are prioritising well-being and sustainability alongside financial growth.

Under **Jacinda Ardern**'s leadership, New Zealand introduced the **Well-Being Budget**, redefining national success beyond GDP. Rather than focusing solely on short-term economic expansion, the government allocated resources to mental health, child poverty reduction, indigenous well-being, and environmental sustainability—recognising that a thriving economy is inseparable from human and ecological health.

Rwanda, meanwhile, has embraced a systems-based approach to governance, integrating environmental sustainability with social equity. With the highest percentage of women in government globally, the country has implemented bold sustainability policies, including nationwide bans on plastic bags, large-scale reforestation, and circular economy investments. By prioritising regeneration over extraction, Rwanda offers a compelling vision of leadership that understands the deep interconnections between governance, ecology, and economic resilience.

Beyond these examples, other nations are also leading the way. **Bhutan's Gross National Happiness index, Finland's Economy of Well-Being strategy, Iceland and Scotland's participation in the Wellbeing Economy Governments initiative, and Wales's Well-being of Future Generations** Act reflect a global movement toward Alma's understanding of progress. In Alma's economy, the invisible hand of the market is guided by its visible heart. We have the tools to redefine success. What remains is the will to use them—to align our policies and investments with what truly enriches life.

Alma's Economy will restore Adam Smith the justice he merits. Too often remembered only as the father of free-market capitalism, Adam Smith deserves to be seen in the full light of his legacy—not merely as an economist, but as a moral philosopher. Alma's Economy will reclaim his thought in its wholeness, rescuing his name from the narrow corridors of self-interest and competition to which it has too long been confined.

Smith's two seminal works—***The Theory of Moral Sentiments (1759)*** and ***The Wealth of Nations (1776)***—are often seen as contradictory: one centred on virtue and empathy, the other on markets and self-interest. But this is a false dichotomy. Read together, they form a coherent vision of a society where economic life is inseparable from moral life. To isolate *The Wealth of Nations* from *The Theory of Moral Sentiments* is to misread Smith entirely.

Modern economics, in its pursuit of abstraction and efficiency, has often reduced Smith to a caricature—homo economicus in powdered wig. But Smith was not a prophet of greed. He never championed markets devoid of ethics. On the contrary, he understood that markets require moral foundations—trust, fairness, reciprocity—to function well and justly. For him, prosperity without virtue was failure.

In *The Theory of Moral Sentiments*, Smith introduced the idea of the impartial spectator—an inner moral compass, an imagined observer who evaluates our actions from a place of fairness and wisdom. To me, this is a profound call to moral consciousness—a reminder that we are not just economic agents, but ethical beings. Alma sees it that way too.

Smith's legacy is not merely about ***the invisible hand of the market***, but the ***visible heart of humanity***. His vision was one of a commercial society governed by empathy, prudence, and justice. He believed in innovation, yes—but innovation in service of human flourishing.

Alma's Economy will honour this legacy—not by rejecting markets, but by anchoring them in moral purpose. It will celebrate commerce that uplifts communities. It will foster entrepreneurship guided by integrity. It will remember that true wealth is not measured in output alone, but in the depth of well-being it creates. Smith understood that economics is not a science of numbers—it is a science of life. Alma does too.

This is Alma's Economy.

An economy where young people can dream again, unburdened by the fear that opportunity belongs only to the privileged. Where parents are not consumed by anxiety over putting food on the table, and prosperity is not a fragile promise, but a shared and living reality.

It is a world where emerging nations in Africa and South America no longer face the impossible choice between repaying crushing debt or lifting their people from poverty. Where markets serve humanity—never the other way around. Where societies are not asked to trade economic growth for human dignity, but are shaped by both. It is an economy where we no longer ask whether we can afford to fight climate change—but recognize that we cannot afford not to. Where the air is clean, the soil alive, and the waters protected for generations yet to come. Where life expectancy rises. Where well-being is built in communities rooted in care, trust, and inclusion. Where democracy is not eroded by digital division, but renewed by shared purpose and collective wisdom.

This is Alma's Economy. An economy that restores balance. That reclaims our deepest values. That reminds us of what we have always known: prosperity is not measured by accumulation, but by dignity. By opportunity. By well-being—for all. It is the world we begin to build when we dare to dream again.

36

A New Approach to Life: From the Hedonic Treadmill to Eudaemonia

Within Alma's Economy—within the broader transformation I envision—there is one subject so close to my heart that it calls for a chapter of its own: the persistent **illusion of more**. An illusion so deeply woven into our culture that we barely notice its grip—yet it shapes how we live, work, spend, and dream.

We briefly touched on this in Block 3, when historian Yuval Noah Harari insightfully noted that capitalism and consumerism have evolved beyond economic systems—they have become modern belief structures, so deeply embedded in our consciousness that we hardly recognize them as such. Like prisoners in Plato's cave, we mistake shadows for reality.

The illusion of more—fuelled by consumerism and materialism—is one of the greatest threats to both our inner peace and our planet. It keeps us trapped in a cycle of endless striving, convincing us that happiness lies just beyond the next purchase, promotion, or milestone. But this chase is insatiable, a treadmill with no exit. It disconnects us from what truly matters and blinds us to the beauty of the present moment.

It is no coincidence that rates of anxiety, burnout, and loneliness have surged in the very societies that are materially wealthiest. The more we accumulate, the more elusive contentment becomes. We are told to dream big, reach higher, and never settle—yet few of us ask: *at what cost?* The **illusion of more** consumes not only our lives, but our planet's finite resources. It erodes community, weakens empathy, and leaves us perpetually unsatisfied.

I have witnessed the rise of this illusion within my own lifetime. Whether it is the world that has changed, or simply that I now live in a large city where this belief system is amplified, I cannot say for certain. Perhaps smaller

P. Ansoleaga Abascal, *Philosophy and Finance: A Love Story*,
https://doi.org/10.1007/978-3-032-22218-3_36

communities still hold on to something more grounded. Something I would like to believe is not yet lost.

And so, in this chapter, I want to pause and reflect on this illusion—how it shapes our desires, how it steals our joy, and how we might, at last, step off the treadmill and reclaim what is profoundly ours: **the freedom to live a meaningful life.**

I grew up between Bilbao—where we spent weekdays—and Sopela, a small seaside town 20 kilometres away, where we spent most weekends. Looking back, I realize these places were small bubbles of integrity and authenticity. Friendships were built on laughter, shared stories, and genuine affection, untouched by utility or status. I still have the same group of friends in Bilbao since I was three years old, and in Sopela since I was nine. For that, I am deeply grateful—they are among my greatest treasures.

I excelled in school, high school, and university, where I pursued a degree in industrial engineering. My studies and career opportunities led me across cities and cultures—Copenhagen, Madrid, Paris, London, Lugano, and finally Milan, where I now live.

Paris was a turning point. I moved there to pursue an MBA and quickly fell in love with the city—not just its beauty, but its essence. I cherished wine and cheese picnics on the Pont des Arts and along the Canal Saint-Martin, enchanted by the depth of French conversation. The people I met were not only knowledgeable but also incredibly welcoming, eager to discuss art, history, and philosophy with a passion that felt second nature to them. There was a richness in their intellectual culture—an effortless intertwining of ideas and daily life—that captivated me.

But something struck me. In social settings, the very first question people asked was, **Que fais-tu dans la vie?** (What do you do for a living?). It caught me off guard. In Bilbao, that question would have come twelfth, maybe even twentieth—never first. There, people wanted to know who you were, not what you did.

Months later, on the trading floor in London, private conversations revolved around expensive bags, Michelin-starred restaurants, and extravagant holidays. I remember a stunning Moldovan colleague confiding in me that she had started dating a man with a Ferrari but was not sure if she should marry him. I was speechless—*Marrying someone you don't know?*

I felt like an outsider sometimes. My instinctive reaction? To fit in. I started frequenting the same restaurants, buying the same designer bags. And yet, each time, I noticed how fleeting these pleasures were—happiness, or rather excitement (though at the time, I mistook it for happiness), lasted from five minutes to half an hour, followed by an enduring emptiness. No problem,

I told myself. I will be happy when I get promoted, when I perfect my financial skills, when I reach this or that milestone.

Luckily, my generous, wise and beautiful mother saw what was happening and placed Epictetus in my hands. Suddenly, everything made sense. His words cut through the noise, reminding me of who I truly was—of my authentic Bilbao years, where friendships were built on laughter, not titles, labels or expensive brands; where worth was measured in kindness, not careers. I was free again. I did not need to fit in anywhere. I was ready to feed my *Eagle* again.

I tell this story because, too often, I feel we live in a transactional, utilitarian world—one where relationships, whether friendships, professional connections, or romantic partnerships, are often chosen for their utility rather than for love, authenticity, or true affinity. People assess their worth through external markers—their job title, income, family's social position, physical appearance—and, based on this *assessment*, they calculate how *high* they can aim. As if human connection were a marketplace, as if the richness of a soul could be measured in status, sizes or euros.

The result? Relationships that are transactional rather than authentic. Marriages that fall apart because they were built on convenience rather than love. Friendships that remain shallow because they were chosen for networking rather than true affinity or shared values.

One of the greatest gifts Philosophy has given me is new eyes—**Alma's eyes**. A complete shift in how I see life, and the ability to find the extraordinary in the ordinary. Among the many perceptions that have changed within me, one has been my understanding of success.

To me, truly successful people do not necessarily have important titles or luxury possessions. They have big hearts, authentic friendships, and inner peace. They are free thinkers. Free spirits. They live in the present moment. They do not conform to society's expectations but think and act for themselves, with great passion, and with the intention of leaving the world a little better than they found it. They remind me of my childhood in Bilbao.

They are those whom the poet Gioconda Belli once called the bearers of dreams—**Los portadores de sueños.** The ones who refuse to accept the world as it is. Who carry visions quietly, stubbornly, tenderly. Who plant hope where others see only barren ground.

They are the ones who do not surrender to cynicism or despair. Who light small fires in dark places.

Who mend what is broken. Who remind us—simply by the way they live—that kindness is a force, that love is an act of courage, and that imagination can still shape reality.

They are the Almas.

The Eliahus.
The Da Vincis.
The Lumeras.
The Hadots.
The ones who believe.
The ones who build.
The ones who never stop.

And yet, so many of us remain caught in a different paradigm: in the relentless pursuit of more. In Plato's cave. We are addicted to the next dopamine hit—whether through social media, consumerism, or status-driven achievements. We have become slaves to fleeting pleasures, constantly chasing new highs that ultimately leave us feeling empty.

Dr. Anna Lembke explores this in **Dopamine Nation**, explaining how modern life overstimulates our pleasure circuits, leading to addiction-like behaviours. We believe the next purchase, promotion, or milestone will finally bring lasting happiness, but we are simply feeding an insatiable cycle.

William Irvine, one of my favourite modern Stoic thinkers, calls this the **hedonic treadmill**—the psychological trap where each external success quickly becomes the new baseline, leaving us perpetually dissatisfied and craving more. We tell ourselves; I will be happy when I lose five kilos. When I get a promotion. When I go on my next holiday. Yet the moment we achieve these goals; our minds simply reset the finish line.

Ancient philosophers warned against this cycle of insatiable desire. The Stoics and Epicureans understood that the endless pursuit of external achievements is not only unsustainable for the planet but corrosive to our inner peace. Instead, they advocated for **eudaemonia**—a flourishing life grounded in virtue, wisdom, and contentment with what is truly necessary. Unlike the fragile happiness that depends on external circumstances, eudaemonia is resilient, deeply rooted in who we are rather than what we acquire or achieve.

The relentless pursuit of more is not just a personal struggle; it is a systemic issue threatening planetary sustainability. The Earth Commission warns that environmental degradation and climate instability, driven by excessive consumption, have pushed us beyond safe planetary boundaries. I am not saying we must suddenly become modern *Diogenes*, living with next to nothing—but we can embrace Stoic temperance, **Aristotle's Golden Mean**. We can redefine success. We can embrace a more balanced way of living, one that prioritizes well-being over excess.

In the future I envision, in Alma's ocean, we transition **from a hedonic life of fleeting pleasure to a eudaemonic life of lasting fulfilment**. We stop consuming blindly and start living intentionally. We shift from chasing external validation to cultivating inner peace, from measuring our worth in titles and possessions to finding meaning in who we are and how we contribute to the world. We step off the treadmill of endless striving and into a life of deeper purpose, harmony, and connection. In Alma's ocean, we do not define ourselves by what we do, but by the depth of our character, the love we give, and the wisdom we cultivate. We remember that our value has never resided in status or accumulation—it has always been in our capacity to grow, to serve, and to honour the vast, immeasurable greatness within us.

37

A New Vision for Finance: Alma's Financial System

I envision a financial industry where every investment is assessed through the lens of impact—Da Vinci's lens. Alma's lens. A world where capital—more than $300 trillion of it—flows not just toward profit, but toward meaningful, measurable, and lasting transformation. A world where every investment is an impact investment. I envision Alma's financial industry.

A financial system built on sound infrastructure, where the measurement of social and environmental impact is as rigorous as the measurement of risk and return. Where investors rely on transparent company reports not only to track financial gains, but to understand the deeper ripples their investments create. A financial system unshackled from rigid labels—no longer confined to ESG, impact-first, or finance-first silos—but embracing a holistic, integrated, as Jed Emerson would put it, *blended* approach. One that sees financial performance and social and environmental impact as inseparable. As whole. One that recognises that **impact is relational**, as are all economic and financial transactions.

I envision a financial industry shaped by people with a relational and systemic mindset. Investors who have shifted from transactional thinking—focused on maximising short-term gain while minimising risk—to a perspective rooted in interconnectedness, in Alma's ocean. In risk, return, and impact.

Investors guided by the Stoic virtues: **wisdom, courage, temperance, and justice**. Investors who have awakened to **Oikeiōsis**—the Stoic recognition that our well-being is tied to the well-being of others. Investors moved by **Agapē**—the highest form of love—not just for their families or their stakeholders, but for humanity, mother Earth and all its wonderful living beings.

P. Ansoleaga Abascal, *Philosophy and Finance: A Love Story*,
https://doi.org/10.1007/978-3-032-22218-3_37

Investors who understand that every investment carries moral weight. Who refuse to treat impact as a niche category or a trend, but as a fundamental responsibility. And most importantly, investors who understand that impact is not a one-directional act of benevolence—it is a reciprocal transformation. This idea is central to me. It was **Jed Emerson** who gave it language: **mutual impact**—perhaps the most profound concept in all of impact investing. The truth that the deeper transformation begins in relationship.

Too often, impact investing is framed as something we do for *others*—measured in the number of lives improved, emissions reduced, or jobs created. But Emerson reminds us that true impact is never one-sided. When we engage in work that heals, uplifts, and regenerates, we ourselves are changed. Our perspectives expand. Our priorities evolve. Our values deepen. Our lives improve. Mutual impact reveals that investing for good is not a sacrifice—it is a source of meaning.

This is the essence of Alma's ocean: interconnected, relational, flowing with shared responsibility and dignity. A place where capital is not merely allocated, but awakened. Where finance ceases to be just a mechanism and becomes a force for human flourishing.

A place where investors are anchored by an unshakable commitment to the greater good. Investors who pass **Socrates' doctor test.**

Let me explain what I mean by that.

Today, unfortunately, **the industry I work in reveals a troubling gap between rhetoric and reality.**

In recent years, the financial world has embraced an ambitious narrative: that it can be a driver of solutions to our most urgent global challenges. *Responsible, sustainable, and impact* investing promise to address climate change, inequality, and poverty—all while delivering competitive returns. This is more than a passing trend; it reflects a growing awareness that every financial decision carries impact—and with impact comes moral responsibility.

And yet, despite this promising shift, a disquieting disconnect remains. Lofty commitments and polished sustainability reports often conceal business-as-usual practices. In financial jargon, this is called **greenwashing** (when companies exaggerate or misrepresent their environmental credentials), **impact-washing** (claims of social or environmental benefit made without real accountability) or **pink-washing** (invoking gender equity for marketing purposes while failing to enact meaningful change). These practices do not just dilute progress—they erode public trust.

Let me offer a few examples.

Take the actions of financial institutions. Despite their public commitments to a net-zero future—and the high ESG ratings they receive in return—major banks have funnelled over **$4.6 trillion into fossil fuel financing** since the 2015 Paris Agreement. These investments are not just sustaining the status quo; they are actively funding projects that devastate fragile ecosystems like the Arctic and the Amazon (Source: *Banking on Chaos*). This contradiction weakens their green pledges, deepens scepticism, and erodes the industry's credibility.

The same pattern emerges in impact investing. While designed to uplift vulnerable communities, many investment strategies fail to include those very communities in decision-making. Capital often flows **to** them, but not **with** them. Without their voices at the table, investments risk reinforcing existing power imbalances rather than dismantling them.

Meanwhile, in the corporate world, sustainability pledges continue to outpace action. Today, 92% of global GDP is covered by some form of net-zero commitment. Yet only 4% of companies have a complete and transparent plan to achieve these goals (**New York Times, "Stakeholder Capitalism Gets a Report Card"**). The result? A growing wave of disillusionment, as bold promises too often dissolve into inaction. And just recently, I was deeply saddened by a report in the Financial Times. More than 200 of America's largest companies have removed references to "diversity, equity, and inclusion" from their annual reports—a rapid and calculated retreat from values they once claimed to champion. Why? Because the political landscape shifted. *Are our values so fragile that they bend with the winds of political convenience?*

If finance is to play a meaningful role in shaping a better world, it cannot be dictated by political cycles, market trends, or PR strategies. It must be anchored in something deeper—**an unwavering commitment to people, planet, and the principles of a just and regenerative economy**. In our human values. This is why *inner work* is essential for financial professionals.

In Alma's ocean, we do not settle for rebranding financial markets with moral slogans like **"People, Planet, Profits."** Instead, we undertake a profound rethinking of how finance interacts with society and the environment. Alma's financial industry—the fuel of our car—will drive systemic change, as finance once did in dismantling South Africa's apartheid.

Alma's Industry Will Pass Socrates' Doctor Test

This brings to mind one of Socrates' most beautiful analogies: **the pastry chef versus the doctor.** A perfect illustration of the tension between comforting rhetoric and uncomfortable truth.

Socrates drew a sharp distinction between **rhetoric**—the art of persuasion, often used to flatter or deceive—and **Philosophy**, which seeks wisdom, justice, and the common good. He criticised the **Sophists** for using rhetoric to win arguments rather than to uncover truth.

In **Gorgias**, Socrates compares rhetoric to **pastry-making** and Philosophy to **medicine**. The pastry chef gives us what we want—sweetness, pleasure, praise. The doctor gives us what we need—bitter truths that heal, even when they are hard to swallow.

The pastry chef tells us what we want to hear—just as companies and investors sell sustainability promises that require little sacrifice. The doctor tells us what we need to hear—urging us to face difficult realities, invest differently, and redefine our relationship with profit.

Pastry, like rhetoric, is instantly gratifying. It appeals to desire, not to health. It feeds pleasure, not well-being. Likewise, many investors proclaim, "*We invest to change the world*," while continuing to fund the very industries that are destroying it.

Medicine, like Philosophy, is different. It is rarely sweet. It demands honesty, effort, discipline—and sometimes sacrifice.
Medicine is refusing to finance new fossil-fuel projects, especially new oil and gas drilling.
Medicine is putting a real price on carbon.
Medicine is integrating climate risk into every investment decision.
Medicine is accepting lower short-term returns, when necessary, to create lasting impact alongside long-term value.

Socrates understood our tendency to choose sugar over substance, comfort over truth. We see this today in the appeal of *finance-first* impact investing, which offers moral validation without requiring transformation. But as Socrates warned, indulging in what pleases us at the expense of what strengthens us weakens both the soul and society. Excess sugar damages the body; empty rhetoric corrodes trust. Greenwashing and impact-washing disillusion the public and erode the credibility of the industry.

The intersection of finance and morality holds extraordinary promise. But in Alma's ocean, it must be medicine, not pastry—Philosophy, not rhetoric; a structural shift, not a slogan; a return to truth, not a performance of virtue.

This is the Socratic test for impact investing.

In Alma's ocean, finance does not indulge in rhetoric. It embraces truth. And so, my invitation is **to reconnect Philosophy and finance, to embrace inner work so that our outer actions are authentic. Only then can finance pass Socrates' test—and become the force for transformation we so urgently need.**

The Forces Advancing the Impact Revolution

As **Sir Ronald Cohen**—one of the pioneers of impact investing—insightfully argues, three powerful forces are propelling us toward Alma's financial industry. Toward what he calls the Impact Revolution. These forces are: **changing values, technological innovation, and radical transparency.**

Cohen believes that finance is undergoing a transformation as profound as the Industrial or Technological Revolutions. But this time, it is not machinery or code driving the shift—it is **values**. It is the demand for meaning alongside money. It is **technology** that enables us to measure what matters. And it is **transparency** that makes the invisible visible—holding businesses accountable not only for their profits, but for their impact.

Together, these forces are reshaping industries, redirecting capital, and redefining the very purpose of business. And as they gather momentum, they carry Alma's vision forward: toward a financial system where every investment is assessed not only by what it earns, but by what it elevates—for people, for the planet, for future generations.

Values

A generational shift is underway. Younger generations are no longer satisfied with financial success alone—they're searching for meaning. As investors, employees, and consumers, they're becoming more intentional about whom they support, gravitating toward companies that align with their values and walking away from those that harm society or the environment.

But this shift is not confined to the young. Across the board, investors are beginning to see that long-term success demands more than profits—it demands responsibility. With more than $40 trillion now invested in ESG funds, the signal is clear: the **why** behind capital matters more than ever.

Technology

Technology is the great enabler of this revolution. Artificial intelligence, machine learning, blockchain, and big data are opening powerful new pathways for delivering, measuring, and scaling impact with precision and reach.

Financial inclusion is one of its most remarkable frontiers. Today, billions of unbanked individuals are gaining access to credit, insurance, and digital banking—often for the first time. AI-driven microfinance platforms are extending loans to small business owners once deemed "unbankable." Blockchain-based decentralized finance (DeFi) is lowering costs and bypassing traditional barriers. With nothing more than a smartphone, a farmer, a vendor, or a student can begin to save, invest, and shape their future.

Technology is also revolutionizing access to energy. Acumen, founded by **Jacqueline Novogratz**, exemplifies this through its **Hardest-to-Reach (H2R) Initiative**—a $250 million project bringing clean energy to remote areas of sub-Saharan Africa. In regions where daily life is defined by darkness, diesel, or dangerous kerosene, off-grid solar and pay-as-you-go systems are transforming communities. The results are tangible: children can study after sunset, clinics can refrigerate vaccines, entrepreneurs can stay open later. A light switch becomes a life switch.

Technology is not just delivering services—it is expanding dignity, autonomy, and opportunity. It proves that finance, when directed with moral clarity, can reach the forgotten corners of the world and offer more than capital—it can offer hope.

Transparency

The final force—transparency—is a game-changer. Sir Ronald Cohen calls it the key to unlocking systemic change, because transparency makes impact visible. And when impact becomes visible, it becomes actionable.

For far too long, companies have focused solely on financial profits, while hiding—or simply ignoring—their social and environmental costs. Pollution, exploitation, biodiversity loss, carbon emissions, deforestation—these were "externalities," conveniently left off balance sheets, passed on to society, and inherited by future generations. But they were real debts, borrowed against our common home, and our common future.

Transparency is changing this.

Thanks to better data, evolving regulations, and increasing public demand, companies can no longer hide harm behind PR campaigns or exaggerate their impact. With clear, measurable data—on emissions, worker pay, supply chain ethics, and more—investors, consumers, and governments can finally make informed choices. We can reward companies that create genuine value and hold accountable those who do not. Transparency gives power back to the people.

These three forces—**values, technology, and transparency**—are the tailwinds of Alma's financial future. Values illuminate the **WHY**. Technology and transparency empower the **HOW**. And at the centre of it all stands a strong and reflective **WHO**: financial professionals committed to inner work, aligned with virtue, and grounded in their deepest humanity. With this foundation, Alma's financial system—and Alma's ocean—is not only possible. It is already beginning to emerge.

38

A New Mindset for Transformation: Creative Courage

Embracing Philosophy as a way of life—beyond utility, beyond career, beyond debate. Feeding our Eagles. Walking the road of being. Nurturing our human values. Committing to deep inner work. Practising the spiritual exercises. Cultivating **Oikeiōsis**—expanding our circles of care and concern. Living **Agapē**—loving selflessly, beyond transaction. And always, Education. Education with a capital E. Lifelong Education. Seeing the interconnectedness of all things, as Da Vinci saw—with wonder, with depth, with wholeness. With a systems mind and a human heart. All embedded in the Love of Wisdom, and the Wisdom of Love.

Each thread is part of the same weave. Together, they help us step off the Hedonic Treadmill—the restless chase for more—and lift the veil of the oblivion of being. They guide us back to our highest states—somatic, mental, psychological, spiritual—so that our choices, our actions, our creations, and our investments align with Alma's way: the path of fulfilment, not accumulation. The path of dignity, not dominance. The path of cooperation, not competition.

A path toward deeper connection—with others, with nature, with the Cosmopolis. A path toward happier, freer human beings. A path that builds Alma's economy—an economy rooted in human values and sacred interdependence, sustained by Alma's financial system.

This path is possible. And it is worth it. But it is not easy.

All over the world, thinkers, doers, and dreamers are working to build Alma's Ocean. Founders are launching social enterprises—*entrepreneurial Almas*—creating profitable solutions to urgent human needs like food insecurity and lack of education. And they are being backed by *financial Almas*—impact

P. Ansoleaga Abascal, *Philosophy and Finance: A Love Story*,
https://doi.org/10.1007/978-3-032-22218-3_38

investors who channel capital with integrity and imagination. They are drops of Alma's Ocean. Proof that it exists.

Today, there are an estimated 10 million social enterprises across the globe, including more than 9500 certified B-Corporations. That's about 3% of all formal businesses in the world. But this 3% speaks only to the number of enterprises—not their economic weight. If we shift the lens to size, revenue, market share, or capital controlled, social enterprises account for far less than 1% of the global economy. Most are small to mid-sized ventures, while traditional corporations—especially multinationals—continue to dominate capital flows, financial markets, and GDP contributions.

So yes, the number of entrepreneurial Almas is growing. But their footprint in the broader economy is still small.

Once again: this path is possible. And it is profoundly worth it—but not simple.

Most entrepreneurs I know are not driven solely by the desire to make money. Profit matters—it keeps the work alive—but it's not what gets them out of bed. It's not what makes their eyes shine.

Entrepreneurs are creators. They see gaps, feel the friction, and bring ideas to life. Their drive often comes from something deeply personal—a wish to fix what feels broken, or to fill a gap that's missing, to express their values, to offer something better or more accessible to the world. Some seek independence from their families. Others want to leave behind something that lasts—a legacy that speaks after they're gone.

Enzo Ferrari did not start Ferrari simply to sell cars. Ferrari was the embodiment of his obsession with speed, beauty, and engineering precision. **Coco Chanel** did not merely design and sell clothes; she reimagined what fashion could be—liberating women from restrictive norms with elegance and rebellion. Many entrepreneurs begin with that same clarity of purpose. Think of **Luigi Lavazza**'s lifelong quest for the perfect coffee blend, or **Francesco Illy**'s pursuit of espresso excellence. And think of **Brunello Cucinelli**, who built a global luxury brand around a marvellous idea: that profit and human dignity are not opposites, and that beauty, work, and ethics can coexist. His vision of humanistic capitalism placed people, culture, and the soul of a place at the heart of enterprise.

These companies did not begin as brands. They began as visions.

But staying true to the original vision is hard—especially as a business grows.

Scale brings pressure. As companies expand, they face rising demands to maximise profits—especially when they go public or bring in outside investors. Financial stakeholders often push for short-term results, forcing leaders to choose between quarterly targets and long-term values. This is why **having the right financial partners matters.**

Growth also brings complexity. Global operations, supply chains, regulations—all these add distance between a founder's intention and the company's everyday decisions. As new executives arrive—people who were not there at the beginning—company culture can start to shift. It's easier to protect your values when you're 50 people than when you're 50,000.

Even companies with a strong mission feel this strain. Take **Tesla**, for example. It was founded to accelerate the world's shift to sustainable energy. And yet, like many growing firms, it has faced criticism—on labour practices, on the environmental cost of lithium extraction. Scale introduces trade-offs. The bigger you grow, the harder it becomes to stay perfectly aligned with your purpose.

The same happened with **Ben & Jerry's**. From the start, the company stood for more than just ice cream. It was rooted in social responsibility—supporting local farmers, fair trade, and progressive causes. Values mattered as much as vanilla. But after its acquisition by a global corporation, the company has had to fight—sometimes publicly—to protect its founding ideals. A reminder that the bigger you become, the harder it is to hold your ground.

When external pressures threaten to pull us off course, it's our inner framework that helps us hold the line. Staying loyal to purpose—aligning actions with values—requires more than good intentions. It takes moral clarity. It takes inner anchoring. This is where a philosophy of life—like Stoicism—can become a real compass. And to me, that's great news. Because when we feel lost, we are not without guidance. The wisdom of moral and intellectual giants—past and present—is always within reach.

We can draw on the Stoic virtues: **courage, justice, temperance, and wisdom**. They shine like constellations in this age of transition.

Courage allows us to act with integrity when it's easier to conform. To speak the truth when silence would be safer. To take a principled stand—even when it might cost us. Courage reminds us that a life lived in fear of others' approval is no life at all.

Justice calls us to ask not just, "Is this profitable?" but, "Is this right?" It makes us refuse to exploit, deceive, or look the other way. It inspires us to act fairly, protect the vulnerable, and contribute to the common good.

Temperance—the virtue of balance, restraint, and moderation—teaches us to resist excess: of power, of wealth, of ambition. It helps us stay grounded. It gives us space to pause, to reflect, and to act with intention instead of impulse.

And **wisdom**—the integrating virtue. The ability to see clearly, to discern rightly, to choose well. Wisdom helps us know what truly matters. It gives us a steady compass in complexity. It teaches us to distinguish between what we can control and what we cannot—so we stop wasting energy chasing illusions.

Together, these virtues form a kind of moral architecture. When we feel pulled by pressure—be it financial, social, or political—they bring us back to ourselves. They remind us that a life of virtue is the good life. And that staying true to our values, even when it costs us, is the only real success.

And in today's world, one virtue shines brighter than the rest: **courage. Moral courage.** The courage to stay true to our values, even when the political winds shift. Even when it becomes normal to look the other way. The willingness to act rightly—resisting fear, greater profits, or pressure from the outside world.

Seneca captured it perfectly: much of what seems insurmountable becomes manageable when we find the courage to face it.

> *"It is not because things are difficult that we do not dare; it is because we do not dare that they are difficult." –Seneca, Letters to Lucilius, Letter 104.26, trans. Richard M. Gummere (1917)*

But there is another kind of courage I want to speak about before this book ends. It goes beyond the Stoic's moral courage—beyond the courage to do what is right. It is **creative courage**: the courage to imagine what does not yet exist, and to build it anyway. **Not just the courage to walk the harder path—but to build a path where none existed before.**

Moral courage might help us scale a business with integrity. But imagining a new kind of business model—that takes **creative courage**. Let me explain what I mean.

We know that sustainable development is the only viable way forward—if we want life on Earth, as we know it, to endure. And yet, sustainable choices remain out of reach for many. Ethical actions are still, too often, a privilege, not a right. We know fast fashion exploits workers and pollute ecosystems. We know industrial farming depletes the soil. We know fossil fuels are accelerating climate breakdown. Even our own savings—managed by our bank, wealth or asset manager—sometimes finance the very things we oppose. And still, choosing better often costs more, or it's inaccessible to most of us.

Ethical clothing is priced beyond reach for many. Healthy, local organic food comes with a premium. Impact investment funds often require a minimum of one million euros just to enter. And even time has become a luxury—time to choose, to cook, to invest with conscience.

But we can ask: *How do we redesign the system so the right choice isn't the hardest one? How do we move sustainability from an elite aspiration to a daily reality?*

How do we democratise impact finance so that every saver can access sound, well-diversified impact portfolios—with their savings, no matter how small?

This is where creative courage comes in.

Building **Entrepreneurial Almas**—companies that balance profit with purpose—is a courageous act. It's easier to cut costs by underpaying workers than by ensuring fair wages. Easier to dump waste into rivers than to invest in cleaner technologies. Yet businesses must still survive. They must remain profitable—ideally, while making their products accessible to a broader audience.

Becoming **Financial Almas**—investors who channel capital into ventures that regenerate rather than extract—is even more demanding. Especially if we seek to open access to small savers. It requires redesign. Innovation. Regulatory navigation. Boldness. It asks us to imagine new financial structures, new investment vehicles, new partnerships—and a reordering of priorities.

Navigating these challenges calls not only for deep resolve, but for even deeper creativity. It is time to invoke what **Rollo May** called "Creative Courage." In *The Courage to Create* (1975), he reminds us that creativity is not mere innovation for efficiency—it is a transformative act that requires courage, self-belief, humility, and openness. His idea remains as relevant today as ever:

For May, **creative courage is the bravery to give form to what does not yet exist**—to bring new patterns, meanings, and structures into the world when the old ones no longer suffice. It is about discovering futures that have not yet been named.

To illuminate this, May turns to **Paul Cézanne**. Cézanne was deeply convinced that he was seeing reality differently—that he was discovering a new way of representing space, form, and perception. He sensed that his work could alter the course of art. And yet, he lived with constant doubt. He hesitated, reworked endlessly, questioned himself relentlessly. His commitment never eliminated uncertainty; it coexisted with it.

This is the heart of creative courage. True commitment does not require absolute certainty. In fact, it is healthiest when it persists despite doubt. To believe deeply while remaining aware that one may be wrong is not a contradiction—it is a mark of respect for truth, which always exceeds any single vision or solution.

Creative courage, then, is not blind confidence. It is not stubborn certainty. It is the willingness to act without guarantees, to remain faithful to a vision while allowing it to evolve. It demands humility alongside conviction, openness alongside resolve.

This insight speaks powerfully to our economic and financial systems today. Too often, we confuse certainty with strength. We defend inherited models—unregulated markets, shareholder primacy, endless growth—as if questioning them were a threat. But this rigidity is not resilience. It is stagnation. When conviction hardens into dogma, creativity withers.

Alma's economy and financial system need leaders who resemble Cézanne more than engineers of control: people capable of deep commitment, yet willing to revise, learn, and adapt. People who hold a vision firmly, but never so tightly that it cannot breathe.

Creative courage calls us to inhabit a delicate balance: **strong belief in the need for transformation, and deep humility about how that transformation will unfold**. Our solutions are not final answers—they are living experiments, always in dialogue with reality.

Just as Cézanne reimagined how space could be seen, creative courage in business and finance asks us to reimagine the very structures that organise value, capital, and success. Not with arrogance, but with patience. Not with certainty, but with care.

This is how new worlds are built.

We need new financial models that make sustainability accessible to all. Businesses that scale ethical practices while keeping products affordable. Companies like **Pact**, offering organic cotton clothing at reasonable prices. Like **Too Good To Go**, reducing food waste while making fresh meals more accessible. Platforms like **Raise Green**, democratising access to clean energy investments. Circular economy pioneers like **Fairphone**, with its modular, long-lasting smartphones, and **Loop**, with its reusable packaging, are showing what's possible. And we need bold government policy—such as tax credits for renewables or incentives for regenerative agriculture—to accelerate the shift.

Reintegrating Philosophy into our world is the idea behind this book—not only as a moral imperative, but as an act of creative design for the future we can build. **Philosophy spurs and ignites creativity because it invites us to question the world as it is and imagine what it could be. It breaks down assumptions. It challenges conventions. And it opens space for wonder—a key ingredient of creativity.** By exploring the deepest questions of existence, meaning, and truth, Philosophy frees the mind from rigid patterns and awakens new ways of seeing.

It nurtures both precision and imagination—making it a fertile ground where reason and intuition meet to give birth to new ideas. Philosophy invites innovation. It pushes us to imagine new systems, new patterns, new meanings. It helps us define value in broader terms—beyond GDP, beyond shareholder returns. It invites us to measure success not only by profits, but by the health of ecosystems, the strength of communities, and the well-being of future generations. **The Queen of the Sciences fosters both morality and creativity.** It expands the boundaries of what we believe is possible, opening space for new patterns of thought, new shared symbols, and new ways of shaping a more humane society.

As financial professionals, entrepreneurs, policymakers, and citizens, we can embody this creative courage. Just as Cézanne's work reshaped the world of art, we can reshape the world of economics and finance. I believe we hold the potential for true transformation—if we have the courage, both Stoic and creative, the integrity, and the humility to pursue it. Because moral and creative courage are not separate. They are partners in transformation.

39

A New Kind of Entrepreneur: The Entrepreneurial Almas

All over the world, entrepreneurial Almas are embodying this kind of courage—designing businesses that challenge systems, reshape norms, and build new ways of living and working. Let me introduce you to one of them. Someone who embodies both moral and creative courage. His name is Petru Capatina—one of my favourite entrepreneurial Almas.

In the heart of Europe's historic cities—where cobblestone streets and ancient architecture whisper stories of centuries past—individuals with disabilities still face steep, insurmountable barriers. Barriers invisible to most of us, yet powerful enough to keep someone from leaving their home. A single step. A narrow doorway. A missing ramp. A noisy supermarket. These obstacles can turn a short walk into an impossible journey.

Tackling this kind of systemic inaccessibility requires more than good intentions. It demands deep moral conviction—and bold creative vision. Petru Capatina and his team are bringing both.

Petru Capatina and WeGlad

Petru refused to accept inaccessibility as a fact of life. To him, mobility should not be a luxury—it should be a right. His response was to co-found WeGlad—short for "Welcome Gladiator"—an interactive mapping platform and social movement committed to making public spaces accessible for people with disabilities.

P. Ansoleaga Abascal, *Philosophy and Finance: A Love Story*,
https://doi.org/10.1007/978-3-032-22218-3_39

WeGlad empowers users to report obstacles in real time and find routes free of architectural barriers. It aims to make travel safer and to strengthen the connection between individuals with disabilities and the places that welcome them. The name "Gladiator" honours those who face these daily challenges with strength and grace.

WeGlad's Purpose is rooted in sharing responsibility and data. This factually happens by engaging retail corporates in mapping and publicly sharing accessibility data of their branches. The same process is done with governments, sharing street data to facilitate the barrier removal, reaching material change. In fact, WeGlad is more than an app. It is a reimagining of urban space. A movement. A call to action. Through features like "Mappathons", communities can come together to identify obstacles and drive local change. It's collaborative. It's hopeful. And it works.

Petru's work embodies the essence of creative courage: the courage to imagine what does not yet exist—and bring it into being. As he rightly says:

> *"Mobility is more than motion; it is the flow that connects talent to its opportunity. Break that, and you will break life."*

This is precisely what Rollo May meant by **creative courage**: the capacity to bring into being new forms of meaning, new ways of organising life, and new patterns through which a different kind of society can emerge.

And in the age of artificial intelligence, this kind of courage becomes even more vital. **We do not need to outcompete machines—we need to out-human them.**

AI can analyse data, optimize outcomes, and mimic language. It can predict trends, automate tasks, and replicate existing systems. But it cannot dream. It cannot imagine. It cannot feel what the world aches for. AI knows **what is**—but it cannot grasp **what ought to be**. AI does not rebel against injustice. It does not love the forgotten. It does not risk everything for a vision of a fairer world.

But humans do. Only humans can look at a broken system and choose to care. Only humans can connect meaning to action, ethics to innovation, heart to structure. Only humans can cultivate **Oikeiōsis**—expanding our circles of care and concern. Only humans can live **Agapē**—loving selflessly. That's the kind of courage we need now—courage rooted in meaning, guided by values, and open to doubt. **The kind of change Petru and his team are working toward demands both moral and creative courage: the moral will to challenge the status quo, and the creative force to build what has never been**

built before. This is not just about accessibility. It's about potential. About talent. About inclusion. Empathy. Dignity. Justice. Belonging.

WeGlad shows us what becomes possible when moral and creative courage meet. It challenges norms. It mobilizes technology for the common good. And it reminds us that systems do not change on their own—we must choose to look, to act, and to ask: *What if there's a better way?*

Petru and his team are reshaping the future. And they remind us that with enough moral and creative courage, we can dismantle the barriers—seen and unseen—that stand in the way of human freedom.

Lucie Basch and Too Good To Go

Across another axis of injustice—food waste—stand, once again, moral and creative courage.

Every day, millions of meals are thrown away simply because they were not sold in time. Meanwhile, hunger persists. Climate change worsens. The system shrugs. But Lucie Basch refused to shrug.

A French engineer with a promising career at Nestlé, she walked away from the corporate path to pursue something deeper. She believed that waste—particularly food waste—was not just a logistical failure. It was an ethical one. An environmental one. A moral one. Her response was to co-found **Too Good To Go**—a platform built on a simple, powerful idea: what if surplus food could be rescued before it became waste? What if waste could be recirculated? What if surplus could become sustenance?

Too Good To Go is the app that grew from that question. It connects consumers to local restaurants, bakeries, and grocery stores with unsold food. Meals that would have gone to landfill now find their way into people's tables. Businesses recover losses. People eat well for less. And the planet breathes a little easier.

This is creative courage: seeing value where others saw none. Daring to redesign the relationship between cost and care, scarcity and abundance. But it also required moral courage: the conviction that wasting food while people go hungry is unjust. That sustainability must serve the many, not just the privileged few. Lucie's work is not about charity. It's about dignity. About reimagining flow, ownership, fairness. As she puts it: "Fighting food waste is the most impactful action we can take against climate change."

Too Good To Go did not invent food. It reimagined how it moves. They did not disrupt the system—they asked us to care enough to change it. And in doing so, they're helping build a culture where surplus is shared. Where good food is passed forward. Where sustainability is a way of being. They remind us that courage, when guided by imagination and values, can reshape the story we tell about what's possible.

The entrepreneurial Almas highlighted in these pages are people I know. And living in Italy, I see that there are countless inspiring stories still untold. If time and space had allowed, I would have included many more of the visionary entrepreneurial Almas who have shaped—and honoured—what we proudly call *Made in Italy*. Take, for instance, **Adriano Olivetti (1901–1960)**, who reimagined industry as a vehicle for social transformation; **Brunello Cucinelli (b. 1953)**, who champions "humanistic capitalism," harmonising profit with human dignity; and **Giovanni Borghi (1910–1975)**, who not only revolutionised the appliance industry but also built an entire village to improve the lives of his workers. These are stories worth telling. Their legacies remind us that business can be a force for good—where purpose and prosperity walk hand in hand.

These entrepreneurial Almas need Financial Almas to believe in their vision, and to back them with capital, care, and courage.

40

A New Kind of Investor: The Financial Almas

Alexandre Mars and Blisce

Alexandre Mars is not just an entrepreneur, investor and philanthropist. He is a visionary—one who believes that business should not just scale, but serve. He is one of the financial Almas I admire most. After a successful exit from the tech world, he founded Blisce—a venture capital firm rooted in ethical alignment. Blisce does not invest only in profitability. It invests in purpose.

Blisce was one of the early backers of Too Good To Go, recognising not just a smart platform, but a cultural shift. Alexandre saw a new model for business—where environmental impact, social justice, and financial return could go hand in hand. This is what a financial Alma does: supports, sustains and champions visions that challenge the extractive logic.

Alexandre is also the founder of EPIC, a philanthropic foundation dedicated to ending child inequality. EPIC brings transparency and accountability to charitable giving, offering individuals and companies a rigorous, curated portfolio of high-impact nonprofits they can support. What I love about EPIC is that it allows donors to align their capital with their conscience—to turn values into action, and generosity into measurable impact. It's philanthropy done with discipline. Capital deployed with clarity and care. Alexandre embraces, Emerson's powerful idea of *blended value*: **"There is no economic performance without social performance."**

When financial capital is paired with moral clarity and creative vision, and guided by Philosophy, it becomes a powerful tool for building the future we want.

P. Ansoleaga Abascal, *Philosophy and Finance: A Love Story*,
https://doi.org/10.1007/978-3-032-22218-3_40

Guglielmo Notarbartolo and PFC

Another example of Financial Alma lives in Milan, through Guglielmo Notarbartolo and PFC Family Office. PFC—Partners for Change—is a single-family office. They invest, grant, and advocate for an inclusive and sustainable economic system.

Guglielmo and his team approach capital with strategic vision and deep intention. For them, finance is not just a mechanism—it is a form of responsibility. They understand that financial decisions are not morally neutral. That impact is not a marketing slogan. It's a commitment. A stance. A way of showing up in the world.

PFC shows us what it means to be a Financial Alma: To see beyond numbers. To ask, always, *what is our money enabling?* And to ensure that capital walks the path of dignity, empathy, and inclusion. I have no doubt they would pass **Socrates' Doctor test.**

Among their many thoughtful investments and donations, two are especially close to my heart: **Wilderness Way**—a team of *Entrepreneurial Almas* caring for traumatised and vulnerable children across the UK—and **Alice for Children**, the NGO I hold dearest, dedicated to protecting and educating children in Nairobi's informal settlements. Wilderness Way offers stability, healing, and long-term care to those who have experienced profound hardship. Alice for Children provides education, nutrition, and shelter to children deprived of basic needs—supporting them all the way from the hardship of the slum to the dignity of a stable job. The former is an investment. The latter, a grant. Together, they reflect how PFC works across the spectrum of capital, and across the spectrum of values.

Family offices like PFC play a vital role in building Alma's Ocean. They are nimble. Flexible. Less constrained by institutional mandates. They can move faster, act boldly, and back the kinds of ventures that are closest to their hearts.

Jacqueline Novogratz and Acumen

Another Financial Alma I deeply admire is **Jacqueline Novogratz**, founder and CEO of **Acumen**.

Jacqueline began her career in traditional finance before realising that markets, left to themselves, too often exclude the very people who need them most. Acumen was born from that insight—and from a bold conviction: that capital, when paired with patience, humility, and moral courage, can be a powerful force for dignity.

Acumen pioneered the concept of **patient capital**: long-term, risk-tolerant investment in enterprises serving low-income communities across Africa, South Asia, Latin America, and the United States. These are not charitable donations. They are real investments—made in businesses providing essential goods and services such as clean energy, healthcare, education, agriculture, and financial inclusion.

What distinguishes Acumen is not only where it invests, but how. Every investment begins with a simple question: does this business treat people as ends in themselves, or merely as means? Dignity is the core criterion. Growth matters—but never at the expense of humanity.

Through investments in companies like **d.light** (solar energy), **Ziqitza Healthcare**, and numerous social enterprises across the Global South, Acumen demonstrates that it is possible to build financially viable businesses while honouring the intrinsic worth of every human being. Returns are measured not only in financial terms, but in lives improved, opportunities created, and communities strengthened.

This is what a Financial Alma looks like at scale: capital deployed with patience, courage, and deep respect for those it seeks to serve. Acumen shows us that impact investing is not about slogans—it is about doing the hard, necessary work of aligning money with moral responsibility. I have no doubt that Acumen, too, would pass Socrates' Doctor Test.

Scaling Impact: Beyond Labels, Toward Interconnectedness

Investing in early-stage companies like WeGlad, Too Good To Go, or Wilderness Way, d.light, or Ziqitza Healthcare, is very impactful but not always feasible for everyone. These private companies often require substantial investments and are considered *illiquid* assets—meaning there's no public market for selling shares if an investor needs to liquidate her position. Such investments demand long time horizons, strong conviction, and a high tolerance for risk, making them typically suitable for family offices, venture capital or private equity funds, rather than the average saver.

Pension funds, for example, manage the life savings of millions of workers. Their primary responsibility is to safeguard these pensions and ensure steady growth over time, allowing retirees to live a well-deserved happy life. This necessitates building well-diversified portfolios that manage risk prudently, distinguishing courage from recklessness—a principle aligned with the Stoic virtue of temperance and Aristotle's Golden Mean. Consequently, they invest predominantly in listed assets—stocks and bonds tradable in public markets. Similarly, bank-managed portfolios handle individuals' savings and future security, requiring financial strategies that preserve purchasing power, manage volatility, and remain resilient over time. Diversification and liquidity are essential, enabling investors to access their funds when needed.

Well-diversified liquid portfolios require public market investments where shares can be bought or sold in milliseconds, directing capital toward sound, well-established corporations. Therefore, a significant portion of global capital continues to flow through public markets. **To build Alma's Ocean, it is not enough to support only small, mission-driven companies; we must also help steer the entire listed world in Alma's direction. Both are needed for systemic change.**

Yes, we can and should scale the business models pioneered by small, innovative Entrepreneurial Almas—like **Too Good To Go**, helping major retailers reduce food waste at scale; **WeGlad**, shaping more inclusive cities; or **d.light** and **Ziqitza Healthcare**, bringing energy and healthcare to communities long left behind. But this is not enough. To build Alma's Ocean, we must also harness the full power of capital markets to regenerate rather than extract. By acting as engaged public equity and bond investors, we can help steer large listed companies toward more just, sustainable, and life-affirming paths.

For context, the impact investing market is estimated at approximately \$1.571 trillion (Source: GIIN). These investments primarily support small, innovative unlisted entrepreneurial Almas. They represent just 0.6% of the combined value of global public equity and bond markets, which together exceed \$250 trillion.

When a small family office invests in a childcare company like Wilderness Way, the impact is deep and immediate—measurable, human, and life-changing. Conversely, when a large activist investor in publicly listed companies engages with a global corporation like Amazon, they can advocate for better wages, safer conditions, and ethical supply chains—changes that can affect over 1.5 million workers and their families, plus their supply chain companies' workers and their families. One approach is local; the other systemic. One is deep; the other broad. Both are essential to building Alma's Ocean.

In financial language, the first is typically called impact investing, while the second belongs to sustainable or ESG-oriented activist investing. But what matters most is not the label. What matters is the intention behind the capital, the human values that guide it, and the real outcomes it enables.

A better future requires both kinds of action: local and global, deep and wide, focused and structural, listed and unlisted. This is not a contest between purity and pragmatism; it's a constellation of efforts, all moving toward the same horizon: justice, inclusion, and environmental stewardship. In other words, Alma's Ocean.

Encouragingly, more financial Almas—investors with a strong philosophical foundation—are emerging within public markets as well. Firms like **Etica SGR**, founded by Banca Etica in Italy, are dedicated to sustainable investing in the liquid, listed space, combining rigorous ESG screening with active shareholder engagement and transparent reporting. **Mirova**, based in France, focuses entirely on long-term sustainable investments across public equities, green bonds, and thematic funds. **Triodos Investment Management**, part of the ethical Dutch bank **Triodos**, channels capital exclusively into companies and bonds contributing to a more just and regenerative society. Across the Atlantic, **Domini Impact Investments** has pioneered values-based investing in public equities, combining ethical screening with active ownership to promote human dignity, environmental responsibility, and long-term stewardship.

These institutions remind us that even public markets, when guided by Philosophy, can rise above short-term profit and become powerful forces in the service of life.

Finance, like life, is a web. People, returns, nature, policies, markets—everything is connected. One decision ripples across many lives, even if we do not always see it. Recognizing this interconnectedness shifts our focus from categorizing investments to asking what kind of future our money is helping to create.

Mistakes will be made along the way, but that's part of the journey. We can approach finance as the Stoics approached life: not as a pursuit of perfection, but as a **commitment to progress**. With humility, clarity, and courage. This is what Alma's Ocean requires: a shared vision; aligned intentions; the wisdom to adapt—wherever we are, with whatever tools we have. Within our sphere of control. Every financial choice tells a story. We can ensure ours is one of justice, beauty, and belonging.

41

A New Choice Before Us: The Future Is Ours to Create

Alonso Quixano may have died, but Don Quixote never will. He rides through the ages, undaunted, reminding us that the true madness is not in dreaming of a better world, but in resigning ourselves to the one that is.

In Don Quixote's eyes, Sancho Panza was not a humble peasant—he was a governor in the making, a man braver than he knew. Dulcinea was not a simple country girl—she was a noble lady, virtue waiting to be seen. The women standing outside a tavern were not prostitutes but elegant ladies chatting, taking the evening air. Don Quixote did not accept reality as it was presented to him; he shaped it with the force of his belief, embellishing it with meaning, lifting others up, seeing the extraordinary in the ordinary.

And so can we.

P. Ansoleaga Abascal, *Philosophy and Finance: A Love Story*,
https://doi.org/10.1007/978-3-032-22218-3_41

Nikole Bozza Ansoleaga

The world will always offer reasons to surrender—to cynicism, to despair, to the cold comfort of saying, *this is just the way things are*. After all, we are told, we are *Homo Oeconomicus*—self-centred, purely rational, disenchanted beings. But Don Quixote does not agree. And neither do I.

Miguel de Cervantes' courageous character reminds us that resignation is the greatest illusion of all. However grim the news, however weighty the world's suffering, we do not need to be spectators. We can be creators of a better world, no matter how small our actions may seem.

The choice always remains.

Let us remember and honour Viktor Frankl, a man who endured humanity's darkest night yet refused to surrender his inner light. From the depths of suffering, he taught that even when everything external is taken from us, one freedom remains inviolable: the freedom to choose how we respond, and who we become, in the face of circumstances we cannot control.

Viktor Frankl is right. Life is a choice. Embarking on the *road of being* is a choice. Feeding our *Eagles* is a choice. Letting our *Wolves* rule our lives is a choice, too.

The first choice—***Alma***'s choice—gifts us calm, possibility, and freedom. It allows us to live in trust and learning mode, to feed our Eagles each and every day. ***Alma***'s choice is a mindset—a way of seeing the world through the lens of creation, curiosity, and connection. Through Da Vinci's eyes.

In ***Alma***'s world, obstacles become lessons. Setbacks are not failures but invitations to grow. Success does not define us, nor does failure. We find strength in our relationships, in nature, and in the steady confidence that life itself is an evolving journey. We care for others, and we allow ourselves to be cared for.

For Alma, every storm carries the promise of a rainbow. Her mindset thrives on love, wisdom, patience, and compassion, balanced with discipline, resilience, and purpose. **Alma's path is not always easy, but it is always worth it.** It transforms life from a series of struggles into an unfolding masterpiece of meaning.

The second choice—***Ega***'s choice—entails fear, envy, and limitation. It keeps us trapped in a state of constant alertness, where threats seem to lurk everywhere. Regret, worry, and scarcity rule the mind, draining our energy and narrowing our vision.

In ***Ega***'s world, failure and success, job titles and material possessions define individuals. ***Ega*** seeks validation, admiration, or security from others. She tries to overcome the anxiety of separateness through conformity, power, or material success.

Alma's mindset defines reality. Ega's mindset reacts to it.

Ega's choices foster competition instead of collaboration, transactions instead of relationships, self-preservation instead of mutual upliftment. Her actions, left unchecked, can injure eternity.

But—as I hope this book has shown—our mindset is not fixed. It can be shaped, nurtured, and transformed. The Stoics understood this long before us. And by feeding our Eagles, we begin to create a life of courage and connection—one that enriches not only our lives, but also the lives we touch.

The future is not written. It is ours to shape. Life is a choice. And love is a choice too.

At the root of our most urgent challenges lies a spiritual truth: the fundamental problem of human existence is our deep sense of **separateness**. But there are two powerful antidotes: Love and Wisdom. Or rather, one—**Philosophy**. *Philos* (love) and *Sophia* (wisdom). The union of love and wisdom. Or better, wisdom at the service of love. The two forces that help us overcome the *oblivion of Being*.

Let us begin with Love.

Love is deeply misunderstood. We confuse it with attachment, dependency, or possession. We commodify it. We treat it as fleeting or passive—as something we receive, rather than something we practice. But love is not an emotion—it is a discipline, an art, a choice.

No one has captured this better than **Erich Fromm** (1900–1980) in ***The Art of Loving***. Fromm, a psychoanalyst, humanistic philosopher, and social psychologist, saw love not as a fleeting emotion, but as an active choice—not something that happens to us, but something we learn to do. Love, he argued, requires effort, understanding, and commitment. Epictetus would have agreed with him.

According to Fromm, true love rests on four interdependent elements, each one making it active. The first is **care**: love as nurturing, as giving—genuine love involves tending to the well-being of another, whether that be a person, a community, or even an impact beneficiary. The second is **responsibility**: love as commitment, as a voluntary response to the needs of another—out of deep, authentic concern. This is key, because love is not merely a feeling; it is a choice we reaffirm each day. The third is **respect**: love as freedom—seeing others as they truly are, not as we wish them to be. Respect is the opposite of control; to love someone (or humanity) is to honour their uniqueness, autonomy, and potential for growth. And finally, there is **knowledge**: love as understanding. To love deeply, we must know deeply. True love demands intellectual curiosity and a commitment to learning. The Stoics understood this well, which is why they placed physics—the study of nature and reality—at the foundation of philosophical training.

Fromm's vision of love is **active**. Stoic. Creative. Epictetus would have agreed with him. Because love without wisdom can become blind idealism. And wisdom without love can turn into cold detachment.

Which brings us to the second antidote: **Wisdom**.

Wisdom is the bridge between knowledge and deep understanding. It is what allows us to see reality as it is, free from illusion or wishful thinking. The great philosophers understood this: to think properly is to cultivate rational clarity, seeking enlightenment through knowledge and reflection. To know the good is to develop moral wisdom and live by virtue. And. . .to ***know thyself*** is the foundation upon which everything else rests. Self-knowledge allows us to question our assumptions, strip away our illusions, and understand our fears, needs, and capacity for growth.

Love to learn, and learn to love.

Philosophy can be the medicine for humanity—the antidote my dear Epictetus would have prescribed. For, as he taught us, we become what we pay attention to.

Reshaping the world—through inner work, education, entrepreneurship, or finance—requires a radical shift in attention. A shift away from passive reaction and toward conscious, loving, wise action.

That choice—Alma's choice—is ours to make.

In the end, it is not love alone, nor wisdom alone, but their union—Love and Wisdom, Philos and Sophia, Philosophy as a way of life—that offers us a bright path forward.

For ourselves.
For economics.
For finance.
For our children.
For their children.

Love and wisdom, together, invite us into a journey:

From Me to We
From Feeding Our Wolves to Letting Our Eagles Fly High and Free
From the *Road of Having* to the *Road of Being*
From Hakim to Eliahu
From an Ordinary Perception to a Philosophical One
From Hedonism to Eudaimonia
From *Ego* to *Eco*From *Ega* to *Alma*
From Head to Head & Heart together
From Knowledge to Wisdom
From Awareness to Consciousness
From External Achievement to Internal Fulfilment
From Pastry Chefs to Doctors
From Me and My Inner Circles to Oikeiōsis
From Observers to Actors
From Aimless to Intentional Living
From a Mechanical Life to a Forever Festival
From Turning Away to Turning Toward
From Passivity to Responsibility
From Bifurcated Value to Blended Value
From a Narrow Lens to Da Vinci's Lens
From Inertia to Creative Courage
From Risk and Return to Risk, Return, and Impact
From Market Values to Human Values
From Fear to Love
And there is only one item we need for this beautiful journey: **Virtue**.

If virtue precedes us, every step will be safe

Step by step, we will release drops of hope, peace and happiness into the world

And what is an ocean, if not the sum of its drops?

Alma's ocean is waiting.

A Shelf for the Soul

Books and thinkers that lit the way on this journey. May they become companions on yours.

Some books arrive as invitations. They open a window, shift a gaze, or plant a seed that changes everything.

This shelf is not exhaustive. It is intimate. These are the works that walked beside me as I wrote, and shaped the questions this book dares to ask. They span philosophy, spirituality, economics, and finance. They show that Alma's Ocean is a direction. A path worth every step.

I offer them to you as fellow travellers—lights to read by, and live by.

Philosophy

Books to think, feel, and live more deeply, and freely.

The Republic: Plato

A timeless meditation on justice, power, and the soul of a city—and of a human being. Plato invites us to question everything we think we know.

Nicomachean Ethics: Aristotle

Aristotle offers a blueprint for human flourishing grounded in reason, habit, and virtue. A clear voice across centuries, guiding us toward eudaimonia.

P. Ansoleaga Abascal, *Philosophy and Finance: A Love Story*,
https://doi.org/10.1007/978-3-032-22218-3

Letters from a Stoic; On the Shortness of Life; On the Happy Life: Seneca

Practical, poetic wisdom from a Roman statesman-philosopher. Seneca writes with fire and clarity on time, mortality, and what truly matters.

Discourses and the Art of Living: Epictetus

The teachings of a freed slave who became one of history's great moral teachers. Epictetus reminds us that while we cannot control external events, we can choose our response to them.

Meditations: Marcus Aurelius

A Roman emperor's private journal of humility and self-examination. His words are a companion for anyone seeking strength and serenity in difficult times.

Groundwork for the Metaphysics of Morals: Immanuel Kant

A foundational text in moral philosophy. Kant urges us to treat humanity—our own and others'—always as an end, never as a means.

Walden; or, Life in the Woods: Henry David Thoreau

A gentle rebellion written in stillness. Thoreau reminds us that the most radical act may be to live simply, and the most sacred economy is inner wealth.

Philosophy as a Way of Life; The Inner Citadel: Pierre Hadot

Hadot rekindles an ancient truth: that Philosophy is not just something to study, but a way to live—with discipline, wonder, and care for the soul.

Sophie's World: A Novel About the History of Philosophy—Jostein Gaarder

A story within a story, tracing the great ideas that shaped Western thought. Ideal for curious minds and young philosophers of all ages.

A Guide to the Good Life: The Ancient Art of Stoic Joy—William B. Irvine

A modern guide to living wisely and calmly. Irvine shows how Stoicism can help us find joy not in what we have, but in how we see.

How to Be a Stoic: Massimo Pigliucci

An engaging, personal exploration of how ancient philosophy can shape modern life. Pigliucci walks the Stoic path with humour and humility.

The Burnout Society; The Disappearance of Rituals; In the Swarm: Byung-Chul Han

A piercing critique of modern hyperactivity, digital life, and the loss of slowness. Han calls us to resist the cult of performance—and return to presence.

Spirituality & Inner Work & Wellbeing—Books that whisper to the soul, and awaken the inner world.

Siddhartha: Hermann Hesse

A lyrical journey of spiritual awakening, blending Eastern wisdom and Western longing. A quiet river of a book about the search for self.

Man's Search for Meaning: Viktor E. Frankl

Written from within the horror of a concentration camp, this book is a testament to the human spirit—and to the freedom we always have to choose meaning.

The Hero with a Thousand Faces: Joseph Campbell

An exploration of the mythic journey shared across cultures and time. Campbell shows us that transformation is the deepest human story.

The Alchemist: Paulo Coelho

A poetic fable about listening to your heart and following your purpose. A story that reminds us that the treasure we seek is often right where we began.

The Power of Now: A Guide to Spiritual Enlightenment—Eckhart Tolle

A quiet revolution. Tolle calls us back to the only moment that truly exists—the present—and to the peace waiting there.

The Art of Happiness: Dalai Lama and Howard C. Cutler

A conversation between science and compassion. The Dalai Lama reminds us that happiness is a skill—and a responsibility.

Untethered Soul: The Journey Beyond Yourself—Michael A. Singer

A gentle but powerful guide to loosening the grip of ego and opening to the vast awareness within.

Silence: The Power of Quiet in a World Full of Noise—Thich Nhat Hanh

A meditation on the sacredness of silence. Thich Nhat Hanh teaches us to listen—to ourselves, to others, to life.

The Book of Joy: Lasting Happiness in a Changing World—Dalai Lama and Desmond Tutu

Two spiritual giants reflect on suffering, joy, and the human heart. A luminous dialogue between wisdom and laughter.

Biologia della Gentilezza: Daniel Lumera and Immaculata De Vivo

Science meets kindness in this exploration of how gentleness is not weakness—but strength in its most radiant form.

28 Respiri per Cambiare Vita: Daniel Lumera

A journey through breath, awareness, and gentle transformation. This book offers mindful breathing practices to restore balance and awaken inner peace.

Fermati e Respira: Daniel Lumera

An invitation to pause. To breathe. To remember that peace begins with presence.

Economics and Society

Books that explore how the soul of a society is reflected in its economics, and how human values shape systems.

The Wealth of Nations; The Theory of Moral Sentiments – Adam Smith In these twin classics, Adam Smith reveals that markets and morality are inseparable, showing that the wealth of nations is ultimately rooted in the goodness of our collective hearts.

Sapiens: A Brief History of Humankind – Yuval Noah Harari Harari offers a sweeping history of humankind, reminding us that shared myths and acts of imagination have guided our journey and shaped the soul of our species.

Reckoning with Markets: Moral Reflections in Economics – James Halteman & Edd Noell Halteman & Noell explore the ethical undercurrents of economics, reminding us that behind every market statistic lie human values and an ever-present need to balance profit with principle.

Capital in the Twenty-First Century – Thomas Piketty Piketty uncovers the forces of wealth and inequality through history, challenging us to confront how economic divides shape the fabric of society and our hopes for a more just future.

Facing Climate Change: The Justice of Climate Policy – Jeffrey Kiehl Kiehl casts climate change as a profound moral challenge, urging us to respond with honesty, justice, and compassion for both the planet and those who will inherit it.

Values: Building a Better World for All – Mark Carney Carney calls for a shift from chasing market value to cherishing human values, illustrating how finance steeped in trust, sustainability, and shared purpose can restore balance and build a more inclusive world.

Accountable: The Rise of Citizen Capitalism – Michael O'Leary and Warren Valdmanis O'Leary and Valdmanis reveal the rise of "citizen capitalism", where everyday investors and consumers hold companies to higher standards, reminding us that the collective voice of conscience can steer capitalism toward the common good.

Finance and Impact

Books that imagine finance as a force for healing—where capital flows to grow a better world.

The Purpose of Capital: Elements of Impact, Financial Flows, and Natural Being – Jed Emerson Emerson reimagines the purpose of wealth, arguing that capital exists not just to multiply itself, but to cultivate freedom, meaning, and harmony with the natural world.

Manifesto for a Moral Revolution: Practices to Build a Better World – Jacqueline Novogratz Novogratz lights the way for a moral revolution through stories of bold changemakers, showing us how to lead with courage, empathy, and a steadfast commitment to building a better world.

Impact: Reshaping Capitalism to Drive Real Change – Sir Ronald Cohen Sir Ronald Cohen champions a new vision of capitalism measured not just by profit but by its impact on lives and the planet, proving that aligning wealth with purpose can drive the change our world needs.

Can Finance Save the World? Regaining Power over Money to Serve the Common Good – Bertrand Badré explores how finance can be reclaimed as a force for good, showing that with vision and moral courage, the power of money can be harnessed to uplift society and serve the common good.

References and Bibliography

Arendt, H. (1958). The human condition. University of Chicago Press.

Aristotle. (1998). Politics (C. D. C. Reeve, Trans.). Hackett Publishing.

Aristotle. (2000). Nicomachean ethics (R. Crisp, Trans.). Cambridge University Press.

Aurelius, M. (2006). Meditations (M. Hammond, Trans.). Penguin Classics.

Bartolini, S. (2014). Manifesto per la felicità: Come passare dalla società del ben-avere a quella del ben-essere. Donzelli.

Buddha. (1985). The dhammapada (J. Byrom, Trans.). Shambhala.

Capra, F. (2007). The science of Leonardo: Inside the mind of the great genius of the Renaissance. Anchor Books.

Capra, F., & Luisi, P. L. (2014). The systems view of life: A unifying vision. Cambridge University Press.

Davies, W. H. (1911). Songs of joy and others. A. C. Fifield.

Deci, E. L., & Ryan, R. M. (2001). On happiness and human potentials: A review of research on hedonic and eudaimonic well-being. Annual Review of Psychology, 52, 141–166.

Einstein, A. (1939). Science and religion. Nature, 146, 605–607.

Emerson, J. (2018). The purpose of capital: Elements of impact, financial flows, and investing. Stanford Social Innovation Review.

Epictetus. (2008). Discourses and selected writings (R. Dobbin, Trans.). Penguin Classics.

Frankl, V. E. (2006). Man's search for meaning. Beacon Press.

Hadot, P. (1995). Philosophy as a way of life: Spiritual exercises from Socrates to Foucault (M. Chase, Trans.; A. I. Davidson, Ed.). Blackwell.

Isaacson, W. (2017). Leonardo da Vinci. Simon & Schuster.

Jaeger, W. (1945). Paideia: The ideals of Greek culture (Vols. 1–3). Oxford University Press.

P. Ansoleaga Abascal, *Philosophy and Finance: A Love Story*,
https://doi.org/10.1007/978-3-032-22218-3

James, W. (n.d.). Quotation on changing inner attitudes (often attributed).
Kahneman, D. (2011). Thinking, fast and slow. Farrar, Straus and Giroux.
Kasser, T. (2002). The high price of materialism. MIT Press.
Laozi. (1963). Tao te ching (D. C. Lau, Trans.). Penguin Classics.
Lembke, A. (2021). Dopamine nation: Finding balance in the age of indulgence. Dutton.
Lumera, D. (2016). La cura del perdono: Una nuova via alla felicità. Mondadori.
May, R. (1975). The courage to create. W. W. Norton & Company.
Meadows, D. H. (2008). Thinking in systems: A primer. Chelsea Green Publishing.
Nietzsche, F. (2001). The gay science (J. Nauckhoff, Trans.). Cambridge University Press.
Novogratz, J. (2011). The blue sweater: Bridging the gap between rich and poor in an interconnected world. Rodale.
Nussbaum, M. C. (2010). Not for profit: Why democracy needs the humanities. Princeton University Press.
Plato. (1997). Apology. In J. M. Cooper (Ed.), Plato: Complete works (G. M. A. Grube, Trans.). Hackett.
Polanyi, K. (2001). The great transformation: The political and economic origins of our time. Beacon Press.
Raworth, K. (2017). Doughnut economics: Seven ways to think like a 21st-century economist. Chelsea Green Publishing.
Sandel, M. J. (2012). What money can't buy: The moral limits of markets. Farrar, Straus and Giroux.
Schumpeter, J. A. (1942/2008). Capitalism, socialism and democracy. Harper Perennial.
Sen, A. (1999). Development as freedom. Oxford University Press.
Seneca. (2004). On the shortness of life (C. D. N. Costa, Trans.). Penguin Classics.
Stiglitz, J. E. (2010). Freefall: America, free markets, and the sinking of the world economy. W. W. Norton & Company.
Tillich, P. (1952). The courage to be. Yale University Press.
Yunus, M. (2010). Building social business. PublicAffairs.
Zingales, L. (2015). Does finance benefit society? Polity Press.

GPSR Compliance
The European Union's (EU) General Product Safety Regulation (GPSR) is a set of rules that requires consumer products to be safe and our obligations to ensure this.

If you have any concerns about our products, you can contact us on

ProductSafety@springernature.com

In case Publisher is established outside the EU, the EU authorized representative is:

Springer Nature Customer Service Center GmbH
Europaplatz 3
69115 Heidelberg, Germany

www.ingramcontent.com/pod-product-compliance
Lightning Source LLC
Chambersburg PA
CBHW050523240926
51846CB00003B/665
* 9 7 8 3 0 3 2 2 2 2 1 7 6 *